An Academic Skating on Thin Ice

For Rex, Holly, and Laura

An Academic
Skating on Thin Ice

Peter Worsley

Berghahn Books
New York • Oxford

First published in 2008 by

Berghahn Books
www.berghahnbooks.com

©2008 Peter Worsley

Library of Congress Cataloging-in-Publication Data
A C.I.P. catalog record for this book is available from
the Library of Congress

British Library Cataloguing in Publication Data
A catalogue record for this book is available from the British Library

Printed in the United States on acid-free paper.

ISBN 978-1-84545-370-1 (hardback)

Contents

List of Illustrations

Preface

Biographies are written by someone other than the subject, mostly from documents, not out of the consciousness of the person being written about. So they are usually linear and prospective constructions: they start with early childhood, then tell us about successive schools; then about whatever happens next.

'Memoirs' (or 'autobiographies') also have linear, chronological frameworks (as this one does). But being written by subjects, they frequently look backwards, and shuttle back and forth.

Memoirs, then, are more akin to Wordsworth's conception of poetry: 'emotion recollected in tranquillity', a take on the past that is necessarily retrospective. It hasn't all been tranquillity, though: everyone's life has passages they'd rather forget – in my case, episodes like the student revolution, for example.

The first thing you are taught in anthropology is the distinction between 'ethnography' – pure, dispassionate description of what happened or what life was like – and interpreting what you have seen within a theoretical framework. Memoirs, then, cannot be just 'ethnography', because the writer always writes from some point of view. Theoretical analysis has its problems too, for we can all recognise when the writer is giving us a Marxist or a Catholic version of what s/he is writing about: when their major concern is not really with tribe 'X' or nation 'Y' under discussion but with using that subject matter as an illustration of the power of their theoretical schemas: to show the dialectic in action (as everywhere else), and the underlying reasons why events unfolded as they did, by using the materialist method of analysis or by showing that it was all a matter of divine dispensation.

Even ethnographic 'what happened' can be problematic, if only because I have had to try hard to rescue some simple facts – the names of people, places, dates – from my memory, sometimes without success. Luckily, my wife can do all this brilliantly. But some things which I thought I had myself remembered very accurately, for the whole of my life, turned out to be quite wrong. And it is only now that I can make sense of innumerable postings from one military unit to another, which, at the grassroots, we experienced simply as the chaotic disbandment and amalgamation of regiments, and to which we reacted with ignorant resignation.

We usually attributed it to the bureaucratic incompetence of staff officers finding ways of filling in their time, or to the stupidity of individual generals. Only later were we able to see what had been going on: that men with great power had been shuffling their resources, managing the wholesale reorganisation of a war machine constructed to deal with the blitz according to the new requirements of the invasion of Europe. Those who did have the knowledge to explain all this not only resorted to 'spin', common enough today, under conditions of open government, but used their far stronger wartime powers of censorship to ensure that we were not aware of their strategies. When dozens of US troops were machine-gunned during invasion exercises at Slapton Sands in 1944, even civilian mail was censored, and we only found out fifty years later. Decades would often pass before even those in power were allowed to write their memoirs, and tell us what their strategies had been.

So I start by describing not just what happened as I saw it then but also with what I now know about what happened then. I begin, too, at the end, not the beginning of my life, and – having just passed eighty – had better write this before it is too late. I begin, indeed, precisely at 4.04 A.M. on the 31st May 2004, when, being old, I woke at cockcrow in the Japanese tea-house in the garden of my friend Alan Macfarlane, at Lode, just outside Cambridge, who finally induced me to write these memoirs.

He's an anthropologist, like me, though very unlike me. He collects everything that has ever touched him: all the memorabilia of his life from birth in Assam on a tea plantation to his current distinguished professorship at Cambridge. Probably because of this overseas upbringing, Alan is very conscious of having to recover his English family roots. He is equally conscious of his intellectual roots, living as he does in the Front Court at King's, which was eventually invaded by the social sciences, though only very recently.

Alan's rooms were formerly inhabited by two other outstanding anthropologists (and ultimately bitter enemies), Meyer Fortes and Edmund Leach. The successive generations which had built the College, though, had not been social scientists. Indeed, there weren't such things, centuries ago, though when social scientists did eventually arrive, one of them, John Maynard Keynes, became better known to the general public even than Alan Turing, who unravelled the Enigma Code.

With his mother, Iris – whom I have never met – Alan has subsequently written a marvellous book on 'the empire of tea'.[1] A fine writer and remarkable person, she won an Open Scholarship to

Oxford in the 1920s – an extraordinary achievement for a woman in those days, but one which her parents never told her about, so she spent nearly all her life as a 'Mem' on a tea plantation in Assam. But she did try to involve herself in the life of the plantation labourers – which explains in part why Alan became an anthropologist. So he collects everything on all these aspects of his life: rooms full of family memorabilia, but also a museum-full of objects made by the peoples of the area: the Nagas and other Assamese peoples, plus a library of thousands of books on everything from the philosophy of the social sciences to his long engagement with Asia, firstly with Nepal, from which he was ultimately driven out by Maoist guerrillas, to an obsession with Asian culture and society.

My life was very different and took me to quite other places. I started my adult life as an undergraduate at Cambridge when Nazi invasion seemed imminent. This made me into what others came to regard as a Dangerous Red; then (despite this Redness) into an officer in the African colonial forces during the Second World War; then into an anthropologist; then, in the McCarthy period, into a victim of that paranoia (none of which, however, landed me in prison or caused me actual physical grief); finally to a Professorship at a fine university, Manchester, and then to a lengthy involvement in the Americas.

An ethnography of what Merseyside was like in the 1930s would only interest people who want to find out about that place and time, or to indulge in nostalgia. I am more interested in writing an account of what the French call the *formation* of one particular person. But I do try to show how that formation – as for anyone else – is the outcome of one's social context: in my case, growing up in a world seaport on the brink of a world war. And I try to adumbrate how it was that a Merseyside schoolboy became an anthropologist though, unlike Alan, I had no direct contact with the Third World.

Acknowledgements

Mervyn Jones and John Saville, fresh from writing their own memoirs, suggested I write mine, but I didn't respond for many years. However, I did eventually react to the rationale they provided: that it is the Great and the Good of the Establishment who write their memoirs, and – 'oral history' apart – ordinary folk don't. Nor does a minority like left-wing academics. So I gave in in the end.

The title was influenced, verbally, by Dirk Bogarde's *A Postillion Struck by Chain Lightning*, and visually by Sir Henry Raeburn's painting in the National Gallery of Scotland of *The Reverend Dr Robert Walker Skating on Duddingston Loch*, a picture which has always haunted me and so many people because he seems to glide on, serene and confident that he will come through safely, though there must have been dangerous patches in the ice all round him. There were dangerous patches in my life too, though I never went looking for trouble – as war-photographers do. Like any sensible person, I knew there wasn't much you could do about the worst things, and I did try to stop them happening to myself and to others. But I also tried to confront, intellectually, why such things happened – which is why I became an academic.

Avoidance, a favourite anthropological topic, is one, universal way of coping with trouble. But, while an Englishman may find the relationship with his mother-in-law difficult, it is not as serious as the mother-in-law avoidance described by one anthropologist who saw a grown man hanging by his wrists over the edge of a steep mountain path rather than come face to face with his wife's mother. So I have only deliberately left out a few things that, while very important to me personally, might hurt or embarrass people dear to me and who are still alive. My sex life may have started late, but it didn't cease as early as this manuscript might seem to imply. I have also omitted one or two things that might invite trouble from people I know to be litigious.

My practical thanks are due to Juliet Webster, Marika Sherwood, Paul Baxter, John Barnes, Martin Walsh, Eduardo Archetti, Len Goldstein, Kevin Morgan, Robert Poller and Bruce Kapferer, and to the greatest guidebook ever written, *The South American Handbook* (Trade and Travel Publications, Bath).

CHAPTER 1

Liverpool, My World

I grew up in Wallasey, Cheshire, in a middle-class environment. Liverpool, I ought to point out, is a shorthand for Merseyside; only, part of it. The south of the Mersey river, though economically dominated by Liverpool, is part of the Wirral, that quadrilateral bit of Cheshire which sticks out into the Irish Sea.

Liverpool might have been the greatest seaport in Europe, but its hegemony had always been challenged; initially by other new industrial cities, notably Manchester and Bristol. One cultural outcome was the rivalry between Manchester United (and even Manchester City), on the one hand, and Liverpool (and even Everton) on the other. More seriously, Manchester was the 'cottonopolis' of the world. But in the later nineteenth century a new threat to Liverpool developed in its very heartland, the Mersey itself, when an insignificant-looking cutting near Ellesmere Port, on the south side of the river, became the Manchester Ship Canal, the outlet for the huge new Trafford Park industrial engineering estate in Manchester. Liverpool, however, was predominantly a commercial centre; there were 'Manchester men' and 'Liverpool gentlemen'.

The south side of the river then developed its own industry, inevitably based on tropical products, in the shape of Port Sunlight – which was not just a huge factory, using palm oil from West Africa to make Sunlight Soap and margarine, but a whole new paternalistic planned town with its own superb Lever Art Gallery, similar to the model estates developed by the Quakers at New Earswick, outside York (Cadburys), and by the Frys at Bournville, in the Birmingham conurbation. The competition with Liverpool increased when the south bank became a centre for the production of Vauxhall cars, rivalling Fords at Halewood on the Liverpool side.

Shipbuilding on Merseyside had been the first major industry south of the river, at Birkenhead, where I was born. In 1801, it had been pure countryside, with only one hundred inhabitants. A couple of generations later, it had grown to 45,000. It was a pioneering model of gridiron city planning (like Middlesborough, another planned industrial city), with the first street tramway in the country, and with Hamilton Square, where my father had his last business, at its heart. When Frederick Olmsted visited it from the

United States in 1850, he was deeply impressed by the civic splendour of Birkenhead Park, modelled on Princes Park and its Palm House in Liverpool, both of which had been built by Joseph Paxton. In Birkenhead Park, he declared, 'gardening has reached a perfection that I had never before dreamed of'. Not only did he revisit it again eight years later but took it as the model for his subsequent design of Manhattan's Central Park in New York City.[2] By the turn of the century, Harold Rathbone, scion of the great Liverpool Unitarian philanthropist, had developed his ceramic business, making the celebrated Birkenhead Della Robbia pottery (at the corner of Hamilton Square where my father had his last business), which he sold to Paderewski and Sara Bernhardt, but mainly to the business class which migrated across the Mersey to the new and more salubrious surroundings of Birkenhead Park.[3]

By my time, though, apart from the area round the Park, Birkenhead had become a predominantly proletarian city, dominated by Cammell Laird's shipyards (where the *Ark Royal* was eventually built). We rented a house on the less prestigious side of the Park. It was respectable enough, but as my father's business prospered – firstly, as an auctioneer, then as an estate agent – we moved to the adjoining, more unambiguously middle-class town of Wallasey: more specifically, to New Brighton, right near the seaside.

Up to the nineteenth century, that part of the river had been dominated by harbour defence – by the magazine near Vale Park where gunpowder for the ships was stored, but above all by the huge, thick walls of Perch Rock Battery (still there), where firstly cannons, then big guns controlled the harbour entrance.

Then came recreational development, as the ferry disgorged thousands of the despised 'trippers', who came with buckets and spades from Liverpool to New Brighton Pier, not for work but to seek fresh air and beaches. Right by the Pier was the huge Tower Amusement Park, which attempted to emulate Blackpool. By the 1930s, the promenade had been extended right up to Harrison Drive, where the Irish Sea began. We called it the 'front' – a word foreigners don't know.

Trippers could drink beer, dance, have tea or sit on deckchairs and watch the Pierrots, and the children could ride donkeys. On the Pier, we had contracts which allowed us to go as often as we liked to hear the same acts – tenors singing the joys of the gypsy life on the open road; little soubrettes; magicians and acrobats; comedians like Billy Leo and Kathleen Hesketh, whose jokes we never tired of, even for the umpteenth time. The smart item for men to wear as they strolled along the front was the straw boater. One bizarre game we children had was to lick our right thumb and plant it on the palm of the opposing hand every time we saw a straw boater, to see who got the most. We also collected old wooden spoons used for cardboard tubs of ice cream. And if you were really lucky, you could walk up to any man and challenge him: 'You are Lobby Lud', whereupon – if you were right – the newspaper which sponsored him would give you a money prize.

It was a wonderful life for a child. We had beaches and a park two blocks away from our house. We could roller skate along the huge prom, row in the Marine Lake and catch crabs with fish-heads bought for a penny. We could witness national and even international happenings: the arrival of the *Graf Zeppelin*, and the passage overhead of the British airship, the *R101*, which crashed in France the next day; the launching of the *Ark Royal*; the opening by the King and Queen of the Mersey Tunnel; or the tragic sight of the submarine *Thetis* sticking up out of the sea, with the bodies of dozens of men still on board her.

Near the Pier was the large, elegant park and entertainment area around the Floral Pavilion, where Frank A. Terry put on shows which were much more lavish than those on the Pier. Then, in the mid-1930s, Wallasey Corporation extended massive seafront walls right up to Harrison Drive, to make a new 'front', with seating and shelters, but looking inland, so that the beaches could no longer be seen. Fooling around with my friend on bikes, I chipped my front teeth on the new concrete. The dentist said they would rot, but they never did. There were new tennis and 'pitch-and-putt' courses. (In the process, they also destroyed our beloved 'Red Noses', small sandstone cliffs where I jumped off and bit through my tongue, sobbing homewards with blood pouring out of my mouth.)

But the heart of the new expansion was the New Brighton Baths, the second largest in Europe, which staged marvellous national-level swimming and diving competitions. (It's now a hole in the ground.)

As the family business prospered, we stopped renting and moved upmarket to a newbuild private housing development on Claremount Road. By 1938, my father could even afford a large, second-hand, square-shaped, Al Capone-type Oakland car, and we all went to the Boulevard Haussmann in Paris for a holiday. We also rented a chalet from the Corporation at Harrison Drive, right on the beach, where we had a marvellous collective life with lots of other children, and saw swimmers stricken with cramps carried in; we attributed it, though, to the red jellyfish we called 'bloodsuckers'.

But the family business was still in proletarian Birkenhead. So, moving between home in Wallasey and my father's salerooms in Birkenhead, I was very conscious of poverty in Birkenhead. One man stood outside the salerooms in Conway Street selling matches from a little tray slung round his neck, with his medals on his chest, and a notice saying 'Blinded at the Somme'. My father himself had been an infantry officer in the First World War. When he was wounded by a shell, he transferred to the Royal Flying Corps, which took him and his Sopwith Camel to Egypt. Like nearly all men who lived through the trenches, he never talked about it. He kept his .45 revolver, though, which I played with for hours, though I was hardly strong enough to squeeze the trigger. He even had some bullets, which he eventually threw down a grid in the street when an arms amnesty was announced. One night a ghost dressed in a white sheet came into my bedroom through the window, and made straight for the drawer where the gun was kept. I fled, howling, to my parents' bedroom; luckily, he never came back.

Wallasey was 'nice' – another all-embracing English word foreign speakers of the language never seem to acquire (apart from Borat). Birkenhead was poor. Today, my grandchildren only know about poverty from TV documentaries about Victorian times. When I asked my grand-daughter, six-year-old Laura, whether she would have liked to have lived in those days, she replied, like a flash, 'No!' When I asked why, she shot back, 'No Play Station – poor!'

Liverpool had been a singularly violent city, like Glasgow, and for the same reasons – ethnic conflict and class struggle. During the Police Strike of 1919 (for up to then, the police could join a trade union), the power and the authority of the State was so severely challenged – not just by the poor but by those who were supposed to keep the poor under control – that the battleship *Valiant* and the destroyers *Venomous* and *Whitley* turned their guns towards the city. During the Depression of the 1930s, the city's poverty fuelled another climacteric as pitched battles broke out between the police and the unemployed.

So, middle-class or not, one was aware of poverty and of ethnicity too, the division between Catholics and Protestants; and of the Irishness of that religious/national division. We had two magnificent cathedrals: Gilbert Scott's red sandstone masterpiece from 1904, and the riposte – the avant-garde Catholic cathedral dubbed by Scouse wits, 'Paddy's Wigwam', not finished until after the Second World War. Irish Catholicism had grown out of the centuries of brutal violence and rack-renting economic exploitation through which the 'Ascendancy' had suppressed the Irish peasantry (though I didn't know anything about all that then). The Merseyside Irish had flooded in with the Potato Famine, when one and a half million had died on the other side of the Irish Channel of hunger and fever, a history still embedded in the consciousness of their descendants. As middle-class boys, we were told to steer clear of the annual 'Whit Walks', separate processions of the Protestants and Catholics, even from 'ours', because, we were told, bricks could be thrown. (We also had to remember to raise our caps when we passed a Catholic Church.) By the 1950s, in Manchester, when I finally saw them from my window in the university in Oxford Road, Manchester, the Whit Walks had become sedate affairs.

Catholicism on Merseyside was, in fact, Puritanism – a rigid cultural resistance which had marked off the culture of the Irish peasantry from that of their rulers. The most shocking sin, for a Catholic boy, I eventually found out, was nothing to do with politics, or religion. When, later, my father mercifully allowed me to change from a Catholic to a Protestant school, in return I was made to attend Sunday morning classes run by the local nuns, together with other boys from 'mixed marriages'. Their main preoccupation was with something called 'concupiscence'. It was something so horrible that we never dared ask what it was.

I was only able to talk to my sister at playtime across the fence dividing the girls' playground from the boys'. The only thing I remember actually learning in two years at my Catholic primary school was knitting, and how to make decorations from raffia and cardboard milk-bottle tops. A lively scamp called Gilbert Gore was expelled – from year two primary school! – for the crime of scrumping vegetables from a greengrocer's shop.

My parents' marriage was 'mixed' both in religious and ethnic terms, because my mother's father was a very English Protestant immigrant to Merseyside from Northamptonshire, but her mother the daughter of a Greek family which made its money in Liverpool supplying other Greek immigrants en route to the US with whatever they needed. The result was that my grandmother, according to legend, spent Friday night counting the gold sovereigns in her pinafore. But I nevertheless thought of myself, and all of us, as thoroughly English (not 'British'; we didn't use that category much then, despite the presence of so many Irish and people from North Wales, which, I am sure, explains why Liverpool has its unique 'Scouse' accent, an amalgam of all these, plus Lancastrian dialect). There was a Worsley family in Yorkshire which produced a Lord

Lieutenant and gave a daughter in marriage to the royal family. And there is a place called Worsley on the fringe of Manchester, from whence came, possibly, the knight, Ralph Worsley, who secularised (stole) lands on the Wirral – including Birkenhead Priory, where the monks had operated the first ferry – and took the title of Lord of the Manor of Claughton.

But we were very humble Worsleys. Though my grandmother was the daughter of a Greek woman from Salonika, we never had anything at all to do with the Greek community. The only family connection ever mentioned was with an important Greek figure, Bishop Papandreou (her family name), an oil-painting of whom hangs in the Greek Orthodox Church near Toxteth. Apart from spoiling me with 'Turkish' Delight and olives, I knew nothing of Greek culture, though she did teach me that people with dark eyes and olive skins (for example, gypsies!) were beautiful. Despite my mother's non-Catholicism, on her marriage to my father, there was no question of her being allowed to retain either her father's Protestantism or her mother's Greekness. Most importantly, she had to give up non-Catholic birth control practices, and was constantly pressurised to join in what, I later found, Québecois called 'la lutte des berceaux', to keep up the numbers of the Catholic population. This left her with plenty of suppressed dissent, though in fact, like many Catholic mothers, she was only to have two children.

But the dividing lines between Protestant and Catholic were by no means absolute. For all the efforts of the priests, there were lots of 'mixed' marriages. My father's mother, for example, was of Ulster Protestant origins and had been forced to convert on marriage (and became a singularly bigoted Catholic), while somewhere along the Irish lines of descent were Catholic forebears as well.

After Catholic primary school, in Wallasey, I was sent to Saint Francis Xavier's College (SFX) in Liverpool, which involved a huge disruption in my hitherto routine life. Now I had to go on an arduous three-stage journey (I was only seven) – firstly by bus from New Brighton to Seacombe Ferry, then onto the famous 'ferry 'cross the Mersey'. There were actually many ferries, bringing thousands of clerks and businessmen from middle-class, residential areas south of the river, and thousands of women, some secretaries, but, mostly office-cleaners – from Rock Ferry, Seacombe, Egremont and New Brighton. In winter, you could keep warm in the enclosed saloon if you could find room; in summer, most people, generally on their way to the city's offices in bowler hats, preferred to walk round the open deck in a ritual anti-clockwise direction for exercise. The ferries took only ten minutes, so the lives of all of us were controlled by the huge clock on the front of the Liver Building with its bird emblems of the city. Together with the Cunard Building, and the Mersey Docks and Harbour Board Building, the waterfront is now a UNESCO World Heritage Site.

They were statements not of direct political imperial power, such as government offices, but of commercial empire, the direct evidence for which was before your eyes – the wonderful ships in the harbour, particularly the beautiful passenger liners shuttling between Liverpool and New York and to the River Plate: the *Georgic*, the *Brittanic* and the *Reina del Pacífico*, sometimes even one of the *Queens*. (Spanish was widely taught in school, in addition to French and German, because it was used in commercial offices.)

There were also the red and white Isle of Man boats, the ferries to Holyhead in North Wales and across the Irish Sea to Dun Laoghaire (then called just 'Dublin'). Any of these journeys could be as bad as any I have subsequently known (including the 'romantic' Mediterranean). Behind the Cunard Building, across the road, big iron rings were let into the pavement, which some people said were slave-rings. I thought they were probably mooring rings for ships, when the riverbank had been much further back from the river. But when I looked in the Victoria County History after the War I could find virtually nothing about Liverpool's involvement in the slave trade. I did eventually find out that Gorée was a small island near Dakar, in modern Senegal, where slaves were kept in holding pens until the time came to funnel them through the 'Door of No Return' into the ships waiting to take them to the plantations of the New World. Their Afro-American descendents visit the House of Slaves, now a UNESCO World Heritage Site, and weep.

A half-century had to pass before the truth finally emerged in books. Today, the Maritime Archives and Library at Liverpool forthrightly acknowledges that 'during the 18th century Liverpool was Britain's main slaving port'.[4] Yet there weren't that many slaves actually in Liverpool, apart from 'trophy' boys dressed in turbans as domestic servants, because Liverpool was part of a 'triangular' trade: the 'Great Circuit', in which merchants bartered for slaves in West Africa with alcohol, beads and cowrie shells; the Africans were then taken, under appalling conditions, to the sugar plantations of the West Indies and the southern states of America (merchants also exported firearms and textiles); while the products of the plantations – sugar, coffee, cocoa, cotton, tobacco and wood –

came back to England. Tate and Lyle's huge sugar factory near the Liver Buildings was the end product. By the end of the eighteenth century trade with the West Indies was four times greater than Britain's trade with the rest of the world. 'Almost every man in Liverpool', it was claimed, 'is a merchant, and he who cannot send a bale will send a band-box.'[5] Yet in *Redburn*, Herman Melville's novel about his maiden voyage from New York to 'the greatest port in the world', he compared the city with Calcutta: 'poverty, poverty, poverty, in almost endless vistas' with people dying on the streets from hunger.

One legacy of this worldwide trade was the presence of many Lascars, plus the restaurants of Liverpool's Chinatown. Most Chinese, however, were laundry workers: our laundry was always done by Mr Wu. At the bottom of the caste hierarchy were the blacks, who survived by self-help and the generosity of a few heroic souls like the Nigerian, Daniels Ekarté, who had arrived from Calabar in the 1930s and was shocked to see the conditions under which not only black people but their white neighbours too were living. With help from the Church of Scotland, he set up an African Churches Mission in Toxteth, the heart of Docklands, with a few beds for the homeless, affordable meals, space for a Mothers' Union and Scouts to meet after school classes, and a small chapel.[6] For black sailors with money to spend, it could be different. 'The Negro', Melville remarks, 'walks with a prouder pace and lifts his head like a man.' He encountered the black steward from his ship 'dressed very handsomely, walking arm in arm with a good-looking Englishwoman'. 'In New York', he remarks, 'they would have been lucky to escape with whole limbs.'

When the gangway came down to let us onto the landing stage, we boys used to shout, 'Mind your big feet!', and scamper ahead of the adults up the road-pontoon to the Pier Head, which could be very steep, as the pontoons rose and fell with the height of the tide; then up Dale Street on the clanking, interminable tram to SFX in Mount Pleasant. We had to hurry – it was all too easy to miss the vital connection and therefore be late for school.

The punishment was to be beaten on the hand (six or twelve times) with a whalebone 'ferrule', rather like a long shoehorn. It was very painful. But the moral tortuousness of the Jesuits went further than their physical brutality. If you did *good* work (e.g. homework), you would be given a Red Bill. This was printed in Latin (of course), on red parchment, and headed 'A.M.D.G' ('To the Greater Glory of God'). It had a numerical value, usually six or twelve. The idea was that you could use it to cancel punishment with the ferrule. But, being Jesuits, you never knew whether they would accept the Red Bill or not. You might still get beaten anyhow. Even at that young age, I thought this was quite immoral: if you deserved punishment, you deserved punishment. But to be completely uncertain whether you would be punished or not was a situation of total moral indeterminacy. So the Jesuits taught me to work out my own ethical principles – which were anything but theirs.

My more unfortunate sister fell into the hands of the nuns, and never escaped. At her convent school she received the non-education appropriate for girls. Even for boys, Catholic education on Merseyside, even at secondary level, was dire.

The religious pressures in SFX didn't stop with the end of the school day. Rather, they became even more intense, for we were expected to stay after school to attend 'sodalities' devoted to the Virgin, or some other religious devotion, a couple of times a week. And to bring pennies too. My mother was very sarcastic about the constant demand for pennies.

The end of the day, though, ultimately brought liberation. We could go to a small shop near school to buy gobstoppers, though the poor children from the neighbourhood couldn't afford even the cheaper sweets. They didn't have any shoes either, even in mid-winter. But whereas, coming to school, we suffered the ordeal of running a hazardous gauntlet, with three precarious connections, we could now stroll back home through Liverpool's splendid civic centre, past the Walker Art Gallery with its memorable painting about the Civil War, 'When did you last see your Father?'; the Picton Library; then into the wonderful museum and the aquarium, where we found Indian totem poles, Japanese giant spider-crabs and Napoleonic memorabilia. I am sure this opened up my anthropological imagination. There was also Strothers wonderful music shop, where, later, I could listen to five jazz records whilst buying only one.

Socially, we lived among mainly lower middle-class business-people and professionals. My father shared their anti-Semitic prejudices, and on his deathbed was terrified because he had a black nurse – a 'darkie'. But Liverpool whites were no Heinrich Himmlers. Theirs was what has been called 'casual racism', like that of my highly-educated neighbour who informed me recently that the people who had bought the house nearby 'had their Sabbath on Saturdays'. My parents would socialise with Jewish families of the right social class, and were not averse to my flirting with the daughter of a fashionable Jewish doctor. Class was more important; Jews were an insignificant minority. It was much more important for my mother and her friends to eradicate the Liverpool accents in their children so that they did not sound like 'wackers'. So I and my sister were sent to elocution lessons: Kipling's 'If', Masefield's 'Cargoes'. It worked: we lost our accents, and it took many years before I lost my own dislike of the Liverpool accent. And in the evenings, the children were made to perform – reciting poems; playing, as I did, on expensive pianos; and the girls doing their ballet steps. To keep us competitive, we all took our piano Associated Board exams.

The presence of my grandfather, retired from the sea, in the house was a great joy. Away on voyages to Yokohama, he had never known which house he would be coming back to, because his wife was always selling the one he had last seen. Now he lived with us, and we did the *Daily Telegraph* crossword together, played chess and double patience, and competed to see who could do the wooden jigsaw of the 'Cornish Riviera Express' the fastest (fourteen minutes was the record). He had an irritating habit, though, of getting up early to filch the weekly copy of *The Wizard*, my favourite boys' magazine, before I could get at it. Sometimes we played Crown Green bowls on the 'front', where he used to take his daily constitutional, sweeping the 'damned dogs' out of the way with his stick.

So our house always had unusual things in it: huge white Indian bath-towels with the traditional blue stripe through them, waxed umbrellas, ceramic plates and cloisonné ware from China and Japan. This gave me – as with so many youngsters on Merseyside – an awareness of the exotic Orient, like the hero of the wonderful *Marius* film trilogy of Marseilles, another world port, in France in the 1930s.

The reality had been very different. 'Pops', my grandfather, had started working on a ship at the age of fifteen, climbing the mast to furl and unfurl sails in gigantic, freezing storms round the Horn. Food was so bad (ship's tack and bully beef mainly) that everyone had boils, which were dealt with by dropping a match into an empty bottle of rum, the vacuum from which sucked out the pus. A lecturer in maritime studies from Cardiff University later gave a talk I cannot forget – the crews, even in the 1950s, were often on the run, whether from girlfriends they had got pregnant, or from the police. When they got to New York or Singapore, they had to turn round in a day or so, and saw nothing of those cities. Full of guilt for having abandoned their families, they bought their children very expensive presents. When they came home, the same children often didn't know them, nor did the presents from a father they didn't know mean very much. But my grandfather had been more fortunate: he ended up as a ship's purser (finance officer), and helped with a share of the mortgage for the new house which my parents would not have been able to afford on their own.

The strain of the SFX regime, and the travelling, took its toll on me. I was often ill. My mother never went out to work, except when she was conscripted as a nurse at Arrowe Park Hospital, and went through agonies attending to the appalling wounds of the men under her care. But she now took the decisive step: I was to go to school on the Cheshire side of the river, nearer home. My father, to his great credit, though scrupulously loyal in his own religious observances, and in seeing to it that we too went to church, was most liberal in his other social attitudes (he was well known enough for the *Liverpool Echo* to publish a cartoon of him, which I still have, typically raising money at an auction for the British Legion ex-service charity, the climax of the performance being the auctioning of a potty for hundreds of pounds). He now gave in to my mother, though it entailed sending me to a Protestant school. At last I could get a decent education.

The school to which I escaped, Wallasey Grammar, was a member of the Headmasters' Conference, and therefore technically a 'Public' School, but it was light-years removed from Eton or Harrow. I was tested by the Headmaster, who found that I was three years ahead in Latin (his subject), and three years behind in mathematics – a shortcoming which has dogged me ever since. The Latin, though, was necessary if you wanted to go to Oxford or Cambridge, which required that you pass a (very easy) Latin paper to enter those universities. (Only in 2004 did all but one Examining Board remove Latin from the list of subjects which they examined for university entrance.) The Grammar School was an excellent, liberal, local grammar school of the day, with inspiring masters – every bit as important in one's life as later university teachers – who first set me on the path to enlightenment: Mr Moscrop; Mr Miller (what a world he opened up in *The Canterbury Tales*, which is still at my bedside); Mr Browning, who traced the story of British and German imperialism; Mr Eggleston, who taught Physical Education (PE) and was a great authority on classical music, even such wild modernism as William Walton; and the highly unconventional Paul Ellison, who invited us round to listen to gramophone records (78s) of Alice Faye, played Elizabethan virginal music on the school Hammond organ, and scandalised our parents by escorting the most passionately admired girl in the neighbourhood to the School Sports Day. He later joined the Birmingham Rep and went off to Hollywood. More importantly, he turned me into a Leavisite, which possibly made me a more interesting applicant for admission to Cambridge than more orthodox would-be undergraduates.

My parents had nothing other than the standard middle-class ambitions for me. My father hoped I would follow his footsteps into his business. He was very proud of his own professional qualification as a Fellow of the Auctioneers' Institute, and always put 'FAI' after his name. But the idea of my going to university was never mooted. He only intervened once to further my career when he saw that I had an interest in and aptitude for something other than his own kind of business. He got me an interview with Ernie Prince, the renowned editor of the *Liverpool Echo*, who only had two questions for me: 'Can you type?' 'No', 'Can you take shorthand?' 'No'. The interview with this ill-equipped youngster was over. At this point, an assistant came in with the news that the first ferry-boat to cross the Mersey with the aid of radar had done so successfully. 'Heavens alive', he said, 'That's not news. Now if she had sunk ...'

I would probably have started behind the counter in a bank in Liverpool like my friend Arnold Curtis, whom I met years later in Shanghai, by which time he had become the head of the Midland Bank there. Only partly in jest, when anthropology had got us into a difficult situation, my wife would say, 'Why couldn't you have been a bank clerk?' My penchant for rather unconventional holidays could backfire too. Once, on an Irish caravan trip, when the horse started to slip backwards down a hill, she flung herself down, exhausted, at the side of the road, and expostulated, 'Why can't we go to Blackpool like everyone else?'

I never did well at sports, though I did win a cup as one of a doubles pair at tennis. I played our Headmaster at fives. But the prestigious, nay heroic, games, were Rugby and cricket. I did finally get into the First Rugby XV, and played a few undistinguished cricket matches in the First Eleven. This modest sports record didn't matter, however, because we could watch the best football team in Britain: Everton, when Dixie Dean scored more goals than will ever be scored again. Then came Tommy Lawton, and I also saw Alex James, in voluminous shorts, in Herbert Chapman's wonder Arsenal team. With some ninety thousand crammed into

Goodison Park, there was a real danger, especially for little boys, of a tragedy like that which killed scores of spectators at Hillsborough in Sheffield, waiting to happen. Eventually, my dad bought seats (what luxury!) for us both.

Mr Allan, my headmaster, had won an M.C. in the First World War (I later met him at the Officers' Club in Belgravia when I was myself a young subaltern). He used to take us for a 'free period', a wonderful hour every week, when we listened to talks on BBC wireless about all sorts of issues of the day. He also exposed us to his sensitive appreciation not only of the usual fine arts, such as music and painting, but of how to appreciate furniture. I also learned a vast amount from a set of seven encyclopaedias, and a volume of photographs of 'Wonders of the World', which my father had bought from a door-to-door salesman. I must have read every page several times – about Triceratops, the solar system, autogiros, anything. We also had a good school library which I used a lot, while Earlston Public Library was a goldmine. I read every one of Alexandre Dumas' novels, and a lot too about salvaging sunken ships: I don't know why – adventure, I suppose, and a Merseysider's pirate lust for gold doubloons. But in those days, our main boyish taste was for Tom Mix cowboy films (we nearly wrecked the cinemas) and, for a laugh, Laurel and Hardy and the Marx Brothers (I took my own grandson to see 'A Night at the Opera' only the other day). When I got a luxurious birthday present of an 8 mm black and white hand-cranked projector, I ran film shows of my three shorts for other boys (Clara Cluck, Pluto and Donald Duck in *Silly Symphonies*) even though these were silents. (I also threw in a three-minute newsreel of the Catholic Eucharistic Congress held in Australia which I had bought because it only cost four pence). The penny admission charge did not compensate my mother for the chewing gum ground into her new carpet. The great films – cowboys and musicals (Shirley Temple, Judy Garland and the Broadway Melodies) – all came from America. America represented the quintessence of modernity, even its rural life (the Hardy Family). We enjoyed Wallace Beery as Pancho Villa, though as Merseysiders we preferred him in films about life at sea – with Marie Dressler in *Tugboat Annie* – and, above all, as Long John Silver in *Treasure Island*. Henceforth, my grandfather was always 'Long John' and I was 'Jim lad'. The lure of exotic climes was as strong in Liverpool as it had been for Marius, who wanted to '*naviguer*' (to go to sea) – to Port Said, Aden, Macassar, Sydney. We watched films about Ali Baba and Aladdin, and read Scheherazade's magical stories about the gigantic Roc bird and the pearls to be found in the Indian Ocean. Other stories, written by white men in Christmas annuals for boys, contained a strong dose of racism and imperialism, like Indiana Jones films today. The hero was always a white man, who fought off savages and wily Orientals with his pistol. My favourite novel was R.M. Ballantine's *The Coral Island*, whose midshipman hero was Peterkin. Re-reading it as a grown-up, I found its pious sentimentality hard to take, but then even Robinson Crusoe is suffused with religiosity. In *The Wizard*, another brave white officer, on the North-West Frontier (up the Khyber), had a loyal native comrade-in-arms, a kind of stereotype of a Gurkha, equipped with an equally deadly weapon, 'Clicky Ba' (cricket bat), with which he cracked the skulls of the enemy. Men of my generation still remember Clicky Ba.

As a middle-class 'lady', with no educational qualifications, my mother never went out to work. Her great pleasure in life was to go to 'town' with me, across the Mersey, have morning tea at Reeces, then lunch at T.J. Hughes or 'the Bon' (Marché), then tea with wonderful waffles at Coopers, all interspersed with shopping. The purchases were wrapped up in brown paper and tied with string, but I was never allowed to carry a parcel; young gentlemen didn't do such a thing. They had to be delivered to our home. Given her immersion in fashion, my father eventually put money into a well-known millinery business on the condition that they gave her a job – which she loved. But when they asked him for more money, he couldn't produce it, so my mother's participation in the labour force came to an end.

My musical tastes broadened. My mother played the piano marvellously, mainly Noel Coward, waltzes from Viennese operettas, or 'White Horse Inn'. My father played a mean 'Kitten on the Keys'. I listened to Henry Hall's Dance Orchestra, Monday Night at Eight with Geraldo, Jack Payne, and even the avant-garde jazz of Joe Loss. From there I graduated to jazz proper via Glenn Miller through to swing with the big bands of Benny Goodman (and the wonderful Quartet), Artie Shaw, Woody Herman and Count Basie. I listened to New Orleans jazz – Jelly Roll, Armstrong – and the Chicagoans: Bix and Eddie Condon. One day, I decided there must be something in this classical music too, so I listened solidly to every programme on the wireless for a whole week. It was a Sibelius anniversary – not the easiest music to begin with – but he is still to this day my favourite. Then I started going to the loveliest concert hall in the world (and I've seen a lot), the Liverpool Philharmonic Hall.

Mr Allan turned out to be the only person who has ever administered physical punishment to me when some of us scribbled insulting remarks about our very nice German master – whom we called 'Krupp' (reflecting the anti-German sentiment of the interwar years, fuelled by the rise of Nazism) – all over a blackboard. I had to bend over and receive cuts from the cane. It isn't PC to say this now, and I've never laid a finger on either of my children, but it made me resolve not to invite any repetition of that experience.

The shadow of Germany was becoming visible in other ways. Mr Allan (who could hardly be accused of lacking patriotism) accepted a Jewish boy from Germany into the school, which was widely criticised, not so much because he was Jewish as because he was German. I later met him in an Officers' Club in India when he was one of the extremely few Germans who had been made officers in the British Army; indeed, few were accepted at any level – most became pick-and-shovel members of the Pioneer Corps. (An Israeli joke of the pioneer epoch has new immigrants passing bricks to each other, saying, 'Danke, Herr Doktor Professor', 'Bitte, Herr Doktor Professor'.) Mr Allan, a classic liberal if there ever was one, even established some 'exchange' arrangements with Germany.

But by 1938 I was helping my grandfather distribute gas masks in the local church tower. Of political note, too, were the activities of 'Dozy' Dorman, an Irish Nationalist boy who burned a Union Jack on the back pitch. I was naïve, and 'oppositional' enough, to ask why it was right for us to have colonies but not the Germans.

When we went to France on holiday in 1938, I had no idea that I wouldn't see it again for eight years. My father was liberal enough to take me and my sister (fourteen and twelve), to see the naked showgirls at the Bal Tabarin. I had enough French to ask for a cab, which, they had taught us at school, was a *fiacre*, but it turned out to be a 'taxi', as in English. Apart from some chat with taxi drivers about M. Chamberlain's umbrella, I found out nothing about French society or political life. When we visited Versailles, we encountered a park-keeper/policeman, badly 'mutilé de guerre', in the company of some people who, by coincidence, lived five houses away in our road in Wallasey. They were all later killed by a landmine during an air raid. Our hotel was broken into one night, and my mother's Persian lamb coat stolen. Somehow, she bought a new and better one and marched through British Customs without paying a penny in duty.

Our next family holiday was very different. People from Merseyside often holidayed in North Wales (close enough for the mountain of Moel Famau to be seen from Birkenhead), especially once the Tunnel was opened, in downmarket Rhyl or more upmarket Llandudno or Colwyn Bay, or to Prestatyn with its beautiful Art Deco swimming pool (where we went). With war in sight, we spent the 1939 holiday in a bed and breakfast in a North Wales village (where our host's favourite occupation was poaching rabbits at night).

There, I listened to Mr Chamberlain's broadcast telling us that Britain was at war with Germany. Everyone was convinced that Merseyside would be gassed and bombed, so we were to stay in Glynceiriog (where my friend, Ronald Frankenberg later wrote a famous study, about which I ungraciously, in a hard Marxist phase, told him was not what he should have written). Life, from then onwards, would be measured out in periods of a few months, often merely weeks – at university, in the army, and in my first and only non-academic employment, in Africa.

I went to school fourteen miles away, which involved more bus journeys, or else trips on my bike, with my fingers virtually frozen to the handlebars in winter. But the road took me to another great school, Llangollen Grammar. What was *really* great about it was that there were *girls*. Before long, I had a sweetheart (not, as now, a 'girlfriend'). I had the joy of sitting next to her, even having to kiss her – paralysed with embarrassment – in a school Priestley play. Yet on the only evening we ever spent together, we didn't end up in bed, but went to the pictures and had fish and chips. After an hour, I finally got round to a fumbled peck on the cheek. How sexual behaviour has changed! But I was leaving the Glyn, and going back to Merseyside. I cycled the fourteen miles back home, from the beautiful Vale of Llangollen, elated but with tears in my eyes. It was worth every yard. I was never to see her again.

I had read that upper-class boys who went to Public Schools were locked into a masculine world, where school was followed by (masculine) university, then perhaps the army or clerical life, and that their social life outside these institutions was spent in (masculine) clubs. After the relative sexual liberation of Llangollen, I little realised that I too was to be similarly locked into a masculine world for the next six years.

I also did not know that for all those years I would hardly ever be at home: firstly, because of university, then the army. I often didn't see my family for months, and, once abroad, for years. I did not even get to my beloved grandfather's funeral.

At Llangollen, we had another set of wonderful teachers, including a lesbian couple (we didn't realise they were) who became our great friends. One of them collected Japanese netsuke; the other made me translate, *into Latin*, one of Chamberlain's speeches, which involved inventing Latin equivalents for 'degaussing girdles' (electric cabling which protected ships against magnetic mines) and the 'Russians', whom I designated the 'Scythii'.

But, by the spring of 1940, Liverpool had not been bombed and gassed, so we went home – just when the War ceased being 'phoney', in time for the beginning of the blitz. One day I cycled to school and from a hill saw things sticking up in the river – ships sunk in the night. Seacombe Ferry was blocked by a sunken ferry-boat which stayed there for ages. Our middle-class area was by no means spared the bombs. The streets were full of unexploded incendiary bombs, ack-ack shrapnel, bomb splinters, and rubble. I never saw any corpses, but there were thousands, and we spent night after night in the shelter, surrounded by hysterical women (men kept stiff upper lips). The worst, though, was listening to appalling banshee wails which people insisted were caused by German pilots throwing empty beer-bottles out of their cockpits. My father was blown off his feet coming out of the pub in Wallasey Village. So, like lots of other people, we sought refuge with friends outside the bombing zone, in Hoylake, hitching lifts on milk lorries or anything else. Things got worse, until, eventually, the back of our house was blown off.

Spending hours tired out after a night's bombing, and days punctuated by false air-raid alarms in the school shelters on the back pitch were not optimal conditions for studying for university entrance examinations. My career at the Grammar School was by no means a story of progress anyhow. I had been put in the third of four Lower Fifth classes on arrival; did well enough to be put into Middle Fifth B the following year, but found the going too hard. I was reduced to tears by a very simple task in long division, because the Catholic school had taught me one way of doing it and the Protestant school another way. No one could help me, including my parents, though they did pay for extra private maths tuition, one hour a week, which did no good at all. I was put down to MVC, where I did well in Arts subjects, but not in maths, chemistry, physics or biology. So the next year, I was demoted to UVD (I think there was an even lower class.) In my School Certificate, I did badly at trigonometry, geometry and algebra. But eventually I did become Head Boy, other rivals having already gone off to the war. Even so, we Catholic boys did not attend the school's morning assembly, but went with the Jewish boys into a side room off the Hall, where we did our homework and told dirty jokes.

The Jewish boys' jokes were particularly sophisticated. The best one was of two travellers on the Trans-Siberian Railway. The train rattles to a halt, so the man asks, 'Where are we?' and the girl replies, 'Omsk'. They travel on for another couple of days, and then the train stops again. 'Where are we now?' he asks. 'Tomsk', was the answer. The train rattles on for two more days, and halts once more. 'And where are we now?' the man asks. 'Vladivostok', she replies. 'Enough of this prevarication', he exclaims. 'Take your knickers off!!'

We Catholics and Jews were finally allowed to enter the main hall after the religious bit, and stood along the side of the Hall, the Head Boy (me) among them. Despite these religious divisions, there was tremendous solidarity, especially at the end-of-term sing-songs by the whole school, not of public-school-style anthems about loyalty to the school but traditional popular songs like 'Ilkley Moor Baht At'.

When I finally got my School Certificate, scraping through even in maths, I could at last shed both maths and the natural sciences altogether. From then on, I never looked back.

The bombing became so bad that my mother and sister lived permanently with friends outside Wallasey, while my father and I stayed at Claremount Road. Finally, I was taken in by my uncle in Birkenhead (odd, because it was near Wallasey Docks, a bombing zone).

It was Mr Allan, a Cambridge graduate from Emmanuel College, who first mooted the idea of entering for an examination for entry to his College. Such a thought would never have crossed anyone else's mind, certainly not mine. If we aspired to go to university at all, it would have been to our local university, Liverpool. But some of the better schools in the north used to act as 'feeders' to Cambridge Colleges (much as lower Division football clubs 'feed' the Premiership clubs), so I was duly entered for Cambridge exams for Scholarships and Exhibitions (like junior scholarships) for the set of Colleges which included Emmanuel.

On the first attempt, in December 1940, I didn't get in. At my second attempt, a year later, I had already passed my Higher School Certificate very well, which entitled me to a Wallasey Borough Scholarship. At the annual Prize Days in Wallasey Town Hall I always got a Book Prize or two. One I chose was D.H. Lawrence's

Lady Chatterley's Lover, so heavily expurgated that it was nigh incomprehensible.

In the December of 1941, I went in again for the Cambridge exam and was awarded an Open Exhibition. Even taken together, though, the Exhibition and the Wallasey Scholarship by no means met the cost of my fees and living expenses, so my father had to pay the rest. He was very proud of me, while my bookmaker uncle Gil used to give me a big black and white five-pound note every year. He also gave me the benefit of his life-experience: 'Peter, I'm a rich man – because bookmakers always win. Never take up betting!' I never did.

CHAPTER 2
Cambridge and the Army

In January 1942, I took the train to Cambridge for the third time, this time, however, to stay for the whole academic year as an undergraduate. I can still remember the names of the stations the porters called out along the interminable route after leaving the main line at Bletchley (oddly enough, the jumping-off station for Oxford too): 'Woburn Sands!' 'Gamlingay!' 'Sandy!' 'Bedford!'.

The first sign that the War had caught up with Cambridge came straight away. No longer was there the prospect of three years of study. We had to join the Cambridge University Training Corps, which involved elementary infantry training on Saturday mornings, resulting in 'Certificate A', and a longer course in the summer vacation (I opted for the Royal Artillery) resulting in 'Certificate B'. You also had to sign up for the Army proper (I took the King's shilling on a fateful visit to Chester with my mother). You were then given one year before you were called up.

My college was Emmanuel. New students ('undergraduates' – you had to learn this language) were put in lodgings near the College for the first year, but had lunch and dinner with their seniors in the Hall, and it was exciting to be surrounded by hundreds of bright young people, some of them from countries I had never had any contact with.

There were lots of people outside College too, because the College, being residential, cuts across the teaching structure, which is run by the University, and takes place in lecture rooms outside the College. Being in College also has the advantage of bringing you into contact with people who are studying ('reading') quite different subjects, and there really is a collegial *esprit* which derives from living together, expressed by proudly wearing the College scarf. One is supposed to say that this promoted interchange between the disciplines, especially between the Sciences and the Arts subjects. I can't say I ever found this. I read English, because, like everyone else, I'd been taught it so well at school, and also greatly enjoyed it.

In the second year, you moved into College, and life became much richer. The only approximation to intellectual intercourse, though, was through meeting other individuals, and from the many voluntary associations in the College – 'clubs' and societies for everything from sports to film shows. Our Film Society even succeeded in electing Ginger Rogers as Honorary President.

The only other social institution with any pretensions to intellectual aims was the Junior Common Room (JCR), open to all undergraduates, where there were newspapers and magazines, and, more importantly, that peculiarly English institution, the 'debate'. Most of this came from Public School models. Some of the debates were frivolous; some were not. We had a notorious left-wing West Indian don putting forward the motion for independence of the West Indies, and our reactionary Senior Tutor calling for the canonisation of Attila the Hun, or something similar. One of the major hazards of life was to get waylaid by him in the Front Quad, while he held forth, at considerable length, about the menace of the trade unions, the Labour Party and the Soviets. His only exiguous contribution to knowledge had been a slim volume on the Durham miners, the area from which he came.

There was also a leather-bound book in the JCR in which people wrote down anything that came into their heads – and utter drivel it mostly was. Some of it was mine, and, to my shame, is still there. It was a jejune flaunting of immature egos.

I had no problem with the Public School boys in College apart from some unreconstructed Hooray Henrys who aimed hoses from the College pond at our window when we invited some Girton women for a Socialist Club talk. (The man who did this was subsequently sent down for toting a gun.) But we were quite isolated once more from women; Girton was miles out, Newnham nearer. We had no contact with the women from the town. 'Town' and 'Gown' were two separate worlds. Luckily, two teacher training colleges had been evacuated to Cambridge, notably Homerton, and I soon had a girlfriend again. I courted her in the usual Cambridge way, mornings and afternoons at coffee shops, and at Friday night dances at the fashionable Dorothy restaurant. Eventually, I broached the subject of sex. It turned out that my predecessor had been captured at Singapore and that she was staying loyal to him. There was no answer to that, was there?

One only met females at lectures. We were policed closely: you had to be in by ten o'clock. Otherwise you could get in only by climbing the walls, which were spiked, or via secret, often perilous, windows. Outside the walls were Proctors – dons (teachers) on patrol, aided by proletarian 'bulldogs', who searched out undergraduates committing serious crimes like not wearing gowns or breaking the ten o'clock curfew hour. If caught, you were fined.

The teaching, I soon found, was abysmal. After our small classes at school, we were now lectured to in very large classes: a couple of hundred. As for the famous one-to-one tutorial system, the quality of this depended on who your tutor was. In any case, it was us who wrote the essays that we then discussed for the rest of the hour, once a week. Many of the younger dons were away on war duties. Those who carried on teaching were free to teach pretty well what they liked. There was no serious attempt to cover English literature as a whole, or even major parts of it. People taught minor eighteenth-century poets while no one was teaching the great Metaphysicals. The only substantial lectures I remember were by E.M.W. Tillyard on Milton. The renowned 'Dadie' Rylands lectured on Shakespeare, but really about producing Shakespeare on stage. My own tutor, H.S. Bennet, was an excellent social historian of Chaucer's England, but he didn't teach us about Chaucer's poetry. To alleviate the boredom, I went to the rooms of the celebrated 'Q' (Sir Arthur Quiller-Couch) in Jesus College at 9 A.M. on a Monday morning for lectures on Aristotle's *Poetics*, where, on freezing days, he offered us a snifter to fend off the Fens.

But the greatest scandal of the Cambridge English Department was that my tutor at Emmanuel strongly discouraged me from attending the lectures of F.R. Leavis, who was regarded as a maverick. I went anyhow, and found only a dozen other people there from the whole university. (After the War, things changed: there were hundreds.)

Cambridge, then, was immensely disappointing as far as academic teaching was concerned. I had learned far more from my two English teachers at school. So we taught ourselves. I did very well, with an Upper Second rating in the exams in the summer exams of 1941, after only two terms.

But, because of the War, it was a wildly exciting time to be 'up' at Cambridge. In my first few weeks, Tommy Beecham conducted the London Philharmonic in Delius' *Paris*; then I saw my first operas, when Sadler's Wells did *La Bohème* and *The Magic Flute* in one week. The New Theatre was also excellent, and two young men called Benjamin Britten and Peter Pears gave us *The Foggy Foggy Dew*. Times were hard for the musicians, though: Constant Lambert had to provide the music for the Ballet Rambert on a piano. The reason for all this was that the war had given a tremendous democratic stimulus to the arts. It seems hard to believe it now, but the great orchestras not only left London for 'the provinces' but actually went into the factories to play to the workers. The only equivalent now is the huge concerts in Hyde Park.

The really exciting ferment, though, was social and political life. Cambridge was fairly cosmopolitan. I met West African princes who introduced me to Beethoven piano concerti, and, in my Cert A squad, Y.C. Ma, the nephew of Chiang Kai-Shek. He was the worst soldier I ever met, but a lovely person. He introduced me to his friend Kenneth Lo, who became a diplomat at the Chinese Embassy in London, and later a top restaurateur. I could never forgive Ma, though, for inviting me to play tennis with Ken Lo without informing me that the latter had represented his country at that sport. It was a humiliating game; occasionally, I saw the ball. When Ma joined the exodus from the mainland to Taiwan, where he held a very high office in the National Bank, I cut off connections with him.

Cambridge University Socialist Club (CUSC) actually had over a thousand members, among them many Communists, in a university of some five thousand. The presence of evacuated students from the London School of Economics (LSE) was also a major stimulus to socialist activity. Norman Mackenzie, who later edited the *New Statesman*, was the leading LSE figure. LSE students attended the same lectures as ourselves, though we retained our separate organisational identities otherwise.

My religion didn't last long. I went to Mass once, and attended one meeting of the University Catholic Society. It was really only loyalty to my father that kept me in that long. In the vacation, my father sent me to see my uncle George, who had trained as a Jesuit in Rome, to try and save me – in vain. As we descended the stairs in his Vicarage, he cast his eyes up to a photo of the Pope on the wall, as if supplicating for help.

Before long, I was writing my first published work for the CUSC Bulletin: a review of *Gone with the Wind*. The next was an assignment to write a piece on the Allied invasion of North Africa. Before long, I joined the Communist Party. To recruit people who had doubts and resistances, they had an interesting, Jesuitical system called 'consulting with Lenin', which consisted of getting two case-hardened LSE Party members to work through those doubts. I envied them because they were studying the 'dream ticket' for lefties at that time – economics and Russian. My sticking point was the Soviet war against Finland.

The Communist Party wasn't like other political parties. You didn't just join, and have a card. You had to subscribe to a set of principles, and – more than that – had to work to implement them. You were required to sell the *Daily Worker*; to absorb and communicate the Party 'line' (policy) to others, especially non-Party members; attend meetings of all kinds, internal and external; and to carry out whatever other multifarious activities were required of you. The result was a formidable machine which coordinated the efforts of all its members. They all voted together (like, later, women's 'caucuses'). They therefore had a force which was far greater than the sum of the parts, which enabled them to dominate large bodies of more diffusely organised people (such as CUSC), not just because of their voting power, but because of their pushing of the same 'Party line' in argument.

Unlike bourgeois political parties, the Party also had much more than a mere programme. It had a distinctive, coherent ideology, called Marxism, which we were expected to come to terms with. To its opponents, this is usually presented simply as an intellectual straightjacket. One learned eventually that it wasn't as coherent as it was supposed to be, but even so it did encourage people to be critical and oppositional vis-à-vis the whole of the rest of 'bourgeois' ideology, which involved a lot of hard thinking – a mindset which would come to be applied more and more to the beliefs of Marxism itself.

You have to remember the situation in which we were operating: a fight to the death against Nazism. Not many of us were dying, but in the USSR they were. In May 1940, only a few months before, in my last term at school, Mr Ellison had come in one day and said: 'Boys, I shouldn't say this – and I could be put in gaol for doing so – but I think that before the end of the month the Germans will be here'.

And let me make one thing quite clear (since people always ask me): we'd never even heard of Guy Burgess and Donald Maclean. As at school, being one year senior or one year junior makes a massive difference: you tend not to interact with those above or below you, and especially with people in other Colleges. It's significant that of the eleven people who were Communists in Cambridge in the late 1930s/early 1940s who recently wrote about their Cambridge days, I knew only one of them.[7] As for people further away in terms of social distance, you didn't meet them at all, especially dons, who were like Greek gods. The only don I later met, and he was only junior then, was Eric Hobsbawm; I also got Wilfred Mellers, of *Scrutiny*, to come and talk to CUSC about modern music. We knew nothing about the John Cornford generation which had gone to Spain only a few years before us, except that they had been heroes. (The Party didn't want them to go anyway; their role, like ours, was to try to be good students.) We did hear that there had been a brilliant postgraduate Communist physicist in Cambridge itself, called Ram Nahum, from Manchester, who had been killed in the only air raid on Cambridge.

And an awful lot had happened since Spain, anyhow, notably the traumatic schisms over the Soviet-German Pact, of which we had no experience. Newer, more massive and very rapid changes made all that – only a few years ago – 'history already', as American students say. Ours was a new world, not the world of the Spanish Civil War, but an entirely new, global alignment of fascist and anti-fascist forces, in which Churchill, Stalin and Roosevelt were (incredibly) Allies, and Japan now threatened in the East.

Communists and non-communists alike had been enormously inspired by Churchill's speeches on the wireless. But the main shield protecting us all from conquest by the Nazis, and the end of civilisation, was the Red Army. I still think this. There were hundreds of their divisions, as against our tens. And, it seemed, too, that their tanks were not made of cardboard, as right-wingers had told us.

In the vacations, the old Cambridge and the new coexisted: we attended our military training, but also had time to read, and to play squash and tennis. When I went home, I found that home was always a new place. My family, via our Catholic connections, were renting a dismal old house belonging to a monastery in North Wales. The monastery had an outdoor 'Stations of the Cross' which the more pious (not many) went up on their knees. Later, we rented a more modern bungalow. Since my mother never washed the dirty laundry herself, I took it to the nunnery to be laundered. When I got to the laundry area a Dantesque sight met my eyes: dozens of pallid young girls in clouds of steam, wearing shapeless uniforms. They were allegedly 'orphans', but in reality often girls who had had illegitimate children and were incarcerated in these places (the last of them closed only in 1996) with the sanction of their parents, and unbeknownst to the general public until the Irish film made by Peter Mullen as late as 2002, *The Magdalene Sisters*. (I later met a middle-class girl who had been evacuated to the same nunnery, and had been waited on – breakfast in bed – by these same girls.)

In Certificate A training on Saturday mornings in Cambridge, we learned very little, apart from how to reduce trees to two types – 'bushy-topped' and 'fir' – to avoid any ambiguity about what we were firing at. But on the summer vacation Certificate B training course, I found out that the Army could teach you, very efficiently, how the internal combustion works, or how to ride a motorbike, all reduced to a few foolproof rules and practical procedures.

I nevertheless stopped going, although one was supposed to continue to do so even after having passed the Cert B examination. (This was a military offence.) But I wanted to be with the workers, so I volunteered to work in the huge Pye electrical factory, the only time I have ever worked in a factory organised on Taylorist lines. The monotony of turning out hundreds of identical electrical components whose end-purpose wasn't clear was stupefying. When the loudspeakers were switched on for an hour of 'Workers' Playtime', it was a massive pleasure. But we were so politically motivated that, we heard later, the regular workforce wasn't happy with us at all: our productivity was more than double theirs!

After fourteen months, I began to wonder if the Army had forgotten about me. I need not have worried. Cambridge was over when a letter arrived ordering me to report to the Royal Artillery Officer Cadet Training Unit (OCTU) at Llandrindod Wells in Wales.

I found myself with men who had already served four years in the ranks, who knew all there was to know about anti-aircraft guns, and who had wives and families. One day, I found one of them, an ex-miner, sobbing on his bunk. When I asked what was up, he said that he found being amongst entirely middle-class fellow-cadets hard to take. I, on the other hand, with only the rudimentary training of Certificates A and B, as a student from Oxbridge (not even a graduate), had nevertheless entirely bypassed serving in the ranks and gone straight to officer training. We were billeted in converted hotels in this old spa, where you could still take the waters.

My inexperience soon got me into trouble. On the graveyard watch (sentry duty between 2 A.M. and 4 A.M.), I used the wrong formula in challenging the Orderly Officer on his ritual round; even worse, I turned out the entire guard. Next day, I was up before the Battery Commander. Luckily, he accepted my excuse, which was that I had never been on sentry duty in my life.

Cambridge hadn't prepared me for being completely outstripped by my fellow cadets in subjects like electricity. As an eighteen-year-old, the physical side wasn't too tough, even though we had to 'double' everywhere. I was even lucky enough to develop an inflamed tendon which got me off lots of duties. (When I told the M.O., 'I've got an Achilles tendon', he replied, 'I hope you have'.) Battle camp, though, was rough. Officers threw thunderflashes around us as we crawled here and there. Or rather, I *thought* this was tough, until I later saw films of Palestine Liberation Organisation guerrillas having Kalashnikovs fired close to their heads in their training. In a freezing Welsh winter, we had to put all our clothes in our ground-sheets, lift our rifles over our heads, and push the bundle across a river. Mine slowly sank as we went across; by the time we reached the other bank, everything was soaked. The worst, though, was having to dry and oil our rifles before we were allowed to put our sodden, stiffening clothes on.

I also had no money. You were paid at the rate appropriate to the rank you came into OCTU with, which, in my case, was that of a humble private, just about enough to buy some razor blades and the odd pint. Eating in the NAAFI was a great luxury. I remember thinking that if I could only get one square meal a day in the NAAFI, I wouldn't ever ask for anything else. And there was one great cultural outlet – the local Repertory Company, where we could even meet the actors in the Green Room after the performance. Everyone was in love with the beautiful girl who became a Rank starlet. The only contribution to cultural life I made myself was to play Chopin and Purcell (easy, slow pieces) for a charity performance.

Despite the black mark against me for the sentry-duty blunder, I was one of the cadets singled out as the best in the graduating elite. (The top Senior Cadet had fought in the Spanish Civil War for the Republicans, and in those pro-Soviet days, I was allowed to talk for half an hour, in a 'free period', about the USSR.)

Full of euphoria, we were sent on graduation leave to our homes, and stopped at Craven Arms. I foolishly jumped down onto the track, and went to get a cup of tea at the platform opposite. When I came out, my train had gone – with all my possessions on it. I was most concerned about my cap, because to be bareheaded in public was a military offence. But by the time the next train got to Crewe, my brilliant comrades had offloaded my stuff in the Left Luggage, so I was safe once more.

My father, in his Home Guard uniform (he was the Quarter-master), was very proud of me when I went on leave. (I don't buy the 'Dad's Army' image of the Home Guard at all, funny as it is; Hitler ordered them to be shot as partisans.) I remember discussing with him the Nazi invasion of the USSR. Now, I said, the war would be won – though I had no idea of the gigantic cost to the Russians.

My first posting was to Erdington in Birmingham, defending a huge tank factory. Some tanks came out with slogans chalked on them reading 'One for Joe' (Stalin). At a British-Soviet Friendship concert in the Town Hall, a tenor in evening dress sang Russian peasant songs and Soviet patriotic ones. More local entertainment came in the form of dances in the neighbourhood, where we met Auxiliary Territorial Service girls who were as interested in sex as we were. I'm surprised sociologists don't write more about 'dances', the discos of their time, which – whether foxtrots or rock 'n' roll – are a very different phenomena from the 'dance' which Alvin Ailey or Sadler's Wells put on. They are one of the only legitimate situations in which young men and women are allowed to approach each other, and, especially, to hold each other, and, not surprisingly, often morph into courtship. (My most embarrassing sexual incident, however, was when I had a medical. I didn't know that when I had to drop my pants, it would be at the order of a most beautiful blonde doctor, and a Captain at that.)

Our gun sites included one on top of Dunlop tower, which can still be seen from Spaghetti Junction on the M6. Legend had it that during one gun drill, the gun-crew failed to clear a round in the loading tray and fired it across the rooftops. (I don't believe this.) I enjoyed Aircraft Recognition more than anything, because it had at least some intellectual content. I also ran the Battery wall-newspaper, using, among the usual orthodox sources, clippings from the *Daily Worker*, which told us, for the first time, about a new guerrilla movement in Yugoslavia led by a Communist called Tito. We also publicised reports about Nazi concentration camps long before their existence was officially acknowledged. I was quizzed about my sources by my Captain.

The army certainly kept you on the move, for reasons which we usually didn't understand. I was sent on courses to Towyn, a very big artillery camp on Anglesey, for Aircraft Recognition, where there were hundreds of WAAFs (Women's Auxiliary Air Force) and marvellous top-rank ENSA (Entertainments National Service Association) concerts. I got a top rating. I expected my next course on predictors at Thirsk to be a similar success, and it was. Predictors were mechanical predecessors of radar, worked by high-precision gears. You fed in three kinds of data – the height of the aircraft, its speed, then its direction. The predictor told you where to fire, and when, in order for the shell and the plane to intersect. I found this very interesting, and worked very hard. But one day, having finished our morning task, I went back to our hut ten minutes before knocking-off time. I was immediately hauled up before the Gunnery Instructor, who proved to be an extraordinary stickler for punctilious compliance with orders. What I had done, he told me, could result in a court martial. I suddenly felt, out of the blue, that I was staring down the barrel of a gun, threatened with severe punishment for something that didn't merit it. I have never forgotten the sense of injustice against which I had little defence. In the end, I got another first-class rating. My last course was at Altcar firing range; I enjoyed the skill involved on the rifle range and was a good pistol shot. Best of all was the precision of the Bren gun. (The cockle-fishermen took no notice whatsoever of our red warning flags, even when we were firing machine guns along the beach.) I also learned that the Regimental Sergeant Major (RSM) was a far more powerful person than any junior Lieutenant, as were the much younger drill sergeants who paraded us for hours. From Altcar, I could not only also go to dances at Southport, but even got home to my parents on the Wirral a couple of times.

Then a posting to Plymouth, along the beautiful Cornish Riviera, the jigsaw picture of which my grandfather and I had done years before. There was nothing left of the centre of the city. The blitz, however, was over, and the sea was blue.

Then we went up north to protect the Rolls-Royce works at Crewe, but there were no air raids there either. So we moved the guns down to Coventry. On the way down, we started out as a convoy in proper military order. But civilian drivers didn't respect our order, and they were in a hurry. Before long, we had a convoy consisting of a gun, a milk-float, a generator, a laundry van, then another gun. On the outskirts of Coventry, I was sent ahead on my motorbike to guide the convoy round a roundabout. But there was an air raid alert, and all road lighting had been extinguished. Too late, at twenty-five miles an hour, I saw the five-inch edge of the roundabout looming up. I flew through the air, and landed on my crash-helmet, personally undamaged, but with a marked angle in the front wheel of the now unusable motorbike. But we were really not needed in Coventry, either. The blitz had finished there too.

One place did welcome us – Neyland, on the opposite shore from Milford Haven – an important port which had never had any 'brutal and licentious soldiery', as the phrase had it, at all. We were billeted next door to a pub in the main street; the landlord immediately sent in a hogshead of beer for us, which we kept between our camp-beds. Across the harbour was a castle full of WAAFs. My girlfriend and I went for walks overlooking the beautiful estuary. She had been in concert parties as an amateur, but didn't like it because the men stared up her skirt.

But there weren't many such places left that needed ack-ack now. What was needed was a supply of subalterns who would lead their men to death and glory invading Europe. (Since the junior officers were in the front of their platoons, their chances of getting killed were much greater.)

So we were sent to become infantry officers on a very gruelling conversion course at Dunbar. D-Day came in the middle of our course. To artillerymen, the infantry was an inglorious step down. As I write, British regiments are being reduced to five, meaning that very historic old ones disappear forever, fused into new, composite units. This means nothing to civilians, but is a scandal to old soldiers, comparable to fusing Liverpool with Everton, or Manchester United with Manchester City, but infinitely worse when the death of loved ones is involved. We were allowed to retain our Artillery insignia for a while; then we had to opt for one infantry regiment or another. I chose the King's (Liverpool), because it had been my father's Regiment. It was a great pleasure, as an avowed atheist, to defy convention and fall out, the only one among a thousand other officers, one Sunday morning church parade. I had an hour to myself.

I never saw the King's (Liverpool), however, because we were suddenly offered the opportunity of joining either the Royal West African Frontier Force or the King's African Rifles in East Africa. I hadn't the faintest idea of the difference, but made the splendid sleep-walking choice of East Africa.

Then another, equally hard, conversion course in mid-winter, in muddy fields in Shropshire, a place I swore I would never visit again – but I did, on holiday with my family on our narrowboat. The muddy fields had now become beautiful countryside. (This is why it is meaningless for people to ask, 'Did you like (whatever country it was)?' It all depends on why you are there, under what conditions (and not just the weather), how much money you have, who you are with, and a dozen other things.) Next up was embarkation leave, in London, where I had a marvellous time, even meeting up, by accident, with my Rank starlet at a theatre. I also had a beautiful Canadian officer girlfriend in the Queen Alexandra's Yeomanry Nursing Service, who materialised for our date at the ballet in a stunning evening gown. I frequently pass the hotel at Marylebone where I was billeted.

We watched the V1 'buzz-bomb' rockets slowly descending, pursued by fighters, with equanimity. You waited for the bang. V2s, the ancestors of today's rockets, were different: they descended, vertically, out of the skies, with absolutely no warning and caused far greater damage.

Then it was off by train to Greenock, on the Clyde, where we joined our troopship en route to Cairo. We were on the *Capetown Castle*, a cruise vessel, now with thousands of bunks crammed into it. The convoy assembled was a most dramatic spectacle: dozens of ships with destroyers, frigates and even battleships protecting us, and aircraft carriers launching Grumman Martlets, and all in glorious weather. Even better was that the U-boat campaign was dying down rapidly. It was all thoroughly enjoyable – and safe – even though a convoy taking supplies to Malta had lost three out of every five vessels only a couple of years before. We never thought then about what the German film, *Das Boot*, has reminded us of only in the last decade: that forty thousand German submariners went out, but only ten thousand came back.

We went westwards towards Canada to escape the U-boats, then headed south, then eastwards towards Gibraltar. On board was a Czech Brigade going to join the Red Army via Iran. The Soviets had occupied the north of Iran; the British, the South. (An apocryphal story of the time was that when the British generals were surprised at the geniality of the reception they were given by their Soviet counterparts, the Russian general said, 'Yes, we like the British military. It's those archaeologists, like T.E. Lawrence and Gertrude Bell, we don't trust!'). Less amusing was the experience of one of the Czechs with whom I became friendly, Ernst Sternschuss, whose forebears, he said, had been given that daft name ('shooting star') in Austro-Hungarian days. I met him again in London after the war, and heard his horrific story of how, when he was eventually wounded, he had to make his way back to Moscow by foot or in peasant carts.

Another large contingent on board – hundreds of WAAFs – however, brought us a fortnight of sheer joy. I took up with a Scottish PE Sergeant-Instructor, and together we won the mixed deck-quoits competition. (Her friend, also an Instructor, whom we beat in the Final, went on to become the 'Forces' Sweetheart' of the Middle East.) We spent our last glorious night, lying on the deck, shamelessly entwined in each other's arms, and then the old Army story – I never saw her again.

We landed at Suez, greeted by the 'galli galli' men who dived for the pennies we threw down, and jokingly greeted any British woman as 'Mrs Simpson'.

It had been wonderful to see the lights of a city again. But we were put into tents in the desert, where we spent sleepless nights trying to foil the 'Arabs' who crawled up silently during the night and tried to steal the rifles which we had chained together. I don't know what they would have done with them, for there were no guerrillas then. Maybe they would have been sold on, via market networks, and ended up with people who might have used them – the desert Beduin. We went out to the Sphinx and the Pyramids at Giza, then seven miles away from the city, though nowadays the city reaches right up to them. Nor are you now allowed today to climb them, as we did; at the top was a graffito carved by Edward, Prince of Wales. In Cairo, we saw wonderful mosques and the quite incredible mummies and statues in the run-down museum. Socially, we had ice creams at Groppi's legendary cafe, or a drink at Shepheard's Hotel, the historic centre of British social (especially political-military) life (later burned down during the Suez War). It wasn't all so pleasant: the heat was so appalling that the Army started very early in the morning, and took a long break over the middle of the day; then started up again a few hours later.

We re-embarked, not on our beloved *Capetown Castle* but on a rust bucket called the *Empire Woodlark*, said to have been used in a Charlie Chaplin film as a wreck in San Francisco Harbour. With my rifle slung over my shoulder, I never made it up the gangway on the side of the ship; I woke up two days' later in the ship's hospital, laid down by some exotic bug. Even in hospital, though, you couldn't avoid the weevil-filled bread rolls. But I recovered soon sufficiently enough to see, like El Orrens and his boy companions in *Lawrence of Arabia*, De Lesseps' astounding achievement, the Suez Canal, cut through the desert.

When I was Orderly Officer, I got talking to the South Africans who had come on board with us. The black troops had been enlisted in the Pioneer Corps as hewers of wood and drawers of water. But at Alamein, when every man had been needed, they had been issued with rifles, and some had been wounded. I was surprised to find that when their skin grew back, it was white, not black. (They also got much darker in the sun, I found, even burned.) The white officers and NCOs were not as bad as I'd feared. In Italy, they had been thoroughly infected with democratic ideas, and when they got back to South Africa, they formed the core of the Springbok Legion, a movement of ex-servicemen led by 'Sailor' Malan, which, alas, didn't last very long. Hundreds of thousands of soldiers of every nationality had been similarly infected. Activists walked up and down British troop trains bound for the front line in Italy, selling Communist literature. The Greek Communists, however, were kept under brutal control, just as Jews had been in the Polish Army in Scotland. But in the Forces' Parliament set up in Cairo, the overwhelming majority of the elected 'MPs' were Labour, then a solid contingent of Communists and another of Liberals.

Finally, we emerged from the Red Sea, with relief, and turned south towards Mombasa, where my fascination with black Africa began. When we landed, my first act was to buy a pineapple, which we ate as the gigantic mountain train pulled us up the railway (built by labour imported from India who had had to face lions, celebrated in the book *Man-Eaters of Tsavo*) through the velvety African night, towards the cool of the capital in the 'White Highlands', Nairobi.

Swahili – My Doorway to Africa

In 1943, Nairobi was a sybaritic delight after wartime rationing in Britain. The settlers lived well, in hotels like the New Stanley or Torrs Hotel, where the settler leader, Lord Lugard, gazed from his statue on a plinth looking longingly, it was said, into the bar. The elite had their luxurious Muthaiga private club. We also had a good Officers' Club, and could afford the occasional steak *au poivre* at Chez Gaby. On a few occasions I did run out of money completely, and had to cable my father for a fiver, which duly arrived.

The colour bar was the omnipresent feature of everyday life: seats in the front of the buses were for whites; those at the back for Africans; the public benches were marked *Wazungu Tu* (Whites Only). So South Africans who had come up to Kenya on the 'Fourth Great Trek' felt quite at home.

The Africans in the main streets commonly wore ragged shirts and shorts with holes in them, and many lacked shoes. The district bounded by River Road, patrolled by Military Police, was strictly off-limits to us, though lovely African girls tried to lure us to go with them. In any case, we had been thoroughly intimidated by the films about venereal disease the MOs had shown us.

As English people resident in North Wales, it had never crossed our minds that we might learn the local language. But the army had the brilliant idea of getting us to learn Swahili on the ship before we even got to Kenya, and on arrival we were sent straight away to Jeanes School, set in beautiful countryside on the outskirts of Nairobi. This had been a school for the sons of chiefs and other African notables whom the British thought would be a useful, pliable, anglicised and elite in the future. (They did the same at schools like Achimota in the Gold Coast.)

I apologise, now, for switching into a bit of linguistics, but that was exactly what happened to us when we arrived. The Swahili teaching, by white education officers, was excellent. In addition, we practised conversation with African teachers, which worked marvellously well, while we walked along roads lined not with African acacia but with Australian gum-trees (widely used in Africa and, I found later, in South America, because they grow so quickly), where woodpeckers were hard at work. The Kikuyu villages, full of women wearing colourful bandanas, were densely populated because the settlers had stolen so much land. It struck me that, even so, a little European technology could still vastly improve life – piped water, dispensaries, drainage, better houses, and so on – an idea which was later the basis of Julius Nyerere's Ujamaa village programme in Tanzania, when he made many hundreds of thousands move into precisely such villages at extremely short notice. At the side of the road, Kamba craftsmen sold their exquisite figurines of people and animals (now much less well done). They soon learned to produce the main form of these figures by turning the wood on lathes in the villages, then finishing them off, in front of their customers, by hand, with knives. It looked like pure handicraft, though. I still have some of these delightful things. Kisii craftsmen also sold their beautiful soapstone carvings, for peanuts, of course.

The downside of life was persistent pilfering, because our dormitories, divided into small rooms, were open at the top, and while we were at class or in town people (our own personal servants, *bois*, or the sentries who theoretically policed the camp) helped themselves to personal items, some of great sentimental value to men serving away from their families. We immediately went to the Indian shops (*dukas*) in Nairobi and bought, with scarce money, 'tin boxes', which were secure once padlocked. I used mine for the next twenty-five years.

Swahili seemed such an eminently logical language, regular in its phonetics, that it seemed that if it had had a better vocabulary, it would have been far better as a world language than that mixture of Norman French and Anglo-Saxon, English, so full of irregularities and so difficult to spell. Unfortunately English, not Swahili, had become the world's number one language instead.

French, I knew, had masculine and feminine nouns and agreements. Latin had an extra 'neuter'. But in Swahili, there were lots more noun classes, and all nouns belonged in one or other noun class.

Living creatures, for instance, belonged to the class indicated by the prefix *m-* in the singular (*mtu*: man) and *wa-* in the plural (men were *watu*). Most trees belonged to the *m-* (singular) or *mi-* (plural) class. Nouns could then be tied to adjectives (and to verbs) by using exactly the same prefixes: a finger was *kidole*, the adjective for small was *-dogo*, so a small finger was *kidole kidogo*. The verb, too, could be reduced to a formula: STROVE (**S**ubject + **T**ense + **R**elative + **O**bject + **VE**rb-stem), which appealed to my scholarly mind, now also exposed to the disciplined ways of thought of the military.

It took me a long time to realise that the linguistic situation wasn't all that different from that of English in the UK. Swahili, like English, was a language of conquest: English, from the conquest of Anglo-Saxons by Norman-French-speaking invaders; Swahili, from the conquest of Bantu-speaking inhabitants of Zanzibar and adjoining islands, and the mainland opposite, by Omani Arabs from the Persian Gulf who had blown down on the monsoon winds and carved out a trading empire on the coast around Zanzibar. At first they traded in that eminently important commodity, spices (cloves); later, in an even more profitable commodity, human beings. Swahili, the outcome of the intermixture of both languages, wasn't therefore all that pure: it was a mixture of Arabic and Bantu – the syntax largely Bantu, and much of the vocabulary, especially words relating to government and work, Arabic. Different dialects, too, were spoken on other islands, such as Lamu, and in the major city of Mombasa. It was European missionaries and colonial Governments who finally adopted the Zanzibar dialect as 'Standard' Swahili.

Under the Arabs, Swahili entered its second stage of expansion: pushing their caravans deep into the interior, the slavers used this language as a lingua franca to communicate with speakers of other Bantu languages. It is still used by millions in what are now Kenya, Tanzania, Uganda and even in the Congo. Those on the coast nearby spoke related languages, so they found it relatively easy to pick up. Bantu languages, too, are spread, not just in the interior of Kenya but across the continent and right down to the Cape. The further you go, the more different they can be – as different as Polish and English are despite the remote common origins of both Indo-European tongues.

After more than a century during which Swahili had been used on the coast and in the slave trade, the arrival of white settlers resulted in a third, even more rudimentary form of the language, reduced to very basic grammatical forms and heavily influenced by English usages. 'Kitchen' Swahili was used to tell farm labourers and domestic servants what to do ('Tote that bale!'; 'Bring another gin!'). You could even buy a book of 'Up-Country' (generally called 'Kitchen') Swahili.[8] In colonial Kenya, this kind of Swahili was more widely spoken than the *safi* ('clean' or 'pure') form taught in schools and which Julius Nyerere – who had translated *Julius Caesar* and *The Merchant of Venice* into *safi* Swahili – made the official language of the new state of Tanganyika when that country got its independence.

Most people, though, don't speak *safi* Swahili. Lots of people in Kenya, moreover, don't even speak Bantu languages at all, notably the Nandi, Kipsigis and Maasai whose languages belong to another language family altogether, and the numerous Luo who belong to yet another family. For all such people, if you want them to understand you, you have to estimate rapidly what their own language is likely to be, then use a simplified form of Swahili.

Knowing even one foreign language – French (plus some Latin) – was an asset. I passed out of Jeanes School with 97% marks. To encourage colonial officers in the colonial Administration to learn a language they could use (and impose) on their subjects, they were rewarded, in cash, for taking first the Lower Standard examination and then the Higher. I took the Lower immediately, and was given the cash.

But I soon realised there was no point in going on to take the Higher Standard Swahili exams in a 'classical' tongue far removed from the world of the Army, urban life and coffee estates. Returning as a tourist years later in the Serengeti, a white tour guide congratulated me on my good Swahili. I congratulated him on his, which he said he'd learned from cooks and drivers. And that's how Africans, too, mainly pick it up, unless they have learned better Swahili at school.

* * * * *

When I left to join my assigned unit, the 2/6th (Kenya) King's African Rifles, I found that it wasn't stationed in Kenya at all but on the borders of what had been Italian Somaliland and Abyssinia (Ethiopia). To get there we had to go through hundreds of miles of country where people did not speak Swahili or even another Bantu language, not the Swahili we had just learned, but Somali. Our jumping-off point for Somaliland was Nanyuki. To reach it, we left Nairobi westwards along the road to the interior. Metalled road gave out after only seven miles, all of which had been built by Italian

Prisoner of War (POW) labour. (An Italian bartender in our Mess told me that there were separate POW camps for fascists, communists, and the rest.) Settlers had made sure, though, that any red-blooded English farmer got a railway spur to pass close to his farm. Then Kenya's main artery became the usual murram road, past the majestic crater of Ol Doinyo Kapuk across the Rift Valley, and past Lake Naivasha, where the houses which white settlers had built on the shoreline twenty years ago were now miles from the water's edge. Nanyuki was a beautiful spot, within sight of the snow-capped peak of Mount Kenya. At 7.30 in the morning, the cloud began to rise around the base of the peak; by 8 A.M. it was entirely covered. We had nothing to do except explore the countryside, where beautiful black and white Colobus monkeys swung from the branches, over a sign which told us we were on the Equator.

Out of the blue, our movement order was changed. We were not to go to Somaliland overland by truck, through the barren Northern Frontier District, but were now sent to embark on a Dutch boat at Mombasa which plied between that city and Mogadishu. The boat had somehow made its way from the Dutch East Indies across the Indian Ocean when the Japanese invaded. It brought with it the famed 'Indisch' luxurious style of Dutch colonial life: pawpaws, bananas, lemon and limes for breakfast, chicken and fish for lunch and dinner.

Mogadishu bore the marks of Italian colonial luxury too, for the first thing a colonial power does is to set up a brewery for the use of its nationals. The Tsingtao beer served in Chinese restaurants today was pioneered by Germans who seized the Shantung Peninsula early in the twentieth century. The Italians had gone a step further. Cioffi's factory made gin, whisky, brandy and liqueurs – all of them out of the bananas which grew on their huge plantations. Alas, I couldn't appreciate any of this, because I was immediately struck down once more with a debilitating diarrhoea which forced me to drag myself every half hour to the latrines. Getting to the sea was a merciful relief.

The US forces who landed there on a 'humanitarian' mission during a famine in 1993 didn't enjoy Mogadishu either. Ismail Kadaré's wonderful novel, *April Spring*, about a feuding society in Europe, Albania, had not yet been written. But Evans-Pritchard's classic studies of two feuding societies in Africa – the Nuer of the Sudan and the Sanusi of Cyrenaica – were available to US Intelligence officers. All of them show that the great cultural invention of feuding societies is political relativity. Small units – lineages or clans – would feud with their neighbours, traditionally also their enemies, but both could combine against a common threat to both of them. In Albania, when a clan had one of its young people killed by a member of another clan, they would exact vengeance by deputing one of their youngsters to gun down someone from the enemy clan at the crossroads. The killer then had to seek safety in one of the large stone refuges owned by local lords, whom they had to pay for the privilege. Their relatives also had to continue to feed them, as they had to stay there for the rest of their lives.

Though the Nuer had no kings or chiefs, they were able to raise a force of warriors, using the age-sets the men belonged to, under the leadership of religious 'prophets', even against the mighty British, when the latter were bombing their herds of cattle in the 1920s. In the Ogaden, a territory disputed between the British, ensconced in the north of Somaliland and the Abyssinians, the 'Mad Mullah' had fought for twenty years against both.

Modern Somalia moved to higher levels of political organisation – not by developing a centralised modern state (except puppet regimes propped up by the Soviets or the US) but by forming alliances which, though constantly shifting, were capable of conducting modern wars – using new military technology, notably the aptly named 'technos', made out of the abundant weaponry the superpowers had left behind (light artillery and heavy machine guns mounted on truck-bodies). Thus equipped, they could be formidable enemies, as the United States found to its cost, when the bodies of American GIs were dragged through the streets of Mogadishu and the invaders were forced to withdraw. This was nothing new: in another feuding society, Afghanistan, the mighty British Empire had had to fight three wars in the nineteenth century, and still had to withdraw in the end. In one of these wars a poor medical officer was the only one spared to walk back with the news that the entire British army had been wiped out. A century later, the Soviets, similarly, had to withdraw. Even 'shock and awe' – the use of overwhelming, high-tech air power – has not defeated these fearsome fighters; in Somalia, the centralised state still does not exist either.

We set off for the far north, British Somaliland, in gigantic seven-ton diesel trucks captured from the Italians; the drivers were Italian POWs. I now had my first experience of yet another foreign language in Africa – not Swahili or Somali but Italian. When we came to a crossroads, my driver asked me what I realised meant 'Right or left?'. I didn't know 'sinistra' or 'destra', but in a flash of revelation recognised a familiar word: 'sinistra' must be the Latin '*sinister*'. From there on, whenever I needed to say something, I tried Latin.

The journey, over hundreds of kilometres of scrubby bush, empty apart from nomads and camels, and belts of giant termite mounds, was not interesting. Every so often there was a river, where people sold us vegetables, fruit and chickens. We never got to talk to the nomads, but were deeply impressed with how handsome most of them were, men and women. Iman, the Somali supermodel, herself the daughter of a nomad, has rightly remarked that girls like her were a 'dime a dozen' in Somalia. The most beautiful woman I ever saw in my life was urging a camel along with a stick. In Ethiopia handsome people are ten a penny too.

We passed through the capital of British Somaliland, Hargeisa, a couple of tens of thousand people, en route to our camp carved out of the bush at Jigjiga, just over the border between British Somaliland and Abyssinia. War, it has been said, consists of long periods of boredom punctuated by bursts of violent excitement. Jigjiga fell into the first category. With the Italians long gone, there was no evident enemy, except an invisible one, sometimes referred to as 'bandits' and sometimes as the *shifta*. So we duly chained our rifles, and counted them every morning and evening to make sure the *shifta* hadn't taken any during the night. Every Sunday we had leisurely curry lunches with many courses, washed down with gin. The greatest alcoholic was the Padre. Otherwise, there was little to do except the hilarious diversion of digging deep latrines into which we had to lower men by rope. When the latrines were fired with petrol, it was even more fun. There was little point in going into the dreary town, mainly populated, it seemed, with girls who were after the money of our men. The askari could be seen in our headlights, swaying the drunken miles back to camp among the gleaming eyes of the packs of hyenas. Junior officers like me had to read and censor the letters of men often older than themselves, but when my British Company Sergeant-Major asked me not to read one to his wife, I didn't, though this was an infringement of military law.

One weekend we took a truck to the historic cities of Harar and Dire Dawa inside Abyssinia, located (though we didn't realise this) on a cultural fault line between Christian Ethiopia and Muslim Harar. The rock-filled road was symbolically perilous, with dozens of hairpin bends so steep that we sometimes had to reverse several times and then go forward, with our tyres at the very edge of vertiginous valleys.

Culturally, Abyssinia was an ancient Coptic Christian society. Politically, though, it had been made into a centralised modern state only in the nineteenth century, about the time when, in Europe, Prussia had transformed a collection of German-speaking states into a modern Reich, by military force, but also by virtue of its new industrial power. Attempts, as early as 1520, to introduce modern industry into Abyssinia had been frustrated by European Powers. Eventually the country came under the domination of one of these land-owning magnate princes, Menelik, whose victorious army, like those of his rivals, was recruited from the peasantry of his particular ethnic group. But the social base of the new ruling class of the new state was still a land-owning aristocracy, with no interest in modernising rural society. Now it governed a state which was totally devoid of modern bureaucratic machinery. Menelik, now King of Kings, simply devoted his energies, and now the state's resources, to imposing the Amharic language and culture of his Shoa heartland on the majoritarian ethnic groups they had conquered, especially the Oromo in the South. His grandson, Ras Tafari, who became Haile Selassie, continued his policy, and in the North, they struggled to conquer and incorporate Eritrea, an entity only newly formed as a result of Italian penetration.

These internal conflicts were further complicated and intensified when Ottoman Egypt, across the Red Sea in Arabia, had sought to spread its imperium amongst the Muslim minority in the north of Abyssinia, particularly in Harar, among the Somali. A new threat to Ethiopia had then come from Europe. On top of the persisting Italian penetration into Eritrea, alliance between Turkey and Germany in the First World War threatened the country from German East Africa to the south, and in the north culminated in the withdrawal from the Dardanelles and the destruction of an entire British Army of forty thousand men in Mesopotamia. It was here, after the battle of Kut, that General Townshend was taken off to comfortable captivity in a hotel in Istanbul while his men starved and died of disease and forced marches in the desert.

My awareness of Ethiopia only dated back to newsreels of a slight figure in Abyssinian garb pleading for his country in Geneva at the League of Nations when that body failed to stand up to Italian aggression, and thereby destroyed that organisation for ever.

Then came Mussolini's revenge. We did not see any bodies dangling from nooses, as during the Fascist era, pioneered in Europe in Muslim Albania in the struggle to impose the ancient Christian civilisation of Roman Catholic Italy on another ancient Christian civilisation dating from the fourth century, Coptic Abyssinia. Italian civilisation now only remained in the shape of the excellent Art Nouveau architecture of their hotels.

When Haile Selassie was restored, he did nothing to relieve the land-hunger of his people. The beginning of that crucial internal reform was left to the left-wing Mengistu regime which overthrew him, but which continued to wage war firstly against Somalia, then against Eritrea. Another Marxist successor regime, that of Meles Zenawi, fought yet another pointless war with Eritrea over poverty-stricken territory on the border with Eritrea.

The arrival of a Brigadier hot from Normandy put an end to our sleepy way of life at Jigjiga. We soon had a full-scale Brigade exercise in the daytime cauldron of a bush which only camel-herders could stand, but which became freezing at night. Two of the coldest times I have ever spent in my life were both in Highland Africa. Luckily, the supply routes established when the South Africans had been there brought us tinned bully beef and guavas, and Castle lager, from Cape Town, and there was also fresh meat. For the first (and only) time, I witnessed the gruesome halal butchery of a goat. (I have never seen the inside of our equally gruesome British slaughterhouses.)

We had had a distinct shortage of enemy with the ack-ack. Now there seemed no good reason to be in the Horn of Africa, either. Our generals had evidently come to the same conclusion, so we were recalled to Kenya. Back we went through Hargeisa, an uninspiring capital, but a lot better then than when both superpowers (and, alas, even the Cubans) were to intervene in a surrogate war. A battle fought near my little Jigjiga had involved hundreds of tanks. Hargeisa, today, is one of the worst places in the world for landmines.

An ancient Belgian troopship awaited us at Berbera, where the temperature was over 100° F by ten in the morning, so we stopped the war, on the Cairo model, and resumed after lunch. The stevedores had worked out a quick method of loading our equipment: they simply dropped our radio sets over the edge into the holds of the barges.

In a couple of days, we were back home, in the bliss of Kenya in a camp at Yatta, near Nairobi. Apart from enjoying city life once more, I found the well-stocked Church Missionary Society bookshop and started to read about the peoples of Kenya: old works like Hollis on the Maasai and the Nandi, which had good grammars of the languages in them; newer ones like Peristiany's study of the Kipsigis; and one that has which influenced me greatly to the present day, *African Intelligence*, by the South African psychologist Biesheuvel – a little-known but excellent combination of theory, method and logic combined with good empirical research.

My battalion was now disbanded. We were stationed at Langata, near Nairobi airport, which was on the edge of the Game Reserve. One day, a soldier brought in a pair of baby leopards, which entertained us mightily, apart from nibbling the feet of the sentry on night duty. Then I realised with horror that the mother might come looking for her babies, so we put them back where we had found them.

While waiting there, I learned quite a bit of Nandi, a non-Bantu language. Like many whites, I was fascinated with the Nandi – largely, I think, because the Nandi had held out against the British for so long (between 1890 and 1906) that the struggle has been dignified by the epithet, the Nandi 'War'. It was the kind of admiration that British soldiers at Gallipoli felt for 'Johnny Turk'.

We were a 'holding unit', waiting to be sent as reinforcements to the East African Division in India. Life was leisurely, but two incidents reminded us just how close army discipline is. Soldiers who had come back late from leave were put into gaol; then the whole camp was made to parade while the victims had a wet cloth put on their buttocks and were beaten with canes. Early one morning, I had to go with the Regimental Sergeant Major of the whole camp – a very powerful person, whose ill temper had no doubt been made worse by being wounded in the thigh on D-Day. The sole occupant of the lock-up was a poor askari arrested the night before for being drunk. He was still hung over and slow to respond when the RSM told him to stand up, and then sailed into him with his fists. It all happened so quickly that I was taken completely by surprise, but eventually managed to calm the RSM down. It showed me how easily one could get involved in situations one completely disapproved of, which might easily involve brutality far more serious that a mere undeserved fist attack.

I celebrated my twentieth birthday with a meal at Chez Gaby. A month later came the news of VE Day. What that meant for us was soon evident – we were off again. We had found an enemy at last – the Japanese in Southeast Asia.

Into India

We played one game of solo all the way from Mombasa to Colombo. It taught me a practical lesson in statistics, because you might be well up one day but wiped out the next. As my uncle had told me, the only constant was that whoever held the bank came out of top. Each of us might lose the bank, and win it back again every so often, but bookmakers hold it all the time. The only public gambling permitted in the Army (because ten per cent was taken from the money betted to be spent on the welfare of the troops) was 'housey housey' (bingo), which I thoroughly enjoyed.

We did not disembark at Colombo but were allowed to swim in the harbour – until a discharge of human excrement from the vessel put paid to that. We disembarked, instead, at Calcutta in the monsoon, at night, and stood in ranks for a couple of hours on the dockside while the rain streamed down our necks. We were as much concerned for keeping our rifles dry as our uniforms or bodies. Then into trucks across the Howrah Bridge, among an incredible press of humanity, to the railway station. The tracks were crowded by hundreds of people who used them as a road. After only a short while, the train halted. Apparently, the engine had hit someone, fatally. It was our first experience of just how cheap human life was in India.

We were then decanted, exhausted, in a field outside the city, where our camp-beds slowly sank into the mud. I woke, after a night with no sleep, my face covered in swellings produced by the local mini-wildlife. When we got into Calcutta, I was appalled by the beggars, the cripples, the lepers and by the sacred cows, which took priority on the pavements over human beings. I could readily have struck one. One admired the great Maidan, but enjoyed far more the relief of getting into an air-conditioned cinema for an hour or two.

Ranchi, the capital of Bihar state, where the 4th East African Division was based, was much better because it was at a higher elevation, and therefore cooler. Even so, when we went into town we played squash at the Officers' Club in over 100° F. In the Army mess there, amazingly, I met the German boy from my school, Kurt Fleischer, who was now an officer in the British Army.

We were pulled everywhere in tongas (rickshaws). There were even dances at which, I thought, the white parents of the lovely girl I escorted might well have been interested in having a Cambridge officer (even if he hadn't graduated yet) as a son-in-law. The same thought had undoubtedly occurred to the only other category of women allowed into the white Mess – the attractive Anglo-Indian girls known as 'Chichis' (who were shockingly treated after independence).

In the 'cantonment', among paddy fields, we were totally cut off from Indian life, so there seemed little point in learning Hindi. Only once was I able to go into the Communist Party offices, where I was courteously received, even though I might well have been working for Intelligence.

By the luck of the draw, I had been sent to a Tanganyika regiment, which, given my interest in Kenyan peoples, didn't suit me at all. My best friend, though, had been sent to a Kenyan battalion next door, the 11th KAR, so I requested a transfer there, and got it. The battalion had fought in the Kalewa Valley in Burma, where, luckily, casualties had not been at all heavy, though several officers wore the Military Cross. Though there were lots of long route marches with full packs, I coped with them easily, enlivened by marching songs and the Acholis' whistles made of African gazelle horns. Life didn't differ all that much from the old life in Jigjiga.

Then the training suddenly started to get a great deal tougher. I don't know why we were not actually trained in beach landings, because that was what we were destined for – the liberation of Malaya, where the Japanese were sitting, dug in with machine guns and artillery on the hills looking down onto the beaches we would have to tackle. But the greatest danger I experienced was on a firing-range when the Sten gun of the askari next to me stopped firing. He swung it towards me, and said, 'Bwana, it's jammed', pointing straight at my chest. I was too annoyed to feel frightened.

The tremendous news about VE Day then reached us, followed by that of the Labour Party's victory in Britain. I had given my father, who was to exercise my proxy vote, detailed instructions: first, Communist; then Labour; then Liberal or Common Wealth; but to abstain rather than vote Tory.

But despite these cosmic events, we were more concerned with what would happen in Asia. We soon found out: some new kind of gigantic bomb had been dropped on two Japanese cities. The actual cessation of hostilities reached me in bizarre fashion. A few days after the Bombs had been dropped, we returned from town a little the worse for alcoholic wear and the jeep stopped. I don't know to this day whether it was there or not, but I thought I saw a tiger a few yards away. I told the driver to step on the gas; then, as we approached the camp, we heard an extraordinary noise – of Africans drumming on whatever they could get their hands on. When I asked what was happening, someone said, 'Don't you know? The war's over'. The first news of the actual cessation of the land fighting had come to me via the 'bush telegraph'.

It has taken all of us sixty years to come to terms with what had happened. We knew immediately that this was even bigger than the firestorms which had already destroyed many Japanese cities, and that this new bomb had totally obliterated two more cities and most of the people in them, but it was some time before the consequent radiation sickness became known. But we were more concerned with what this meant for us, here and now, and our immediate response was one of relief: instead of the trauma of a beach landing in Malaya, with a very high chance of being killed in the process, we would now be able to go home to our loved ones.

As far as our superiors were concerned, when you've won a war, and once the alcohol has worn off, the first thing to do is to reassert discipline and keep the troops occupied. So we immediately had to scrub off the black boot polish from our webbing equipment and replace it with white blanco. Every rock in the camp-area had to be realigned and whitewashed. Then followed elaborate drill-parades for the entire regiment, to the accompaniment of a military band.

By a great stroke of good fortune, I was appointed Battalion Welfare Officer. My principal duty was to see to the brewing of vast quantities of maize beer, which involved frequent journeys into town in the company of our jovial Luo master-brewer. The beer was consumed by officers and men alike, at night, often in the men's tents. There was a great atmosphere of relaxation. Evening after evening, we played no-holds-barred games of *karamoja*, which makes rugby or even American football look like girls' rounders.

Our men then put on a spectacular display of African dancing, which went down wonderfully with the Indian audience: the Kamba with their whistles and acrobatics, the Nandi, Kipsigis and Maasai with their leaping, graceful warriors' dances. Head-dresses and costumes were ingeniously improvised and drums made out of four-gallon petrol tins.

My major contribution, however, was organising a team to take on the nearby British and Indian Divisions in cross-country relay-racing. I selected largely tall, lithe Nandi and Kipsigis runners, and, at first, ran with them. Then, when they proved too fast for me, I coached them from the comfort of the back of a Bedford truck. All was going well until the very morning of the race, when I found two of our runners badly hung over. My desperate pleas, though, had their effect – they ran all the same. At the end, they were so far ahead of the British and Indian competitors on the last stretch that our last Nandi runner simply stopped running and started doing his high tribal leaps, whooping in disparagement at the poverty of the opposition. It is quite possible that this was the first time Kenyan long-distance runners were exposed to international competition – and won easily.

Stuck in the countryside outside Ranchi, we had seen very little of Indian life – the occasional public festival like Holi, when people sprinkled each other with coloured water, or the lights during Diwali – even less of the numerous 'Tribals' of Bihar, apart from cock-fights at the side of the road. We did not even have any contact with the Indian Brigade nearby, except when we were foolish enough to try to play hockey against a Sikh team.

But with peace came a chance to see the great cities of Mughal India – the Red Fort at Delhi, and Lutyens' New Delhi. There were few books in the shops about Indian history. But we didn't need books – we could visit Fatehpur Sikri and climb the minarets of the Taj Mahal at Agra, where craftsmen were still replacing semi-precious stones using the bow-drills their ancestors had used for centuries, or the palace at Lahore where chess had been played with human pieces. Finally, the long drive from Rawalpindi to Srinagar, capital of Kashmir, in a taxi driven at high speed, sharp bend after sharp bend, on the *outside* edge of the Jhelum Valley. It was a relief to stop occasionally and listen to the wayside musicians playing their enormous hurdy-gurdys.

Lake Dal was a joy to behold. We were escorted to a houseboat by the *shikari* who selected us, and spent our time paddling kayaks, so easy to use, within distant sight of the snows of the Himalayas, to the floating vegetable gardens, and to the place my mother had always sung about at her piano – Coleridge-Taylor's 'Pale Hands I Loved, Beside the Shalimar'. The high point was a Persian banquet of some twenty dishes.

The post-war idyll was rudely interrupted. In February 1946, the Indian Navy mutinied, right in Bombay harbour.[9] During the War, Subhas Chandra Bose, a Congress leader, had been taken by submarine to Germany, and had returned to form the Indian National Army which, a Division strong, had fought alongside the Japanese in Burma. (When the Japanese army collapsed, they were left to starve.) But there had been enormous support for them in India, and when the British foolishly put a Muslim General, a Hindu Colonel and a Sikh Colonel, who had fought for the Japanese on trial for treason after the war, anti-British sentiment was unified in one stroke. Defended by Nehru, such was the outrage that they had to be released.

All of a sudden, to our horror, we found ourselves being trained in 'riot drill' (first fire above their heads, then at their legs, then at their bodies). Whatever use was planned for East African troops, the main force meant to hold down India suddenly became totally unreliable – the British Army. Demobilisation had begun, but not fast enough for men who had served out there for years, many of whom had never seen their children. Demobilisation strikes broke out across India. One British Communist, Norris Cymbalist, was sentenced to ten years, later reduced to two and a half. Even less reliable was the better-educated and more progressive RAF. When bodies of aircraftsmen marched on their headquarters, ingenious methods were devised to prevent officers from identifying and picking out strike leaders. Instead of shouting orders ('Halt!' 'By the left!'), as usual, by someone positioned outside the body of troops, the orders came from some invisible person placed in the middle.

We ourselves soon left Bombay, a city I had found every bit as horrific as Calcutta, for our second home, Kenya. Watching a mongoose fight and kill a cobra on the fashionable beach was absorbing enough, but as the officer appointed to inspect the train we were to leave on, I encountered a terrible smell. I looked under the train and found a dead body covered with flies. We had entered India with a death on a train; now we were leaving it with another death on another train. I swore I would never go back – and I never have. This last death, though, was nothing compared to the Bengal Famine which had happened just before we arrived and the even worse deaths of millions at the Partition of the subcontinent.

Back in Kenya, there followed another period of regimental disbandment and amalgamations, out of which I ended up in the historic 5th battalion of the King's African Rifles. The inevitable Army response to disbanding a regiment was to make people do more unnecessary things, like going out running at 5.30 in the morning, in the hills around Gilgil, which we thoroughly enjoyed. I hardly saw my new regiment, however, for I was given a wonderful job – taking soldiers back home on long journeys across East Africa. The first trip was down through Tanganyika, past Mount Meru and the even more majestic snows of Kilimanjaro, fifty miles away. Game – giraffes, Grant's gazelles, Thompson's gazelles – in their hundreds, were all around as, even though we were a long way from the heart of the Serengeti. (When I went to the Serengeti as a tourist in the 1980s, they reckoned the numbers of the game in their millions, as far as the eye could see, for days on end.) There were starbursts of colourful weaver-birds, startled out of their hanging nests as our trucks passed under them.

The reason for this abundance of game soon became apparent. Across the road was a large wooden building through which all vehicles had to go. The doors were then shut while men used handpumps to spray on the pesticide DDT (*'moja, mbili, tatu'*: 'one, two, three') to kill off any tsetse flies which might carry sleeping sickness into a tsetse-free zone, as well as malarial mosquitoes. Rinderpest also made it impossible to raise cattle. So, devoid of both humans and cattle, a whole huge zone ultimately became a 'Game Reserve' for tourism. (DDT was eventually banned, after I had spent a further three years inhaling it in Australia every night, often under mosquito nets.)

Then we saw something odd. I had a map of the 'tribes' of East Africa, issued by the Army, with nice, neat army-style lines dividing one tribe from another. These people on either side of the road *looked* like Maasai – they wore Maasai clothing, beadwork, coiffures, and spoke Maa, the Maasai language. But they were not herding cattle, as they should have been, according to any tourist brochure; and, unlike the proud, dominant Maasai, they did not live mainly on the blood and milk of their cattle, because they had long lost them to rinderpest disease or to other Maasai. So they had had to take to growing vegetables to survive; they had become *agricultural* Maasai, called 'Arusha'.[10] But they hadn't lost all of the Maasai culture, notably the language and the induction of their young boys into Maasai age-sets. But when the time came for the initiation of the boys (like Catholic confirmation, or Jewish bar mitzvah), they didn't retire into the seclusion of *manyatta* villages, as pastoral Maasai boys did, but were sent out to forage for what they could get, using blunt-headed arrows to bring down birds. The boys daubed in white at the side of the road, who happily took our cigarettes, were precisely such initiates, but seemed more interested in the cigarettes than our food.

Normally, we just camped at the side of the Great North Road, though there were occasional African *hotelis* which sold delicious curries at the side of the road. It was all very sociable. My delightful Kamba driver soon taught me how to double de-clutch. Occasionally we could spend a pleasant night in an old colonial hotel – at Arusha, then in Iringa, where we could even play tennis. In the evening, my fellow officer talked about missing his wife (and not only sexually) – something rarely discussed in the Army. Finally, we descended the escarpment leading out of the town, and passed a place where I was destined to spend nearly a year of my life – Ifunda.

When we drew near our destination – Songea, home of the famous warriors, the Ngoni – we halted outside the town while the men put on their best jungle-green uniforms and their medal-ribbons, and we entered in triumph, with hundreds of ululating women and massed drummers welcoming us.

My next trip was to Juba in the Sudan, via Uganda. Life was a lot more comfortable once the war stopped. I even had a collection of gramophone records, so Delius and Muggsy Spanier filled the bush at night, while on the Sudan trip I even got my own train. We could pull into a siding and brew up tea for everybody with hot water from the engine. There were said to be thousands of elephants towards the border with the Sudan, but we only saw piles of steaming dung. (Later, most of the game was wiped out by groups armed with Kalashnikovs.)

Then it was back to the fleshpots of Nairobi. Men who had served a long time were getting demobilised, and those who remained began to think about women. One of the demobilisation schemes was for 'compassionate' leave for white other ranks (there weren't many of these in the colonial forces). We were required to vet their applications; it appeared most people had interpreted the term to mean 'passionate'. The Officers' Mess resounded to continuous playings of Mary Martin singing '*Do It Again*'. The Africans had their torments too. When the famous Baganda women dancers came to perform, we officers were seated on camp chairs at the front – at first. But the gyrating buttocks of the women proved too much for the African troops. They surged forward, rushing the stage and sweeping us aside in the process.

I managed to spend a short local leave in the beautiful Highlands, in a hotel near Kericho, where I foolishly volunteered to escort a truckload of young white schoolgirls who were on holiday from the Sudan, where their fathers worked for the Railway, to the local cinema to see *Lassie, Come Home*. This was a mistake; they cried all the way back; so did I.

I then spent two or three days on a farm which took in tourists, and decided that, since I was so nearby, I would go and visit my demobilised comrade, 'Frankie' Simotwa, who lived in the Native Reserve nearby. After walking the several miles, I realised that I couldn't get back that night, so I stayed with Frankie and his new family, one of the only two times I ever spent in an African hut. It was not comfortable. Sad to say, he was no longer the smart young soldier I had known. As normally happens, his relatives had cleaned him out of everything he had brought back, and he was wearing clothes in holes and a battered hat. As I made my way back, a search party – sent out from the tourist farm in great alarm to look for a white man whom they thought must have been mugged – found me.

It was quite incredible for them to hear that a white visitor had actually spent a night in an African Reserve.

Demobilisation

Out of the blue came a letter telling me I was going home, as I was eligible to resume my university course. This time, we were taken by Dakota over the Sudan, where we could see the Nuer, Shilluk and Dinka with their herds, from only two thousand feet, as well as giraffes and elephants. At Wadi Halfa, on the Egyptian border, the erks had placed a notice:

AT THE END OF THE WORLD, LITTLE MEN SERVE AND WAIT.

Next stop Cairo, and into a troopship which took us through very rough seas to Hyères, near Toulon, which had once been a spa with its casino.

I was demobilised at my regimental headquarters of the King's (Liverpool) Regiment (which I had never seen). Then, for some reason, I was sent across the Pennines to collect my very prickly demob suit, which, like most people, I hardly ever wore subsequently. Then I was home again, in North Wales.

Home had changed frequently during the war, sometimes mysteriously and suddenly. It was now the twelfth-century Black Lion pub, later listed in the *Good Food Guide* (though not while my mother ran it). She loved being back at work in a very congenial job, where she dispensed the hospitality which made the pub famous for its (illegal) after-hours singing around the piano – this attracted people even from Merseyside (all the more easily when my mother charmed the local Special Constable into joining us as a regular law-breaker). On one famous night, there were twenty-four Americans from the nearby airbase sleeping on the floor of the bar. When the Yanks left, they dipped their wings over the 'Black' in salute.

Then my father suddenly sold the pub, and bought an expensive house back in Prenton, Birkenhead. We assumed that these sudden moves were caused by fluctuations in my father's business. But there seemed no pattern to it. During the War, he had actually prospered from being employed in making valuations of the numerous blitzed houses for the Government. So we sometimes moved to a better house. Yet we soon ended up back in New

Brighton, renting a flat across the very road where we had started out – though now, not as house-owners but as tenants, and this was only one of the unexplained moves we made.

I have never found out why my father kept selling our successive homes. My mother was never consulted about any of this. 'I run my business and bring in the money', my father said; my mother ran the house. He didn't interfere in how she ran it, so she shouldn't question how he ran the family finances. My hunch now is that he had been winning – and losing – money, not in business but in betting on the horses. Coming from a gambling family (he had worked with my uncle in his betting business for a while, and we went as children to lots of meetings at Bangor-on-Dee, Chester, and other race-courses), he must have periodically accumulated serious gambling debts. Gambling men, I have found, have two standard gambits: normally they say they have 'broken even' (they claim never to have lost much), or else they are on the verge of 'cracking it': a big breakthrough – which never comes.

CHAPTER 3

Peace and the Cold War

Then it was Cambridge once more – 'Bletchley!', 'Woburn Sands!', 'Gamlingay!', 'Sandy!', 'Bedford!'

Men of my father's generation never talked about the trenches of Flanders. At lunchtime back at College on the first day, though, I sat down at the Refectory table with another officer, also still in uniform. (He later became a Tory MP.) He asked me what kind of a war I had had, and I said I had to admit that it hadn't been bad – hadn't had to fire a shot in anger, and I'd seen a lot of interesting places. 'My war was very different', he said. 'I went in at D-Day; by the time we ended up on the Rhine our officers had changed three times.' (Another ex-colonel I met said they'd lost a thousand men in his battalion alone.) The Second World War, however, had been a war in which more civilians died than armed forces. My best friend at College, Karel Reisz, a Czech, never told me what I only learned from his recent obituary – that both of his parents had been killed at Auschwitz.

And war was not yet done with. I received a great shock when a leaflet came through my pigeonhole from the Cambridge University Socialist Society (which I hadn't even had time to contact) warning us of the danger of a Third World War. I had only just got back from the Second. Churchill, I knew, had announced the beginning of the Cold War in a notorious speech at Fulton, Missouri, the year before. At home, political life under the new Labour Government was very exciting – and problematic. There was a terrible shortage of coal, and the Tories were attacking the miners for leaning idly on their shovels. Every day, the output of coal was headlined in the papers. And it was very cold indeed. The class struggle broke out in the respectable public domain of a Cambridge tea shop, with bitter wrangling as the bourgeoisie flung accusations from one table to another about the lazy miners, and we Red students stoutly defended them.

But before I could settle down to the class struggle at home and the Third World War abroad, I had to sort out my course. 'You ex-servicemen', my Senior Tutor muttered, 'Ninety per cent of you want to change your courses.' When I asked if I could switch from English to my new-found interest, I wanted to say 'anthropology', but I didn't dare ask for that, so I said, 'sociology'. 'There's no Sociology at Cambridge', he replied. 'You could do Social Anthropology, though.' This was exactly what I wanted to hear.

My excitement soon subsided when I found that social anthropology was as badly taught as English Literature had been. Only the peripheral courses such as physical anthropology and archaeology were interesting. There was, however, a brilliant course, meant for intending Colonial Cadets, which we were allowed to attend, given by Evans-Pritchard from Oxford. This was, in fact, the material he had used in the Introduction to his celebrated *African Political Systems*, where he developed the distinction between state and stateless systems. We also learned a great deal from H.A.R. Gibbs, who lectured the Cadets on Islam.

The mainstream anthropology courses, however, were a disaster. The theory course, for instance, was given by Professor Hutton, an ex-Indian Civil Service official who had written the standard work on the Indian caste system, but who seemed mainly interested in the Nagas of Assam, especially their practice of taking heads with the expectation of acquiring their 'soul-stuff'. He had an unfortunate habit of emitting bleats when excited. When dealing with Freud, a particularly extended bleat prefaced an argument intended to demolish one of the great theorists of the twentieth century. 'Sigmund Freud believes that sex drives human behaviour – a ridiculous notion', he pronounced. 'Who's ever heard of people making love when they were seasick?'

The course on Material Culture was so antiquated that it was simply an occasion for farcical fun and games. A lot of it was 'practical', as when Frank Girling (who later became a professional anthropologist) succeeded in sending up a column of smoke from his fire drill. We also fired blowguns across the hall of the museum, and hurled Australian spear-throwers to nearly deadly effect as the spears cleared the quadrangle buildings and fell among cyclists in the street outside.

So there was general excitement when we heard that what we called 'modern' anthropologists were to join the staff. The first was Reo Fortune, known for his book, *Sorcerers of Dobu*, on a New Guinea people near the Trobriand Islands classically studied by Malinowski. But Reo was also famous for having gone to the field in Melanesia as the husband of Margaret Mead, who, during her fieldwork, had taken up with another well-known anthropologist, Gregory Bateson. With the cheek of youth, I asked him was it true that both couples had come home with different partners. 'Yes', he replied, in that strange mixture of New Zealand and US accents, 'We didn't see eye-to-eye over theoretical matters' – an excellent put-down (and possibly true).

Reo's book was celebrated because it had been used by the eminent American anthropologist and poet, Ruth Benedict, in her influential *Patterns of Culture*, as a type-case of a culture saturated with paranoia. There had been scholarly murmurings that this curious cultural pattern might, in fact, have reflected Fortune's own bizarre personality. It soon began to look like this.

His first lecture began on the relationship between physical anthropology (the study of the human body and its evolution) and social anthropology (the study – in those days – of 'tribes'). 'In the Chin Hills of Burma', he announced, 'people dance at mortuary ceremonies with the bones of their ancestors round their necks. That's how physical and social anthropology are related to one another.' We looked at each other with incredulity. This proved to be no aberration.

I immediately asked for Reo as my supervisor. For my first essay, I was asked to compare the organisation of the ancient city of Kano in Nigeria with the kinship system of the Ankole of Uganda. I was gobsmacked. What connection could there possibly be? Was this a joke, or some deep insight I couldn't fathom? But I, a mere neophyte, quietly accepted the task. The connection became evident the next day when I went to the offprint section in Heffers' Bookshop and found, for sale, an article on the social organisation of the ancient city of Kano, and, next to it, an offprint on the Ankole kinship system. The connection was that they were side by side on a bookshop shelf.

I was evidently in the presence of a true eccentric, but one who, from time to time, showed great flashes of penetrating insight and scholarship. The trouble was that one never knew which one was getting.

The second modern anthropologist to arrive was G.I. Jones, a former colonial officer who was a great expert on Nigerian land tenure, although not a theorist of the stature of Reo. I switched to him, nevertheless, rather than put up with the unpredictability of Reo Fortune.

I was learning nothing of modern social anthropology. But in Africa, I had run across the work of the Rhodes-Livingstone Institute in Northern Rhodesia, and finally tracked down their 'Occasional Papers' – not on the normal library shelves but locked in a bookcase in the professor's room, from whence I borrowed them. It was a revelation – a whole series of studies based on first-class empirical fieldwork, but infused with theoretical analysis. I also followed up Evans-Pritchard's lectures by reading both of his classics, *The Nuer* and *Witchcraft, Oracles and Magic among the Azande*. I began to feel that I was really getting into modern social anthropology proper at last.

The new arrangements for us ex-servicemen were designed to compress three years of the university course into two. I began mine in October 1946, so was expecting to continue till the summer of 1948. I had already passed a Preliminary examination back in 1942, in English Literature. Now I had to do another Preliminary, this time in Social Anthropology, which I duly did in the summer of 1947, and was delighted to find that I'd got a First. Because of success in this examination, my College Exhibition was elevated to a Scholarship. I was now in the strange situation of having passed *two* Preliminary examinations – neither of them, though, the principal components of the normal degree, the Part One and the Part Two. However, after this exam success, I suddenly received a notification that I had been awarded a BA (Wartime Regulations), something which I hadn't been expecting at all. This was to cause me trouble later on.

With an unexpected degree under my belt and then, a few weeks later, a very good result in my examination, I could take life a bit easier. When we spotted a notice on the 'screens' (College notice-boards) asking for volunteers to play the double bass and the timpani, with the arrogance of youth, a friend and I immediately signed up. I bought a book from Millers about 'How to Play the Bass', which started off by saying that there had been several different kinds of bass – such as the now archaic three-string variety – before the instrument settled down into its modern form. I looked at mine – it had three strings. We were due to play the *Idomeneo* Overture, which has some pretty fast passages. There aren't any frets on the finger-board of a bass, as there are on a guitar, to help you hit the exact right spot for a note, so I was often a bit out. This didn't matter when the whole orchestra was playing – no one could hear my mistakes – or that I was only playing every other note in the fast bits. But the conductor would rap with his baton, disgustedly, in passages where I was alone and exposed – and a semi-tone out!

A group of us started singing madrigals in the tunnel between Front Court and New Court, because the acoustics were good. We even made a record. One afternoon, Karel and I bunked off to see a re-run of *King Kong*. Next day, punting up to Grantchester, we covered ourselves in mud, and communicated only in Kong-like grunts. When he later left colloid chemistry for film-making, I was almost offended at his film *Morgan – A Suitable case for Treatment*, for it included excerpts from *King Kong*. I felt as if our intimate secrets were being plastered across the screen.

But my major activities during my next few months were political. With an American monopoly of the atomic bomb, we were terrified of their using it to crush the USSR. (Later, we were equally terrified when they were both menacing each other with nuclear war.) Our main concern was to keep the ties formed in wartime in being. So when we heard that a World Youth Congress was to be held in Prague, many of us went, together with a hundred thousand other young people from both Eastern Europe and the West.

The journey took us through appalling sights. It was tough. We joined the train at Paris with little to eat and nowhere, apart from the luggage-racks, to sleep. People lived amid the ruins of Cologne in cellars only lit by hundreds of candles; the same scene was repeated at Nuremburg, sights which subsequently led Edward Heath to attempt to eliminate them forever by taking Britain into the European Community.

For sheer excitement, the Youth Congress was hard to beat. We were greeted at the station in Prague by Džina, a young woman with grey eyes who had spent the war in England. We were housed in a secondary school, controlled by Les Cannon, a humourless Communist trade union (ETU) official who tried to get us to march in step. He later left the Party and became the Right-wing hammer of the Left in the ETU as Sir Leslie Cannon. We ate in a huge hall where we waited for two hours, very hungry, queuing in proper English fashion to get something to eat, but hadn't reckoned with the thousands of Italians who arrived in very large numbers wearing their pointy student caps ... and pushed in ahead of us. When we were asked to contribute to a cultural entertainment, the Soviets sent top ballet-dancers; all we could do was to sing 'D'ye Ken John Peel?'

It was an exhilarating experience, real camaraderie, meeting Russians and even Koreans. We were taken to Mariánské Lása3ně (Marienbad) and Karlovy Vary (Carlsbad), and housed in a convent, where the local partisans threw a party of little else but slivovitz for us. They described for us how the Red Army had charged machine guns head on. I played two hands of boogie-woogie piano duets all night, but for the next two days was completely unable to get out of bed. Even more disgraceful scenes occurred as drunken youngsters rang the front doorbell and vomited to the horror of the hospitable nuns.

Then our British contingent was invited to join an 'International Brigade' going to a work camp in Slovakia, at Bálažye, a village which had been the headquarters of a partisan unit, where the entire population had been wiped out by the Germans. The stream was still full of cartridge-cases. A Greek Communist youth brigade was with us. We were tired out enough with the hard manual labour, but they got up at 5 A.M. to climb the hills and paint rocks with white political slogans. (They later went to Communist schools in the USSR. I saw a documentary about their return to their natal villages, where they pointed to people who had been firing at them from nearby houses during the civil war. Now they had to live together.)

Then we were invited to go on another project – to rebuild a railway in Yugoslavia. We crossed into Hungary, where the Chain Bridge at Budapest was still lying in the water of the Danube. The plate-glass windows of large department stores displayed ... maize cobs. At Subotica, on the Yugoslav border, we were greeted by a kindly Yugoslav officer who bought us slices of watermelon. The work on the railway was done with primitive wheelbarrows, carting soil and rocks all day long. The latrine consisted of a log across a stream. I thought it was kindness itself when a Yugoslav comrade handed me large leaves in lieu of a toilet roll. Our non-vegetable food largely consisted of tins of stewed steak supplied by the UNRRA *(United Nations Relief and Rehabilitation Administration)*. Most of our companions were Czechs, delighted to get abroad for the first time, and very light-hearted (anarchist, we rather thought). But when we visited the British Brigade, down the road, we thought they were too strait-laced. Dorothy and Edward Thompson were there. At the memorable wake for Edward's funeral in London, Dorothy recalled that the only song they all knew, when called upon to contribute to an international show, was 'My Old Man Said Follow the Van', which Tariq Ali thereupon made us all stand up and sing.

I was very touched when a Belgian girl (not a Communist) reached up to the truck taking us out of Yugoslavia, and said, 'Peter, danke für die Kameradschaft'. Leaving Yugoslavia, wearing the blue army fatigues and boots we had been given, we arrived in Trieste, a city disputed between Italy and Yugoslavia. A day or two before, the Italian Fascists had stormed into a hospital ward at Gorizia full of Yugoslavs ... and machine- gunned the patients. We were invited to their funeral. I couldn't understand why shopkeepers were closing their shutters, until vehicles full of Italian Celeri ('Swifties') riot police poured out and started to baton everyone in sight. Gorizia remained divided along each bank of the river until the accession of Slovenia into the EU, as late as 2004. The boundaries of each state still remain, but people can now move freely from one side of the river to the other.

Arriving in Venice was a relief. We slept on the floor of the local CP office, and ate scampi for the first time in our lives. And saw the wonders of the city. Then Rome, where I went instantly to the Czech Embassy for a visa back to Prague to collect my luggage from Džina. When I left that city we had an 'understanding': we were effectively engaged.

In Vienna, a scene of desperate destruction, with 'roads' bulldozed through the rubble of the city centre, we saw our first Red Army soldiers, and learned how to say, 'Do you speak Russian?', and the words for 'money' and 'cigarettes'.

I had expected to take one further examination at Cambridge in the following summer, and thereby receive the normal BA degree. But a friend of mine drew my attention to an advert in the paper for posts on the new 'Groundnut Scheme' in East Africa, a fast-track, high-tech and large-scale strategy for coping with what was perceived as a world shortage of fats, notably soap and margarine, under the aegis of the Minister of Food, John Strachey, noted for his socialist – indeed, at one time, Marxist – views. (Whether there would have ever been such a shortage is still debated.)

So poor was the university teaching that the idea of an interesting and well-paid job back in East Africa appealed to me. It also seemed to promise not only to solve a world raw materials problem, but to do so in a way consonant with the values of a Party that was introducing the Welfare State at home, especially in the spheres of education and health, for the Scheme was to be based on the latest agricultural techniques involving the use of high-tech (for those days) army surplus machinery, worked by an African labour force, but one which would be taught English, not like the traditional colonial-style plantation relations in which skilled white men gave orders to the workers in Swahili. To this end, a concentrated English language programme would be established immediately.

The techniques for this were based on a very special way of teaching English – Basic English, as developed by William Empson and I.A. Richards, which I knew about from my English studies. There was a distinctly progressive dimension to this innovatory way of approaching English, redolent perhaps of the League of Nations' idealism of the interwar period when people had seen Esperanto as a universal tongue of brotherhood. Naturally, this suited me down to the ground.

These had been developed, successfully, by a very interesting intellectual entrepreneur, Adolph Myers, who had been a key figure in the Army Education Corps in India. He used direct methods of language-teaching based on intensive face-to-face interaction, using specially produced texts which gradually introduced new words and grammatical forms, using subject matter related to the tasks required of soldiers in their everyday lives. There were also lots of drawings of Indian troops wearing turbans, which for some strange childish reason my baby daughter later used to make me read interminably to get her off to sleep. Though a simplified form of English, it did make it possible for those who learned it to go on to more elaborate use of the language.

The implementation of the Scheme was given to the United Africa Company. Applicants like me found themselves at Unilever House in London, where we were thrown into the deep end – required to give a lesson, using Myers' methods, after only the briefest exposition of what that entailed. I somehow came through.

They needed a mix of skills: we had a very sophisticated professional avant-garde Jewish artist from New York, a graphic designer/photographer, an American linguist and an experienced schoolteacher. As the only one with any knowledge of anthropology and East Africa, I was to be responsible for the content of the course, as well as taking on some of the teaching.

The shadow of the Cold War fell on me even before we left for Africa. I was told I had been appointed, but a week or so later was called for interview by one of the senior Directors. He'd been told by Intelligence that I had strong left-wing inclinations, which, he said, he'd also had at my age. But he hoped I would be 'sensible'. (I suppose my having been an officer in the KAR helped.) So that first hurdle was surmounted.

We were flown out to Dar es Salaam – me in my heavy winter coat at just under 100° F (because I knew it got cold in the Southern Highlands, where we were heading). The headquarters of the Scheme was Kongwa, near Dodoma, in the centre of Tanganyika. We arrived there by ordinary bus, covered from head to foot in red dust. What we saw was an astounding sight – mile upon mile, as far as the eye could see, of groundnuts already flourishing.

Near Iringa was a monument which the Germans had erected to commemorate German soldiers who were killed by the Hehe in the great battle there, at Lugalo, in 1891.

> On a huge hill [John Donne had written],
> Cragged and steep, Truth stands, and hee that will
> Reach her, about must, and about must goe ...

The truth that stood here was colonial truth. But 'hee' that would reach Truth proper would have to look further than the German version of things. It recorded the German losses – the commander of the German expedition, Zelewski, plus nine other Europeans, including three of his officers and six NCOs, were killed. But it did not record that it was their African allies who suffered most, as did the Hehe, who lost seven hundred men out of their large army of some three thousand, or that the Hehe actually won the battle and made the German forces retreat, leaving their dead on the field. In the words of one historian, it was 'the only battle in the colonisation of German East Africa in which an African army defeated a substantial force under German command'.

Ifunda, where we were to live, was twenty-five miles south of Iringa. Originally a German Lutheran Mission station, it had then been converted into a camp for Polish Displaced Persons. (I don't know how they got there, and I don't like to think about what happened to them when they were sent back to Europe.) Now they were moving out as we moved in. It was extraordinary, in colonial times, to see Europeans, hundreds of Poles, many with blond hair and 'Slavic' cheekbones, trading their meagre possessions, mainly European clothing, such as karakul hats, for a few shillings to the local Africans, for there was little to distinguish either side in economic terms.

Our accommodation was in quite decent brick huts, each even with a garden. Most of the staff were engineers, training the Africans to become mechanics, drivers, and so on. There was great camaraderie all round. But Tanganyika, nominally a UN 'Trust Territory', was effectively still a colony, and our liberalism was not universal. When I pulled up at the Iringa Hotel with an African teacher beside me, a drunken white man spilled out and proceeded to insult me for having an African in the front seat.

We buckled down to the task of designing a textbook to be used in teaching the Africans English, on the lines of the one Myers had designed in India, and were well equipped with the latest technology for producing the textbooks, including the newest device, the wire recorder (tape recorders didn't exist yet). We were virtually a self-sufficient publishing house in the middle of Africa.

We were getting on well with our course design when the first intimations began to trickle through that all was not well with the Groundnut Scheme. It was impossible to know what was true, but it all sounded very bad. Local gossip reported that pyramids of petrol cans had been stacked at Dar to which the local population helped itself; more seriously, that the famous United Africa Company had had no adequate financial/administrative records or controls for most of the first year. The Tories made maximum use of this scandalous state of affairs, notably in a pamphlet by 'Josiah Wilkes' entitled *How to Lose 36 Million Pounds* which played a big part in bringing down the Labour Government in 1951.

But it was the agriculture that proved to be the major disaster. The advice of Lord Rothschild's scientific experts had been the basis of the agricultural policy, but the machines, including the massive chains and bulldozers used to clear the bush, had been tested in Britain, not on the local African soils, which were full of carborundum which wore out the metal. As an anthropologist, I was particularly annoyed that no one listened to the local people, the Gogo, or observed their practices. A pastoral-cum-agricultural people, the Gogo only used the plains for their herds; they planted their crops in the lee of the hills round Kongwa, which had a much more reliable rainfall. For the first two cropping seasons, the plants burned up. When John Strachey visited the Scheme, groundnuts were imported from South Africa, like 'Potemkin villages', to impress him and the hordes of journalists.

Sweeping economies were now introduced, and affected us more than most. We were no longer to design English language textbooks, but to produce Swahili teaching materials for white men to use.

So we set to work, and the main responsibility for the new Swahili textbooks fell to me. After testing them, and training the African teachers, the first classes arrived. Within three weeks, the class walked out perfectly able to communicate as they needed. I didn't know at the time, but two of the first class were CID men sent to check on what Worsley was teaching. They reported that I was teaching Swahili. They still went on opening my mail, however ('Found Damaged in the Post', the GPO sticky tape said).

There was little to do in Ifunda, certainly – living in such a camp – not 'participant observation', the main technique used in anthropology. So I started recording Hehe music, from contemporary hits to ancient war-chants – which turned out to be in the language of the adjoining former enemies, the Sangu, from whom the Hehe had borrowed much of their military organisation.

I often walked to the nearest village, and became friendly with a most dignified old man, Mamfugale – a Bena, living like so many Bena in Hehe country. Walking down the river valley nearby one day, I found myself going up and down with regularity. These were, to me, obviously ancient plots of land, once irrigated and much bigger than the contemporary ones. I found miles of them in other valleys nearby, but the Hehe couldn't tell me anything about them; they were simply made by the 'people of long ago'. Eventually, I wrote my first anthropological article about them, with a map so that others could find them.[11] Only Basil Davidson subsequently visited them, though, apart from a professional archaeologist who was very dubious about our theory.

I was also introduced into a new field of study, which I came to know as 'alternative medicine', via the intestines of a little baby. My servant was a very polite man, so respectable that he named himself 'Pardon'. One day, he told me that his child was seriously ill with a snake in its tummy (*nyoka ndani ya tumbo*). Had I got any *dawa* (medicine)? All I had was aspirin, but I had to do something, so I cut one in half. Two days later, he came up with a shining face. The medicine had worked marvellously. 'Look', he said, pulling a cloth from behind his back. It contained a two-foot tapeworm. He had been open-minded enough to try Western medicine – and it had worked. But there had indeed been a snake in the child's stomach. From that moment on, I learned to take very seriously African and other non-Western diagnoses of illness.

African Resistance

My main activity was collecting quite a large vocabulary and working out the grammar of the Hehe language, helped by my linguist colleague, Joe Rumberger. I also recorded Hehe history from key informants, notably two princes, one of whom had actually fought at the battle in which the Hehe capital, Kalenga, had been captured by the Germans. He was now blind. Taking him back from Iringa to make recordings in our camp, the back wheel fell off our clapped-out vehicle, and careered past us at high speed, landing us on the back axle-stub. 'What was that, bwana?' he asked. 'Oh, nothing', I said, 'Just a puncture.' It is not often one thinks of being blind as an asset. Later I was able to go through my scrappy historical notes with Adam Sapi, the Chief of the Hehe.

The definitive study of the meteoric rise of the Hehe kingdom, though, was not carried out until 1964 by an Oxford anthropologist, Alison Redmayne.[12] It had begun in the middle of the nineteenth century, and was therefore well recorded by the Germans, who found the Hehe a formidable enemy, beginning with the consolidation of a group of tribes in what became central Tanganyika who based their military organisation on that of the Ngoni, to the south of Hehe country. The Ngoni's own origins went back to southern Africa, where one segment had split off from the Zulu Empire and moved northwards, most famously, under Mzilikazi and Lobengula, into Matabeleland, but periodically splitting off many more times to form new, smaller states. John Barnes, the anthropologist, has described this movement as 'The Long March', and – as a former naval officer – further compared it to a fleet of naval vessels cruising the ocean and attacking ports (villages) and seizing booty: in this case, women, slaves, food and ivory. It was, he says, a state alright, but a 'snowball state'.

Other, non-Ngoni, peoples used the formidable Ngoni military organisation as their model, notably the adjoining neighbours of the Hehe, the Sangu and the Bena. They then struggled for hegemony over the region.

Within a few decades, the Hehe had become a centralised kingdom with a big army, based in a strong fortified camp at Kalenga, just outside modern Iringa. Like other such well organised and militaristic societies, they not only raided their neighbours every year but attacked Arab caravans coming from the coast to trade guns and powder for slaves and ivory. Then the Hehe took on the Europeans.

African armies had defeated European ones on several occasions. The British had to fight several bitter wars and suffered several setbacks before they finally defeated the Ashanti in 1901. More important to the British Empire was the mineral wealth of South Africa, the final obstacle to British dominance being the Zulu Empire. The film *Zulu*, celebrating the undoubtedly heroic defence of Rorke's Drift in 1880, has proved to be continuously popular. The film *Zulu Dawn*, commemorating the Zulu victory at Isandlhwana on the very same day, where an entire British Army was destroyed, has been less so.

But the greatest defeat of a European army by an African one has been comparatively ignored. A British army had defeated the Ethiopians at Magdala in 1868, when the Emperor had been killed. His successor then had to fight a war on two fronts, against the

Mahdists in the Sudan, and against a new threat from another European power, Italy, which occupied the Red Sea port of Massawa (encouraged by the British), and now started to move into the interior of Eritrea. But they faced a new Ethiopian Army of 196,000 men, half of whom had European rifles, plus fifty-six guns. In the 'Dogali Massacre' of 1887, the Italians lost 430 dead and eighty-two were wounded. Then, in 1896, came the great battle of Adowa, when General Balatieri (alas, one of Garibaldi's Thousand Red Shirts), who had sworn to bring Emperor Menelik back 'in a cage', experienced 'the greatest defeat inflicted upon a European army by an African army since the time of Hannibal',[13] losing about seven thousand European dead with fifteen hundred wounded. Many Europeans were tortured to death until Menelik put a stop to it. Their askari allies had their right hands and left feet amputated. The remaining Europeans were ransomed for ten million lire. Crespi, the Italian Prime Minister, had to resign. But seven hundred Ethiopians lay dead, ten thousand had been wounded, and Ethiopia had to accept the loss of Eritrea. The humiliation of Italy was only avenged by Mussolini's conquest of Abyssinia forty years later. (In the KAR, we had arrived at Jigjiga only shortly after the Italians had been defeated in their turn.)

Though not on the same scale, the defeat of a German expedition by the Hehe, under their chief Mkwawa in the battle of Lugalo, in 1891, has also been ignored. All that remains, for the record, is the German monument at the site of the battle, celebrating not the victors but the losers – apart from the memories of the Hehe themselves.

The Germans had steadily been crushing other large African polities – the Nyamwezi, the Maasai, the Chagga. The very year after Lugalo, the Hehe mounted a huge attack on an Arab caravan. Mkwawa began to think that the Germans would retire to the coast. The Germans, on the other hand, feared that Mkwawa might attack the coast itself. They determined, therefore, both to avenge Lugalo and to wipe out the growing Hehe menace.

Some said that Mkwawa thought he would be defeated if he ever saw a white man (though he may have shaken hands with one German – in the dark). His gigantic *boma* (fortress) at Kalenga had taken four years to build. It had stone walls, with gates, palisades, military stockades, ditches and watch-towers, a permanent water-supply, food stocks, cattle and cultivation, which, like other menial tasks, was carried out by captives and bondsmen. Inside were thousands of seasoned spearmen, including three hundred men armed with European guns (which, however, Mkwawa did not make good use of). There was an elaborate division of military labour, with spies, frontier forces and messengers.

Mkwawa was a singular despot. The Germans, however, had a Maxim gun, and though the battle raged for over two days, this single weapon was crucial, and the outcome inevitable. Yet Mkwawa escaped, and carried on a guerrilla campaign for four more years, despite a huge reward for his capture, until he was finally tracked down and committed suicide. His head was cut off, and a skull removed from the site of the graves of chiefs (which may not actually have been his) was taken to Germany. So important was this campaign in the whole history of German colonialism that a special clause was inserted in the Treaty of Versailles requiring the return of the skull of Mkwawa to Tanganyika – which eventually did happen, though only as late as 1954.

Compliant Hehe aristocrats were now installed in Mkwawa's place; others were hanged. Children were taught to sing 'Heil dir im Siegekranz', the German national anthem – still sung with enthusiasm by some old people in the 1960s, when Redmayne recorded Bonifas, the son of Mkwawa's successor, Sapi, singing 'German songs and German and Latin hymns in a mixture of muddled German and Latin and Kihehe'[14].

After the death of Mkwawa, the Hehe had had enough. The Germans took Usangu off them, and when the huge Maji-Maji Rebellion swept through the Colony in 1896, they never joined in, though in the rest of the country thousands died, believing that German bullets would turn to water (*maji*).

Yet such was the persisting prestige of the Mkwawa dynasty that the Germans themselves toyed with the idea of appointing Mkwawa's son, Sapi, as his successor, even though Sapi had borne arms at the battle of Kalenga. He had then been educated by the Germans for three years at a monastery on the coast, but it was the British, who had taken over the colony in 1919, who actually took this step in 1926. But with the outbreak of the Second World War, he was regarded as too pro-German, and was removed once more in 1940, and died in exile at Mwanza. Mkwawa's other son, Pancras, whom I recorded singing Sangu war-songs, was also educated at a mission on the coast. But it was still a member of the Mkwawa dynasty – Sapi's son Adam, educated at a British school for chiefs' sons at Tabora and then at Makerere University College – who succeeded Sapi. During the Second World War, Adam was even sent to the Middle East, largely because many Hehe were serving there, and remained Chief of the Hehe until, at the independence of Tanganyika (later Tanzania) in 1961, he lost his administrative powers, but kept his title as Chief of the Hehe, and was also appointed Speaker of the first Parliament.

*****

At weekends we explored everything within reach – tea plantations, mission stations, the town of Mbeya. We visited the tiny capital (a large village, really) of the neighbouring Sangu. Since whites never went there, they took us for government officials, so our arrival caused pandemonium. Singers and food were produced, and the Chief was seated on his throne. We made polite excuses, and extracted ourselves from this diplomatic difficulty. On another occasion we drove up into the mountains of the Nyakyusa. I found it a significant example of the importance of culture over mere physical environment that the people who lived on the hot plains were swaddled in cloth, while those up in the cold mountains wore extremely little. The rest house provided for District Officers and other whites on tour was occupied. Then a white man, with what I thought was a rather strange look in his eye, offered us somewhere to sleep for the night, pointing to a track in the darkness through a banana plantation. His servant duly gave us beds. When we woke up we found we were in a leper colony. I'm sure this was a rather morbid joke on the white man's part, as we found ourselves shaking hands with people whose fingers were missing. More attractive was a visit to Lake Rukwa, where gigantic crocodiles launched themselves like torpedoes from the banks; seconds later, they were just a pair of eyes. When we bumped into submerged hippos, they emerged looking like very offended old gentleman.

We soon found that dotted lines on maps didn't necessarily mean that there was a road there. It could be a washed-away track full of big rocks. As in Australia and South America, crossroads which looked impressive on the map turned out to be a motley collection of run-down buildings. On one muddy mountain road the front wheel of our truck slid over the edge (*The Italian Job* on a less dangerous scale). The cinematic analogy turned out to be apt. Looking for a village to get help, we ended up instead being helped by a European girl with flaxen pig-tails, straight out of *The Sound of Music*, who calmly hitched up eight oxen to our vehicle and pulled it back onto the road. She was one of the last surviving German agricultural settlers.

By now, the Groundnut Scheme had collapsed. The first thing to be axed, of course, was the liberal fringe of the Scheme – our linguistic unit. So we had the opportunity of a last long leave, and decided to drive our ageing Ford V8 estate wagon to South Africa. Rounding a bend just over the Northern Rhodesian (Zambian) border, the whole road was suddenly full of cattle. We hit one, which pushed our radiator backwards, and was to give us trouble, in the African heat, for the whole journey from then onwards. We only stopped at one town on the Copper Belt. But the next day the light-hearted chat came to a dead stop as we saw, fifteen miles away, the truly spectacular sight of the mist rising from the Victoria Falls. I called in at the Rhodes-Livingstone Institute in Livingstone (which was to prove fateful), asking them to let me know if there were any research posts going, and later did the same in Johannesburg.

Crossing into Southern Rhodesia (now Zimbabwe), a prosperous white settler farming country, the road now had two metalled strips, one for each wheel – better, but full of potholes, and when a vehicle was coming in the opposite direction, both parties had to bump off the strips onto the dirt sides of the road, then bump their way back onto the strips again. Then we saw the city lights of Bulawayo, which, like Salisbury (now Harare), proved to be a kind of very large Tunbridge Wells-near-the-Zambesi, basically a very boring, provincial English town, but with thousands of African servants and workers.

Though we had a mechanical engineer in our party, the damage caused by hitting the cow meant we had to leave the V8 for repairs and proceed to South Africa by rail. It certainly was 'Goli', the City of Gold, as the Africans called it, as I found when I visited one of the more comfortable mines where it was 90° F at four thousand feet down.

Then I called in at Witwatersrand University, and at the Communist Party offices, where I was put in the hands of a young, beautiful and highly intelligent journalist called Ruth First, who worked for the Communist Party newspaper. Ruth had taken a Diploma in Social Science at Wits, but had opted for a harder life, having already written a famous searing series of articles exposing conditions on the white farms. She showed me my first shanty-town, and the graveyard opposite, which had only been open for a year, but was filling up fast. That night, returning from a Communist Party meeting, we were jeered at in the street because we were whites associating in public with Indians and Africans. I was surprised that Janie Du Plessis, who gave the talk, found it necessary at all to try and whip up enthusiasm against what was to become, the very next year, State-legislated apartheid.

The Communist Party in South Africa was a party of heroes – Indian, black and white. After a period of ghastly imprisonment, including torture, Ruth eventually came to England; her husband, Joe Slovo, became an outstanding white minister in the post-apartheid government. Ruth was eventually blown to bits by a letter bomb sent by South African Intelligence to Maputo, where they had been living in exile. The torture and killings went on right to the end; our graduate student in Manchester, David Webster, a delightful person, an expert on rock music, who belonged to a liberal pressure group which organised support for the families of victims of apartheid, was shot in the back. The three-mile march at his funeral was the biggest turnout in the main downtown area of Johannesburg since the Emergency had been declared in 1986.

The Indians were less well known to us in the UK, but we did know about the blacks and about whites such as Bram Fischer, an eminent lawyer from a distinguished Afrikaner family who was only released from gaol so that he could die. When Solly Sachs, a leading Afrikaner trade union leader, visited me in Manchester years later with his son, Albie, I had a foreboding that Albie was heading for a grim life; he too was indeed eventually imprisoned, tortured and eventually the victim of a bomb blast which cost him an arm and sight in one eye. Solly once said to me that liberals were people who were 'so open-minded that their brains fell out'. But even being a liberal, in that political climate, took immense courage.

We collected the car in Bulawayo and headed for another Tunbridge Wells, Salisbury, and then to see the stupendous, brooding ruins of the ancient gold-mining city of Great Zimbabwe – so stupendous that for generations it was stoutly denied by whites that Africans could possibly have built such structures. It must have been the Phoenicians – or anyone other than the Bantu. We again found the border shut in 'Portuguese East' – they had a month's worth of saint's days every year. So we returned northwards via the excavations for the new hydroelectric dam at Kariba, which was to serve the needs not of the surrounding rural zones but of the mines and cities of southern Africa.

At the Tanganyika border we were greeted by a complaint that we had damaged a cow. Since the cow, with hundreds of others, was wandering along Africa's equivalent of the MI, I felt no guilt. Back across the border, in the dark, in an area I knew well, I suddenly spotted a tree trunk right across the road. There had been an outbreak of cattle disease and this was a control point. I swerved violently round the end of it, then down into a ditch and up again back onto the road. The people on duty had decided to go to rest for the night, and not bothered to light any warning lamps.

We had a magnificent return to the UK via Rome – with one major, miserable exception. I had immediately gone to the Czech Embassy, asking for a repetition of my visa of a year before but was refused. 'Didn't I know that there had been a change of government?' (the Communists had taken over Czechoslovakia), he asked. Džina waited for me a few months further, but I then got a letter at Cambridge telling me she had got married to her childhood sweetheart. I realised that I had been too unpredictable. It was my fault, I knew. How could she know I wouldn't go off to remote parts again? I had lost my Džina and the Cold War had descended upon Czechoslovakia.

I had no option except to go on to Florence, in time for the Maggio Music Festival and a May Day procession of over half a million people. When I took my wife there three decades later, we got up early and found ourselves in the company of a few hundred others. Then the Giotto frescoes at Padua, Venice, Paris and finally home, where I had no job.

Max

After a couple of months, out of the blue, came a letter asking me to go for interview at the Colonial Office in London, for a research post at the Rhodes-Livingstone Institute (RLI).

The interviewing committee consisted of a Colonial Office official and the former Director of the RLI, Max Gluckman. He proved to be such an amazing personality, uniquely responsible not just for a watershed in my life but for bringing into being, in no time at all, a second 'Manchester School', not of economics but of social anthropology.

The research post was for research into race relations in Southern Rhodesia. 'What is your attitude towards the colour bar?' asked the Colonial Office man. I said that I was opposed to it on scientific grounds, on ethical grounds and just about any other grounds that I could think of. Needless to say, as Max told me on the phone next day, I didn't get the job. But, he said, he had just been appointed to a new Chair of Social Anthropology at the University of Manchester, and would I be interested in applying for a Research

Studentship? Would I?! It was a dream come true. Manchester was a great city, and I could even go home to Merseyside for weekends.

Shortly afterwards, I met my future wife, Sheila, at a meeting of the Wallasey United Nations Association, where the Chairman, Mr Allan, my old headmaster, had invited me to talk on my Tanganyika experiences, since Tanganyika was a UN 'Trust Territory'. There I was greeted by someone who seemed to me the sophisticated model of French Left Bank chic, a Juliette Greco in Wallasey. Luckily I was commuting home every weekend, and able to see a lot of her. By an amazing coincidence she turned out to be a Communist too (there weren't many of them). We were married six weeks later and duly went to … the Left Bank for our blissful honeymoon. This was the first time I had slept with a woman; she too, incredible as it now seems, was new to sex. (Other women told me later they had started at fifteen.)

We lived in the converted roof-space of a Didsbury house – which I thought also the very epitome of Parisian romance. The family was Mancunian/Armenian, and for many weeks I called the father of Adriné, my 'landlady', *haireg*, which was what she called him, thinking this was his name (it means 'Daddy'). Discussing the dangers arising from the breakaway of Yugoslavia from the Comintern, he said it was serious, but the Armenians, he said, would take advantage of the situation to revenge themselves on the Turks.

Max was an upper-class South African of Russian Jews who had immigrated to South Africa. (There was said to have been an Admiral somewhere in his genealogy.) His father had been a lawyer, numbering among his clients Clements Kadalie, the flamboyant leader of the Industrial and Commercial Workers Union. Max, too studied law at Witwatersrand University, then switched to the new subject of anthropology and went as a Rhodes Scholar to Britain, where he attended Malinowski's famous seminars at the London School of Economics (anyone who was anyone, including Jomo Kenyatta and Paul Robeson, attended) and quickly won the strong support of Radcliffe-Brown and Evans-Pritchard. He was very progressive on colonial issues, but, for the record, was never a member of the South African Communist Party or the British one – though his wife Mary, was, which influenced Max considerably.

Max had succeeded Godfrey Wilson, a Christian pacifist confronted with the dilemma of a World War, which drove him, so Max told me, to suicide – though I have never seen this acknowledged in print, even in authoritative sources.[15] The records of the interviews for Wilson's successor as Director of the Rhodes-Livingstone Institute, published over forty years later, reveal that they hadn't even thought of appointing a social anthropologist at all, but a malariologist or an archaeologist. When they eventually did decide on having a social anthropologist, Gluckman had actually been quite low on the list of candidates. K. Oberg, a Canadian of Swedish-Finnish descent, was ruled out for not being a British national. Gluckman, like Meyer Fortes (who later became Professor at Cambridge) was further considered to have two kinds of impurity – South African nationality and Jewishness.

That left my old tutor, Jack Trevor, a physical anthropologist, who decided against the post. Then the famous archaeologist, Louis Leakey, was offered it but refused.

Because of the Nazi-Soviet Pact, Gluckman had at first voiced opposition to the war. Then he did a volte-face and asked to be released from the post to which, at long last, he had been appointed so that he could return to Britain to enlist. This was not allowed.

For a long while he tried to work with the Government as a provider of scientific advice, an 'applied' anthropologist, not because he was a colonial stooge but because he had come to believe in Soviet-style planning, which he saw as rationality in action, and called his major project for the Institute the 'Seven Year Research Plan'. Such was the prestige of planning at that time that even Lord Hailey, the architect of 'Indirect Rule', approved of the 'Five Year Plan of Research' adopted by the International African Institute and funded by the Rockefeller Foundation, which played a major role in developing anthropology under Radcliffe-Brown and Malinowski.

One striking instance of the kind of practical research Max participated in involved cooperating with agriculturalists, notably Bill Allen and his colleagues, Trapnell and Clothier, who produced powerful refutations, based on careful research, of the view widely held by whites that African 'slash-and burn' agriculture – which involved cutting down and burning the bush so as to produce fertilising ash – was the very epitome of African irrationality. He showed, instead, that given a stable population and enough spare land to permit periodic rotation from one area to another – once its productivity began to go down – this kind of agriculture worked very well. But when populations rose and land could not be left to recover, as was beginning to be the case under colonial conditions, soil-exhaustion and erosion could indeed ensue.

There was widespread opposition, though, to what was felt to be RLI interference with Government policy. One reactionary

Provincial Commissioner declared that research workers, 'full of strange ideas', should not be allowed to discuss political questions or criticise Government officials unless closely supervised by a District Officer. Gluckman in particular – he had it on the authority of his mother's first cousin, Professor H.M. Chadwick, a 'foremost anthropologist at Cambridge University' – was 'quite irresponsible' and 'can talk in a language quite unintelligible to the ordinary human being'. Then, among his next people – the Barotse – Max, clumsy and gangling as he was, accidentally shot and killed the Lozi dignitary in charge of the Royal Barge, for which he was committed for trial but was discharged. On top of that, he was hauled before the Governor following complaints about his political loyalty. Wilson was reduced to writing a fairly grovelling letter in Gluckman's defence.

Far more significant was the opposition to the RLI from the mining interests – 'a state within a state' which operated under 'extremely favourable conditions'. They did what they liked in the mining towns and controlled the economy. In 1937, they earned £300,000, 'merely by existing', from copper royalties alone. It was nothing to them to pay a bit to the RLI, though with much foot dragging. Even Max, as Brown (the main authority) noted, though intellectually fully aware of their impact on the rural areas, 'showed remarkably little direct interest in [the mines], and ... never paid the Copper Belt a proper visit'. Godfrey Wilson had won grudging permission to carry out first-hand research there himself, though in the end his penetrating *The Analysis of Social Change* had to be based on published materials. When it was further drawn upon by Leonard Barnes, in a popular Penguin with the title *Soviet Light on the Colonies*, alarm bells rang.

The Copper Belt had long been highly unstable. In a major strike of 1935, six miners had been killed by the police. By 1940, a particularly ominous strike of white miners sparked off another by blacks, resulting in the deaths of seventeen of the latter at the hands of the military. Provisional research permits were now withdrawn and work in progress suspended. When the RLI did finally send Bill Epstein to carry out a study of a mining town years later he was banned from entering the mining compounds because he had dared to stand on a platform with a leading trade unionist.

Max's position was fast becoming impossible. He had always avoided letting research become centralised (effectively, in the hands of the Colonial Office), arguing instead for locally-based research institutes such as the RLI but with the crucial provision for anthropologists to write up their reports in South African or British universities. He now gave up applied anthropology and opted for academia in the UK, though still keeping one foot in Africa.

I arrived at Manchester to take up one of the new Research Studentships not long after Max had started to set up the new Department. The interview was interesting, and quite unlike the Colonial Office ones. One Economics professor, who had served in the KAR, asked me whether I thought there was any validity in the common view among whites in East Africa that some tribes were 'warlike', and others not. I said I didn't agree with that, and that it probably stemmed from initial resistance, or absence of it, to the British colonial regime.

Manchester had long been the seat of the famous 'Manchester School' of Economics, with people like Arthur Lewis, and that Department outnumbered all the rest. Yet the whole Faculty was so small that staff and research workers together could all get into a small room for coffee. It is PC to say that this led to intellectual interchange with other disciplines, but I can't say this really happened, the Government Department excepted.

All the disciplines were now being expanded. Two of my fellow candidates, in Government and Social Administration respectively, both ended up as professors at Manchester. The anthropologists I found myself among were a small handful of new boys in a new discipline – Ronnie Frankenberg, Freddie Bailey and, by far the most brilliant of all of us, Victor Turner. (When Vic and I were at Brandeis University in Boston years later, when he had just returned from a few months in Mexico and had given several papers, including his famous one on pilgrimages, one Mexicanist turned to me and said, 'Now I can see what I should have been studying for ten years!')

I was writing up my field data for an MA on the Hehe language and giving my colleagues some seminars on the structure of the Bantu languages when Max suddenly asked one day whether I wanted to be a linguist or an anthropologist. 'An anthropologist', I said. 'Well', he replied, 'you don't really know much, and you'd better start finding out. You've read Evans-Pritchard; now go away and read Fortes' two books on the Tallensi.' I was shocked. I had no higher opinion of the teaching at Cambridge than he did, but I did, after all, have what I had been told was a very creditable degree in the subject from Cambridge. But he was absolutely right. So I sat in the Manchester Reference Library and worked my way through the difficult Fortes volumes. I was duly very impressed with them – yet unhappy at the same time, and said why in my MA dissertation. Fortes' analysis seemed to me an idealist model which assumed that everything was determined by kinship and clanship. Today, I recognise that there is no economic reason why patrilineality should be so central to Tallensi culture (other people, for example, have matrilineal kinship systems), and that this is indeed a cultural not an economic fact. But Fortes' analysis of the kinship and clanship system seemed to me to be too algebraic, to hang together just too perfectly as a system of 'kinship-(and clanship)-in-themselves', and to give no weight at all to economic relations in generating social solidarity (though it was Max who made me express this in the manuscript more forcibly than I had intended).

Max started with a major advantage – not only a lifetime's knowledge of Africa but years directing research at the Rhodes-Livingstone Institute, where a whole series of people had passed through his hands and done first-class fieldwork. He was also able to juggle finding research posts for new people in Central Africa, while ensuring, very assiduously, that there were posts for them at Manchester, and eventually teaching posts, when they came back from the field. Manchester was also very generous to its new professors – when they arrived, they were given one or two 'honeymoon' posts, and from year to year there were others. Then, from the early 1960s, the whole university system expanded as the 'Robbins' period began.

In Manchester we had one major additional advantage over other universities – a special fund for the social sciences endowed by Lord Simon – a big engineering magnate and Liberal – backed by his wife, who had her own distinguished career in family planning and other social welfare work. They eventually gave their home at Didsbury, Broomcroft Hall, to our Faculty as accommodation for visiting scholars. It was run by their butler, 'Mac', who masterminded sumptuous dinners a couple of times per annum for all of us. On these occasions people were presented to Lady Simon, in audience, as she sat in a large chair. It was rather like approaching Queen Victoria's throne.

This munificence meant that we had a stream of distinguished visiting scholars, usually from overseas, who were glad to come to such a comfortable place where the academic demands on them were far from onerous. They usually spent a term with us and were only expected to give a couple of papers, or a series, about their latest work. Many of them were Africanists (and not all of them, like Solly Sachs, were academics). So we were exposed, day after day, to superb extracts from work in progress, usually before it hit the Press, from people like M.N. Srinivas on the Coorgs of South India or Kathleeen Gough on the amazing kinship/caste system of the Malabar coast. Most of the papers, though – notably Max's pioneer work on Barotse jurisprudence and Emrys Peters' research into the Beduin of Cyrenaica – came from our own internal resources. Given an audience at the Emir's court, the courtiers politely laughed behind their hands at Emrys, a Brit who spoke in a dialect of desert nomads very different from their own courtly speech. (The same thing happened to John Barnes, who reduced the population of Norway to hysteria by giving a broadcast in the 'hick' dialect of Bremnes, the offshore island he had studied.)

Kathleen, who had been at Cambridge in my time, where she was adored by all the men, was to suffer as much as I did in the McCarthy epoch, being fired from her university post at Brandeis. In the UK, Ronald Frankenberg was also refused permission to disembark from his ship after travelling to the Windward Islands to do field research, while Frank Girling, who did his fieldwork in Uganda, was unwise enough to invite an Indian Marxist colleague to visit him in Uganda and was forced by the Colonial Office to remove an Appendix in his work discussing the theories of Friedrich Engels. In the US, two fine anthropologists, Irving Goldman and Gene Weltfish, I found out much later, also lost their university posts. It is important to remember, though, that it was by no means just intellectuals who suffered during the McCarthy epoch. George Clooney's fine film about Ed Murrow and his CBS colleagues in Manhattan, *Goodnight and Good Luck*, should not allow us to forget that most of the victims of McCarthyism were much less important and famous figures, who also struggled for a more equitable society.

In weekly seminars, those of us who had no fieldwork to draw upon were put to work as well, and Max expected us to work as hard as he did. One Friday afternoon he told me to read Junod's two-volume *The Life of a South African Tribe*, plus another volume, and give a paper on the lot next Monday afternoon. I did, and gave up a concert by what my dear landlady, Mrs Walters, called the 'Ally Band.

So there was a price to pay for all this stimulus. Max was, as everyone recognised, what passes for the stereotype of an authoritarian African chief. Not for nothing had he worked with the Zulu, though his relations with the royal family had actually ended in disaster, when, he told me, he had intervened to stop a

Zulu prince flogging a man to death, and was therefore thrown out of Zululand – which was why he never produced a monograph on that people.

He was also an upper-class white South African, used to having servants to do what he wanted, including working in his garden. When visitors arrived from Africa we would be summoned to Cheadle Hulme to talk to them – five of us once jammed into, literally, a small broom closet, when his house was being decorated, to meet Ian Cunnison.

Max prided himself, rightly, on his style as a writer, preferring short, Anglo-Saxon words to long, Latinate ones. His manuscripts were covered with crossings out where he tried one adjective after another. This lucidity gave him the ability to communicate with readers other than anthropologists, notably on the radio. His series of talks on the highly prestigious Third Programme of the BBC, mostly about quite arcane African anthropological topics such as witchcraft, were immensely popular but never 'dumbed down'.[16] His commitment to writing, too, infected me, so that I've always felt a little restless if I'm not writing something (like this).

One thing anthropologists are good at is myth, and they duly concocted one about our Department. Where the Tallensi were believed to be held together by kinship and clanship, our social cement was said to be our subscription to a common ideology introduced by Max – football. It is true we were all leaned on heavily to go as a gang to Old Trafford, as were visiting scholars. But many of us had been watching football from childhood, and Vic Turner and I stood on the ruins of the Stretford End and watched the rise of United long before Max ever tried to organise us.

The football model of Manchester departmental solidarity is also sub-intellectual. It neglects how important Max's *ideas* were, for he had something other departments didn't have – a coherent theoretical position. The analysis of 'the social situation', and not solely of larger-scale structures, was also one of his methodological emphases. More widely, to him, conflict was basic in any society or social situation. Those who were opposed in one sphere might, however, be aligned with quite other people and have different opponents in other spheres. Division in one sphere 'cut across' divisions in another, and these did not overlap so as to form one absolute kind of generalised opposition dividing people across the whole social order. These cross-cutting ties and overlaps therefore made possible the overall persistence, even the integration, of the social order. And since there were many kinds or sources of social opposition, no one of them (such as class struggle) was any more determinant or 'ultimate' than any other.

Marxists such as Ronnie Frankenberg and myself were inoculated against this doctrine because we saw contradiction and conflict not only as basic elements in Nature; not only because we accepted a more evolutionist view that new forms of life emerged; but because we saw these changes as resulting from revolutionary, disjunctive ('qualitative') changes of kind, not just cumulative ('quantitative') transitions. In society, class struggle was the ultimate, decisive kind of conflict. Raymond Firth (no Marxist) also observed in a perceptive 'Memoir' about Max, that social conflict became a 'mechanism of integration' 'not only within groups, but also between them'.[17] It was a kind of functionalism by the back door.

Max was in great demand from publishers, and generously introduced them also to the work we were doing. Before long, our Department, new as it was, was as good as any in the country and, I thought, in my more euphoric moments, in the world!

But the Cold War was still with us. I applied again for a post with the RLI, and this time, Max told me by phone, I had got the appointment, but MI5 had put a block on it. The viciousness and omnipresence of the Cold War is hard to recall from this distance in time. Max told me, for instance, that Evans-Pritchard, the professor at Oxford whose work I deeply admired, had said that he would do his best to ensure that I, as a Marxist, never got a post in anthropology – and he (and others) succeeded.

We made one last effort to circumvent British colonialism by applying to the Horniman Institute to study an eminently apolitical topic (double descent kinship systems) in an even worse colony, Angola, which was backed by Radcliffe-Brown, who was Visiting Professor at Manchester, but it came to nothing. After eight years of concentrating on Africa, that continent was now obviously closed to me. Max therefore advised me to apply to a new department in the new Australian National University in Canberra – a real gamble since I had to admit that I knew nothing about that continent or about the Pacific, to which I would probably be sent, apart from Firth's own work on the Tikopia and – what every anthropology student had read – Malinowski's books on the Trobriand Islands of New Guinea. Despite this ethnographic ignorance, Raymond Firth, the doyen of Pacific Studies and Professor of Anthropology at the prestigious London School of Economics, appointed me to a Research Studentship. Firth himself was going out to Canberra to start up the Faculty of Social Sciences, within which was the new

Department of Anthropology, headed by an outstanding intellectual, Siegfried Nadel, a man with a track record of distinguished research and publication on Nigeria, Eritrea and the Sudan.

I had therefore to convert myself, overnight, into a student of the Pacific. I also had to say to Sheila, to whom I had become engaged, and had duly warned of my fieldwork plans, that now we would be going, not to Africa, but ten thousand miles away from her family, especially from her beloved, ageing grandfather (who did indeed die while we were in Australia).

CHAPTER 4

Australia: Into the Lion's Den

Going to Australia, I realised, might mean an interesting job but it would also be walking into trouble because I had visas from East European countries in my passport. Australia, under Sir Robert Menzies (known on the Left as 'Pig-iron Bob', because he had sold that commodity to Japan – which duly returned it to Australia in the form of bombs on Australia's Far North), made Britain look like a liberal Paradise. It was great visiting Gibraltar, Ceuta, Naples, Sorrento, Herculaneum and Pompeii, then, once more, Suez, where I had first entered the Empire (I hadn't popularised the term 'Third World' yet!). Now Sheila made the same journey down the same street from the ship. After fifty yards, overwhelmed by the beggars and the donkey shit, she turned to me and said, 'Could you take me back to the ship? I don't think I can stand this'. But she stuck it out, not just then but for a lifetime of the sometimes exciting, often tough life of an anthropologist's wife.

Then she had better experiences for a while – Aden, Colombo (where she saw the remarkable spectacle of magicians who could make plants grow up, out of the sand, before your very eyes) and, finally, Fremantle and Perth. On board our ancient ship, the *Maloja* (wisely broken up soon afterwards), we had splendid companions – miners from Newcastle and nurses who were all emigrating to Australia on £10 tickets. Life on board was like one of Goffman's 'total institutions'. People fell in love, got married or, less pleasantly, threw themselves overboard.

At the very moment that our ship sailed into the Great Australian Bight the result of Menzies' national Referendum to outlaw the Australian Communist Party was announced. We might well have landed only to go straight into jail. But the Referendum produced a majority of 'No' votes – only, however, by a hundred thousand votes out of the entire population.

We were met by friends of Sheila's and experienced our first encounter with corruption in Australia, for they were living in a flat provided by their relative's trade union and we were then driven up to Canberra by a chauffeur in a union car.

We were obliged to live in a very comfortable hostel provided by the ANU (Australian National University), which was fine except that it cost us more than our Studentship provided for total living. We were about the poorest people in Australia, the Aborigines apart. Australians used to stagger out of the butcher's with half-sheep across their shoulders while we ordered a couple of chops. And I had to go off to the Department every morning leaving Sheila, who knew nobody at all, crying more than she had ever cried in her life. There were a few dreary shopping centres – and she couldn't afford to shop. Around us was a social and cultural desert, the capital of Australia, named by local wits, after the vast deserts of the interior, the 'Dead Heart of Australia'.

Australia was not the country it is now, which all young Europeans want to visit, and Canberra, to put no finer point upon it, was a dump. It was a vision of a garden city by an American urban planner, Walter Burley Griffin, but unfortunately it hadn't been built yet. (We were lucky enough, later, to spend a week in an 'atrium' house built by him at Castle Crag, Sydney.) Despite his vision, Canberra, at that point, even in the Civic Centre, still possessed largely underdeveloped 'paddocks' or fields and a population of only thirty thousand people. I regularly developed conjunctivitis from the dust that swirled across the city. Nor, like the whole country, was it all that prosperous then. There was only one decent restaurant, though that scarcely mattered to us, since we were only able to afford to visit it once (I remember it was Chicken Maryland), and a few cinemas. (Visiting, years later, our hostess rang a friend from our restaurant and told her we were 'just' having a Vietnamese banquet). Even worse, virtually all the employment was in the Public Service and, worst of all, if a woman married she had to give up her Public Service job.

Canberra also suffered, like the whole country, from the legacy of English culture. If ever a country needed Germaine Greer it was Australia. What Canberra did have, however, was marvellous Australians, especially Communists, who we discovered were virtually underground.

We house-sat for friends who were on holiday until we were allowed by ANU to leave our hostel. Eventually our lives were saved by two of the most delightful people I have ever met, Gwen and Mac Dickins, who remained friends for half a century. The Department was very small and new, just like Manchester, and was housed in old but perfectly satisfactory wooden buildings which had been a Nurses' hostel – and are now preserved as a cultural heritage.

Like Manchester, ANU was a new department; indeed, the whole university was no bigger than the Manchester Faculty. It was conceived of as a kind of high-level think-tank which would produce young scholars who would go on to staff other universities in Australia. Full of youthful energy, one of the first things the handful of new Research Students did was to form an ANU Students Association, which turned out to be one of the best things we ever did, because when I fell victim to Australia's version of McCarthyism, our affiliation to the federation of student organisations across the country won us support from them and it was the only organisation which ever helped me.

In such a small university, one could meet people like Marcus Oliphant, the country's leading nuclear scientist (who spent his retirement years campaigning against nuclearism), or Frank Titterton, who took time off to show us his linear accelerator. Closer to our discipline was the geographer, Oskar Spate (not as well known as he should be in the UK), who had already produced a major work on India (which included a characteristic reference in the index to 'Census of India, damnable deficiencies of'), and went on to produce three superb volumes on the exploration of the Pacific. C.P. Fitzgerald had recently produced a magnificent survey of Chinese history and culture.

We were therefore exposed to leading Australian teachers who had returned to start up new faculties at ANU but who, at that time, didn't have a lot to do. There were more chiefs than Indians. So Paddy Moran was happy to give a tiny group of us Statistics lectures, and Geoffrey Sawer lectured on law.

Nadel was an outstanding intellect. He had studied music as a performer and had taken his own opera company on a tour of Czechoslovakia; had written several works on music, including one on musical typology and a biography of Busoni; had broadcast for Radio Vienna on ethnomusicology, all before the age of thirty. He then switched to anthropology, taking his doctorate in Psychology and Philosophy.

As a Jew, he was then driven into exile in England. Though an Austrian, his style was Prussian. He had worked among the Nupe in Nigeria and the Nuba in the Sudan at a time when 'punitive military patrols were common',[18] and had access to a police squad, and could summon informants at will. He told me that he had never had any difficulties with finding informants – he simply told the sergeant to line them up whenever he needed them – and wrote unashamedly about the 'bullying technique' he used.

My tutor was Bill Stanner, who had worked in East Africa, was scholarly and approachable and had also worked on the Aborigines of the Kimberleys in Western Australia in the 1930s. He hadn't published a lot, but made up for this in later life with a set of pioneering articles on Aboriginal religion. He was also a friend of leading liberals (i.e. conservatives), and could therefore entertain us with fine Hunter River wines.

Seminars were an intellectual pleasure. Nadel, having already written *The Foundations of Social Anthropology*, gave us a superb set of papers which became *The Theory of Social Structure*, light-years ahead of his more pedestrian anthropological colleagues, if only in its use of notation developed in symbolic logic.

As we got to know people, life improved. Sheila got a job in a bookshop, and as Canberra had little public entertainment, we spent our evenings drinking and singing bush ballads with Communist and other progressive friends. (It is a mistake, however, to try and play tennis against Australians.) We could also escape to Sydney from time to time, which was immensely pleasurable.

In such a place, your social life is more important than commercial entertainment. Our friends included some of the finest people I have ever met: some war heroes like Bob Michell, who had flown Catalinas around the South Pacific, and Mac Dickins, who never told me until a year or two before he died that he had been on the deadly Kokoda Trail in New Guinea. (The Japanese themselves lost a quarter of a million men in New Guinea.)

I was to work among a people in the Central Highlands of New Guinea (only penetrated by white men in the 1930s), neighbours of the Gahuku-Gama already studied by Michael Read. I had read the Patrol Reports in the Department of Territories (Australia's equivalent of the Colonial Office), thanks to a suggestion of my friend, Frederick Rose, himself an anthropologist who had worked on Aboriginal kinship on Groote Eylandt, an island in the Gulf of Carpentaria. Everything was ready. We had been down to Sydney to order a year's supplies (how much pepper would we get through in year?) from Horderns, the big department store. These stores were now waiting on the boat we would embark on, in the dock at Sydney.

I had already got into a quite non-political kind of trouble. I had carelessly put down on my application form for the ANU Research Studentship that I was a 'BA(Hons) (Cantab.)'. I thought all Cambridge degrees were Honours Degrees, but mine (which I hadn't solicited, and therefore paid little attention to) wasn't. (Cambridge, in those days, wasn't that punctilious about its degrees anyhow, I thought. To get your MA, for example, you just had to pay up.)

My BA was a BA (Wartime Regulations). So I was virtually accused of making a false declaration. I could only plead (a) carelessness and (b) that my tutor, Jack Trevor, had said that they would have given me a *starred* first, but that starred firsts were not awarded for the preliminary exam. Firth, the Dean, reproved me, but forgave me.

Next, I went down to Territories to collect my entry permit for New Guinea – a formality, I thought. 'Not for you' was the response of the official I saw. MI5 had struck again. I had been banned once more, from another continent.

So I decided to go public. After five years' preparation, I would never be allowed to do fieldwork, and without that you couldn't become an anthropologist. If I was to go down, I thought, I might as well go down fighting – and pull the temple down with me. Being besieged by the odd paparazzo was nothing compared to what celebrities have to put up with nowadays, but it was nevertheless an experience I would not like to repeat. Sheila was in tears. My photo was printed in the *Sydney Morning Herald* and the case was debated in Parliament.

But the ANU did keep my Studentship going and continued to finance my planned fieldwork. I was saved, not by colleagues in the ANU (one, who had proposed to employ me as an interviewer, was only concerned that my participation might prejudice her research project) but by someone outside the University altogether – Fred Rose. He looked and sounded like a dinkum, one hundred per cent Aussie – except that he wasn't. He had studied biology at Cambridge; then took a Diploma in Anthropology; then, in the hard times of the 1930s, emigrated to Western Australia and got himself a job as a meteorologist in Broome. From there, he moved to Groote Eylandt in the Gulf of Carpentaria – a stopping-off place for seaplanes on the London-Sydney run – because the airbase was across a small bay from an Aboriginal settlement, Umbakumba, where another English immigrant, Fred Gray, had established a settlement with Aborigines he had previously employed diving for trepang (a sea-slug which lives on the coastal floor and is highly prized by the Chinese because it is said to be an aphrodisiac).

When the trepang industry collapsed with the outbreak of war, Fred Gray got himself recognised as a 'Protector' of 250 Aborigines, which entitled him to a small Government subsidy. Fishing and hunting, in a rich environment, brought in food.

Though whites from the airbase were not supposed to go onto the Reserve, Fred Rose, obsessed by Aboriginal kinship (largely because of Friedrich Engels' *The Origin of the Family*) proceeded to study them. He was full of nineteenth-century evolutionist ideas. But he was also meticulous in the use of scientific method and a scrupulous fieldworker, and devised a method of recording the kinship terms used by every Aborigine on Groote towards every other on a matrix pro forma.

While I was in Canberra he published an authoritative study of the cattle industry in northern Australia. But it was the research which he did on the Groote Eylandt kinship system[19] which has been described by the eminent Dutch anthropologist, Josselin de Jong, as 'not only a new contribution to kinship studies, but a new *approach* to them'.[20] Yet, Fred told me later after his book had ultimately been published in East Berlin, it was still never reviewed in academic journals either in Australia or in the Soviet Union.

So he suggested that they couldn't stop me doing field research within Australia, and offered to write to Fred Gray for me. Security is never perfect, and once Fred Gray had agreed, the machinery was set in motion for us to go to Groote, by train and plane to Burketown, then by a boat, the *Cora*, which took supplies to the mission stations round the Gulf.

The line stopped at Townsville, where the streets were lined with mango trees from which you could pluck fruit as you walked along. Less pleasant were the thousands of cockroaches which came out when the sun went down, or the sand flies which you didn't notice biting you until you were unable to sleep for a week. I met my first Aborigine at Palm Island, which was used as a dumping ground for Aboriginals who had broken the law or were deviant in other ways. I couldn't understand the man who talked to me in what I thought was pidgin, probably because he was simply a mentally unstable inmate.

Outside Townsville some jokers had built a museum which included two strange 'aboriginal' torsos carved in wood, completely unlike anything recorded in the books. I took full details and photographs, wrote them up and sent them to Sydney to the brilliant linguist Capell and the archaeologist Fred McCarthy, both of whom unhesitatingly said they were fakes by white men. I'm sure they were right.

Aborigines had eaten shellfish for thousands of years at the coast, and built up what archaeologists call 'kitchen middens'. Australian gangers on the railway lines had accumulated middens of beer bottles. The end of the line was Cloncurry, a copper-mining town which had had a population of twenty thousand in the 1920s. Now it had a few hundred and one hotel instead of the many it had had in its heyday (you were still made to wear collar and tie in heat of over 100° F). Shown round the town, I commented on the number of burned-out buildings. Was it, I asked, due to the terrible heat? 'Hell, no!', said my guide, 'when the town started to go downhill, people burned down buildings in the night to collect the insurance!'

Sheila had never flown before, and had been looking forward to stewardess service. Instead, she had to sit on mailbags being delivered to the giant cattle stations by our little Cessna, in between vomiting due to the waves of heat. (One of the Vestey-owned stations was said to be as big as Wales.) A Land Rover drove out to collect mail and gave us coffee.

Burketown, with eighty residents and a geyser pouring tens of thousands of gallons of hot mineral water down the middle of the only street, made Cloncurry look like St Tropez. A handful of Aborigines slumbered under the wooden stilts which kept the termites at bay, while balls of lantana, like tumbleweed, bowled all over the place.

Queensland had a good policy of requiring new public servants to spend a year in the outback. But since no one wanted to be there they were boiling with resentment, and backbiting seemed to be the main sport. I was warned not to believe a word the Matron said and the Matron warned me not to speak to the teacher. Sgt. Hegarty, the policeman, gave me my first lesson in role-compartmentalisation. 'When I have to put an Aborigine on trial', he said, 'I put on my hat and sit on this side of the table. Then, in my capacity of Protector of Aborigines, I have to defend him, so I take off my hat and go round the other side of the table'.

The pub was filled with jackeroos going on annual leave to points in the South. After drinking all night they shot off into the bush on wild horseback races; some came back with broken legs. It was pure *Crocodile Dundee*, or (another wonderful film) *Outback*. They might dream of their girlfriends in the surf at Bondi Beach, but some of them never got there when they lost all their money at 'two-up' to some local Chips Rafferty.

The *Cora* was a 200-ton vessel which regularly got stuck in the river-mouths of the shallow Gulf so we had to wait for the tide to float us off while the captain swung the lead. We used charts first made by Matthew Flinders in 1802. At 6.20 P.M. precisely, clouds of mosquitoes, the bite from even one of which could go through a shirt and was very uncomfortable, descended from both banks. We retreated under mosquito nets to our camp-beds on deck, and ate kingfish steaks which we caught on long lines. The crew hauled in a monstrous hammerhead shark on a huge hook baited with a leg of meat. There were six perfectly shaped foetuses inside it.

First stop was Mornington Island, where David McKnight was to carry out classic research, starting in 1963, for a total of more than six years spread over fifteen years. When I began, anthropologists only did a year or two in the field and often never went back, then spent years writing up their material. Now, with more money available, they keep going back time and again.

The missionaries immediately impounded the pet cat one Aborigine had brought ashore and had it destroyed. Fred Gray did the same with a wholesale cull of cats and dogs at Groote. Why they were so concerned was explained to me later by a friend who had been brought up on a New South Wales sheep station, where feral cats had grown big and savage enough that they attacked sheep.

Borroloola had once even possessed a library; now a few dugout canoes manned by Aborigines ferried goods up to a collection of run-down buildings.

The Aborigines of Groote Eylandt

Then the mighty Roper River; then across to the mission station at Angurugu, Groote Eylandt, where we were not allowed to disembark because the Christian charity of the Church Missionary Society (Church of England) did not extend to us.

Rounding the island, we arrived at Umbakumba, our destination, a cluster of solid wooden buildings with kitchen gardens and a large dam for water, maintained by 250 Aborigines. Our only communication with the outside world was by boat or foot twenty miles to the Mission, or by using the radio which was powered by a treadle, like an old-fashioned sewing machine, and put isolated spots like ours in touch with other similar settlements round the Gulf at six o'clock every evening. It was from this that we learned of the death of Stalin and of the Coronation.

We were given a room in a splendid concrete building, with running water and a lavatory, and an open-sided room which gave onto a garden of orchids. Not for us the sufferings of fieldwork. We had a kerosene oven, and Fred had a kerosene fridge. The Aborigines lived on the beach, in the open; in the dry season they warmed themselves with fires; in the wet season they took cover beneath sheets of stringy bark.

Then I was introduced to two marvellous informants – Kulpidya, one of Nature's diplomats – and Mini-mini, already recognised by the leading authority on Aboriginal art, Leonhard Adam, as one of the very best bark-painters in the country. I only had to pay them for their services as informants in the universal medium of exchange, 'sticks' of compressed tobacco sweepings from the factory floor.

The majority of the tribe (of only 450 people), however, lived at the Mission, which was a very considerable drawback for our research. It might be thought that this tribe, with so few people, divided into two, with most of them in another settlement which I could not visit, was too tiny to be studied and too degraded by white domination. It turned out to be a very complex and persisting culture, with a formidable kinship and clanship system, a religion that proved difficult to get into, and knowledge systems we call ethnobotany and ethnobiology that I only became aware of as my research progressed. The article which I subsequently published on the latter subject[21] was eventually superseded by a study of world stature, based on fifteen years research into the biology, linguistics and ethnology of Groote Eylandt, by a missionary, Dr Julie Waddy.[22]

I had argued with the leadership of the Communist Party (who invited me to speak to their Central Committee on the subject) that Aborigines were by now proletarians, not nomads.[23] This might seem a non-issue, since one can be committed to the class struggle and be religious at the same time – culture is not confined to economic position or political identity. But at that time Aboriginal tribal cultures were still disappearing rapidly. Richard Chenhall records the tragic case of one old man in northern New South Wales, the last survivor of his tribe, who buried the remaining ritual objects of his people – forever. But he also records, as late as 2002, that once they secured rights to land and once they had acquired a new 'Black Pride' the tiny remnants of several former tribes, scattered and small as they were, came together to form a new kind of Aboriginal community out of the cultural scraps left to them.[24]

On Groote, the first thing I had to do was to tackle the language. I had two advantages: one, a very good outline of the grammar, written by a missionary; secondly, through Bantu, a knowledge of languages with plenty of noun classes. Of the five hundred Australian languages, many are not difficult to learn, but about a dozen are complicated in the extreme. I, of course, had one of these latter. To take merely one example, pronouns distinguish not only plurals but duals and trials, plus inclusive and exclusive forms (distinguishing 'you-and-I' from three or more people). I continued working on one problem I had just discovered at the end of my stay – that of 'secondary particles' – up to the very last day I was there.[25] Next day, as the dinghy pulled away from the shore, I thought to myself 'I shall never use this language again'.)

At the beginning, we had a unique opportunity when, within a few days of our arrival, several senior ritual experts arrived from the Mission to attend a circumcision ceremony, for the one and only time during out stay (such pagan rituals not being allowed at the Mission, the obverse of the policy the Aborigines dubbed 'No pray, no tucker'). I wasn't able to communicate with the religious specialists even in Pidgin; nor, in the dark, could I make out what was going on in the complicated sequence of dances.

My main focus was upon the kinship system, the heart of any Aboriginal culture. I followed Fred Rose's model – firstly, because I knew so little about Aboriginal culture; secondly, because he had done it so excellently. I did add something, though: genealogies written on sheets of kitchen paper which stretched out sideways many feet, a technique suggested to me in Manchester by Elizabeth Colson, the only time I received any formal teaching whatsoever in fieldwork techniques. This enabled me to add to Rose's matrix method the more usual techniques of the genealogical method.

This kept me busy until Christmas, when we had a party and sports. I was in charge of the sprint races. The fleet of foot soon outpaced the slower ones. But at the end, they all came in pretty much the same, in a long line. They didn't want to disgrace one another.

Then came the wet season, a period of monsoon weather so hot and humid that Sheila once lay down where the wall met the floor of our concrete building, like an animal, because it was a few degrees cooler. Then we found ourselves 150 miles away from the epicentre of a hurricane, which brought the sea two hundred yards up to the dunes on which our buildings were built. Sheets of corrugated iron were flying at waist-height and would have cut anyone in two.

Fred Gray had purported that he was taken aback because the *Cora* had brought no supplies for him. (I later became convinced that he had simply run out of money, and had ordered nothing.) Our limited supplies had therefore to be shared, and the Aborigines had to be sent into the bush to fend for themselves on 'bush tucker'. They came back sleek and fat through not having to live on 'damper' flour and tea as usual.

When it cooled down, I immediately went out with groups of Aborigines to explore the island. I'd given the children a map of the island, with nothing other than the coastline shown (because there was nothing man-made on the island, apart from the two settlements), and asked them to put down anything important. Their maps were covered with spiders' webs. 'What are these?' I asked. 'Roads, of course', they replied, referring to tracks virtually invisible to a white man.

I thought I was reasonably fit until I went out with the Aborigines. They loped along with ease, mile after mile, breaking off only to run after goannas or dig out (delicious) wild yams with their spear-throwers, while I was dying to rest my leg muscles. They walked as if flat-footed, on top of the sand, whereas my boot prints showed a deep impression of the heel, then a push-off from my toes. Aborigines didn't normally go walkabout at all, as they had to work in the settlement, but we did two major trips with them in the bush. On the first, I went to Central Hill (a mere two hundred feet high, but the highest point in the whole Gulf of Carpentaria). That's what whites call it. To the Aborigines, it is Yandarrnga, a mythological Being who came from the mainland during the Creation time, accompanied by Sawfish, Shovel-nosed Ray and other companions, giving rise to sacred sites as they went and establishing the territories of the clans.

'On top' was a huge, dramatic overhanging cave covered with rock-paintings, many of them scenes of the annual visits of the Makassarese, who had come down from the Celebes for hundreds of years fishing for trepang until Australia, as part of its then white Australian chauvinism, stopped them in 1907. There were the praus, their rigging, sails and double-rudders and the crews.

One benefit, for the white anthropologist, of the colonial *pax Australiana*, was that you were not likely to get speared any more. Another was that a white person was able to go pretty much where s/he liked, so I was able to photograph and make good copies of the paintings on kitchen paper. I was then asked by C.P. Mountford, a well-known popular writer on the Aborigines, if I would make them available for a forthcoming volume he was publishing for UNESCO. A great entrepreneur, he had persuaded the *National Geographic* magazine to finance a joint US-Australian expedition to Arnhem Land, and UNESCO had already published a lavish edition of the first volume of the resulting papers. But when I reviewed it for the *Journal of the Royal Anthropological Institute*, I had to say that it was an 'old-fashioned, ethnological' collection of facts, with 'no coherent theoretical analysis whatsoever'; that though the main interest of Arnhem Land was that it was an Aboriginal reserve, there was not a single professional anthropologist among the seventeen members of the expedition; and that Mountford's own contribution was no substitute. His transliteration of texts in Anildilyakwa, the language of Groote, for example, was amateurish in the extreme: thus he used the (misspelled) term for the stringy-bark 'shades' (*auwarawalja*) which the Aborigines constructed while they were performing their major religious rituals as the name of the rituals themselves – rather like, I said, referring to Queen Elizabeth's recent coronation as the 'Westminster Abbey'! Then followed the usually sort of academic barney – I was 'foolish' and 'incapable of understanding the purpose and subject of the book'; he was merely 'collecting facts', 'free from "academic bias"'. I retorted that facts didn't make sense of themselves and that theory was not some extra frill to be added in later, and even queried his interpretation of Aboriginal art.[26]

So he refused to publish the article I had specially produced for him. I still haven't published it, but donated it to the archives of the Australian Institute for Aboriginal Affairs in Canberra, where it is there for the record – a pity, because still nothing has been published about this site, quite as magnificent as anything in the whole of Arnhem Land. When an archaeologist, a few decades later, did go to Groote specifically to study sites connected with the Makassarese, by that time the Aborigines had the power to control her movements and did not allow her to visit Central Hill. Ritual barriers were placed across access paths in the bush which led to such major sites. They wanted her, instead, to study sites on the coast of more modern relevance to them, because they were places where their recent forefathers had lived.

We visited one of these, Dalimbo, in the southeast of the island – the farthest point eastwards in the Gulf used by the Makassarese for trepang fishing, as the name indicates, for it is Makassarese not Aboriginal (Daeng being the title of Lompo, the captain of one of their praus).

There was nothing to hunt or collect that night, except a rotten coconut that had floated over from New Guinea, so we had to broach our emergency bully beef not-so-'iron' rations straight away and drink brackish water from near the beach.

Walking down the beach, Sheila was reduced to having to lift one thigh after the other with her hands. (Sand is also very hard to sleep on.) We slept in a cave with a very low roof – a mistake since, waking with a start, your head hits the rock and you end up covered with blood. The myriads of flies which constantly flew into our eyes and infected them, despite the veils we wore, now enjoyed an extra banquet of our blood too. We had also tidily thrown empty cans behind rocks at the back of the cave, which were immediately competed for as a new kind of 'des res' by hermit crabs, which rattled them all night.

Fred had loaned us a ·303 rifle, which was used once to fire at a dingo that hurtled through the camp. But when the men took the rifle into the bush they came back with an amazing prize – one of the feral cattle that had got loose from a station started by white men way back in the 1920s and were still living out there thirty years later. The steaks were wonderful. I wrapped the tongue in a plastic mac; it went off in a day or two, so I said to Kulpidya that we'd have to throw it away. Ever the diplomat, he professed equal disgust (it was 'stinky'), until I found him two days later eating it, maggots and all, with relish.

Groote, for hunters and collectors, was as rich a country as you could wish for. After the first night, we never experienced any shortage of food. Fish were easy to catch in water so clear that even I could pick out which particular grey mullet or a vividly coloured parrotfish I wished to catch and bring it in with just a hook, a line and a bit of bait; the Aborigines used spear-throwers and wire-pronged spears. Flying foxes, very tasty, were equally easy to catch – you simply set fire to the tree from which they were hanging.

But the best value for effort was hunting turtles. I never went on this operation because I would have been a hindrance to men hurling huge harpoons. But we shared in the catch, cooking the beheaded animals in sand ovens with red-hot stones. Equally remarkable was the women's knowledge of how to remove the deadly Prussic acid from 'cheeky' yams by boiling them, and then to leach out the acid by immersing the slices in running water for two days

With such an abundance of food, we could afford to rest instead of hunting and collecting. But so ingrained is the habit of searching for food that for some this only meant that instead of looking for basics they now devoted their energies to luxuries like pandanus nuts or, best prize of all, 'sugar-bag', the honey of wild bees.

We crossed a small bay in dugout canoes left at strategic points by the Aborigines, and were highly alarmed when the huge rocks just below the surface turned out to be stingrays. That didn't worry our companions – with water lapping the gunwales to within an inch of the top of the hull, they cheerfully balanced, up and down, amongst all our clobber (including bone-boxes in which women kept bones of their deceased children), passing each other pipes of tobacco.

On the way back, a messenger brought us mail and fresh bread – I had never before had such a wonderful meal. That night we had to cross a small river (the tail of the Stingray, actually), holding our goods on our heads just out of the water like African porters in a Tarzan film, and spent the night being rained on. Everything, apart from the rifle, was soaked. Next morning, when I went to look at our crossing-place, there was a grey nurse shark.

Back at Umbakumba, the language and the kinship system took nearly all my time. But one day we had an unexpected visit from a Medical Officer from Darwin, on his annual visit looking for yaws, syphilis and TB among the Aborigines. I now had the chance of doing something with the entire population, without their having to go off to work. So I decided to replicate a test devised by an American psychologist, Porteus.

Porteus was dubious about tests which involved the use of symbols, notably words and pictures, because these privileged people who could read, so in cross-cultural tests whites usually came out best. (When you give illiterate people a photo, even of themselves, they often turn it this way and that, trying to figure it out – for it is a black and white, two-dimensional reduction of life-size in a strange rectangular shape.) So he opted for a test based on something quite familiar to those who had to do it, not a 'culture-free' test but a 'culture-*bound*' one, in other words part of their culture. In the case of one Aboriginal group he studied, he used photographs of footprints; then cut each pair into left and right, shuffled them, and then asked the Aborigines to pair them back up again. I still felt that using photographs of any kind privileged whites, so I got the Aborigines to make their footprints in the sand.[27]

Rose had called Aboriginal society 'gerontocratic', for Aboriginal society is not, as is still commonly believed, some kind of 'primitive communism'. It is not a class society based on private ownership of the means of production, but it is doubly inegalitarian – firstly, because men dominate women; secondly, because older men dominate younger ones.

I had assumed, therefore, that adult men would not only be best at recognising others' footprints, because of their hunting skills, but would also be recognised most often, as indeed they were, especially the senior among them. Conversely, young girls were least recognised and least good at doing the recognising. Yet some individual results are difficult to explain just in terms of collective categories of age and sex – the best recogniser (twelve out of thirteen matches!) was a twelve-year-old girl.

But it was collecting kinship terms which filled nearly every day. I'd given each term (such as 'younger sister') a code letter to save having to write long words like *dadiangamadja* every time). Suddenly, 12-year-old Nakinyapa, who was translating for me, came out with a code-letter – 'O'. He had cracked the code merely by listening. I heard later that this highly intelligent boy served a term in gaol, like so many of his contemporaries.

It took months to collect the kinship data, and there was scant time to work out the logic underlying these masses of terms. Rose had collected nearly twenty-five thousand identifications; I collected another eleven thousand, concentrating on people Rose hadn't been able to interview or who hadn't been born then. Analysing this mass of data would have to await my return to Canberra, but by running quick samples I could already see that there had been great changes. Roughly eleven per cent of the terms of address people were now using were different from those they had been using a dozen years ago when Rose had been there.

Basically, Rose had been right. There was not an 'algebraic' perfectly fitting system of kinship terminology, as the functionalist school had argued. Kinship got out of kilter, if only because men took women who did not belong to the right 'marriageable' category (they even kept 'harems'), then started calling them and their immediate relatives new terms for 'mother-in-law' or 'sister-in-law', whatever they had called them before. But they didn't then rearrange all the other terms they used for *everyone* else (an impossible task), so the terms used as a whole were often inconsistent. In the midst of this disorder, there were only what I called 'islands of order'. The next (highly competent) anthropologist to visit the island, David Turner, then proceeded to construct a model of the kinship system which restored an extremely coherent kinship system![28] (Not to be outdone, a Dutch Surinamese and a Hungarian anthropologist came up with even more coherent models.)

We came to the end of our stay and I still hadn't introduced communism to the island (how would one do that, even if the great hero among the Aborigines was a youth who had stood up to Fred Gray, spear against rifle, in a quarrel?). I myself had only had one quarrel with Fred, when some children stole turkey eggs and he made the fathers beat them as punishment. I protested and was told to leave the island – difficult, since there were only two boats a year.

But our time had come to an end anyway. At Thursday Island, Sheila went to the obstetric clinic and found out what we'd suspected – that a baby was on the way. It would have belonged to the North-West Wind clan (Bara), because Kulpidya was my 'brother'.

Down the Barrier Reef (largely invisible because most of it was at night time, and most of what we saw only just protruded above the surface) we saw the huge abandoned American airbases on the Atherton Tableland which had played such a crucial role in winning the Battle of the Coral Sea and thereby decisively changed Australian defence policy away from its traditional reliance on Britain to reliance on the US. A less serious sign of modernisation was having our very first colour photo taken (still my favourite) by a Chinese photographer from Mackay, Mr Pang Way. I was also treated to a display of Australian egalitarianism when I got up early one morning, and very deferentially and ostentatiously skirted the handiwork of the crewman swabbing the deck, only to meet with the response, 'And where d'you think you're going, sport?'

Having spent no money for a year, we had enough to pay for plane tickets from Brisbane to Sydney. Even in those days we flew over dozens of illuminated tennis courts everywhere. We found a romantic little hotel in Rose Bay where we saw Chaplin in *Limelight*.

Back in Canberra my main preoccupation, having had only ten months in the field, was to write it all up for a Ph.D. – and again only had ten months in which to do so. Despite my experience with the faked Townsville statues, I did allow myself though to be distracted briefly when C.P. Fitzgerald, our great sinologist at Canberra, got so excited by discovering that an unquestionably Chinese statuette of a Taoist immortal had been found, half a century ago, wedged in the roots of a banyan tree in Darwin, that he raised the reasonable question as to whether the Chinese had discovered Australia before the Europeans. I concluded, however, after reviewing the material in several languages, that the statuette was probably brought there by much more recent Makassarese trepangers.[29]

The whole issue was revived in 2002 when a former US submarine commander wrote a book claiming not only that the Chinese, during the period of the famous Ming voyages, had discovered Australia, but indeed most of the world.[30]

They did undoubtedly reach Africa. But, though the book was crammed with data, I was dubious about its reliability when I found my own work used to buttress the claim that the Chinese had reached Northern Australia when, in fact, I had asserted the exact opposite!

The statuette, far from being several hundred years old when it reached Darwin, was subsequently dated as early nineteenth century. Far from being an extremely valuable object made of jade (and therefore 'worth a lifetime's wages to the crew' and probably, therefore, so the book claimed, having belonged to 'a wealthy Chinese captain or admiral of a great ship') it was made of steatite, not a costly material.

I had become increasingly interested in the famous Cargo cults in Melanesia, so, only the week before, had been to the house of Mr Karkhovets, the Soviet Cultural Attaché, for the first European to land in northern New Guinea had been a Russian, Baron von Mikloukho-Maclay. Back in Manchester, I had taught myself a bit of Russian, on the number 42 bus between Didsbury and the University. I now went through the five volumes of Maclay's diaries, recently published in Moscow, enlisting the help of Rimsky-Korsakov's grand-daughter (one of our Librarians) whose parents had been part of the White Russian expatriate community in Shanghai. I translated some extracts which described what sounded very like Cargo cults going on long before any other Whites, notably missionaries, had arrived.[31]

'Baron' is the rather misleading title Mikloukho-Maclay bestowed upon himself. As well as being a prolific polymath, he was also an 'operator', if there ever was one. In an epoch when all the imperialist European powers were jostling to establish colonies in the South Pacific, Maclay had been landed on the northern coast of that huge island from a Tsarist naval vessel with an ominous 21-gun salute from the ship's guns. His first act was to surround his camp with a minefield, though once he had learned his lesson he avoided letting himself and his weapons get used in internecine local wars. He spent two periods (1871–72 and 1876–77), entirely apart from any other whites, carrying out biological, ethnographic and much other research. The ethnography was not very good (he was more interested in fish than people). After two months, he could not say 'yes' or 'no', 'good' or 'bad', 'hot' or 'cold'. But his notes did record that some kind of Cargo cult was going on. Later on, the cults were commonly blamed on the influence of whites, especially missionaries bringing ideas about the Second Coming of Christ. Maclay's notes showed that cults of this kind had occurred *before* whites in any number had established themselves.

I wanted to know if anything else was available in Russian about him, so had a rather sordid, vodka-soaked lunch with Mr Karkhovets.

Then, a week later, all hell broke loose when Vladimir Petrov, the top Soviet official in charge of MVD secret operations, defected – and I had just been socialising with a Soviet diplomat! In an

Obituary of Fred Rose I wrote for the *Guardian* (18 February 1991), I described Fred as 'both persecuted and paranoid'. I used to laugh when he went over to the window and drew the curtains shut, or at his insistence that there were strange noises emanating from his phone. But when I rang from a public phone box to see if the baby had arrived, Sheila had just been told by a nurse that 'They've arrested all the Commies' – not good news in the middle of giving birth. When I got to the Gollans, where I was staying, they were digging a big hole in the garden in which to bury Communist literature.

Fred had been only too right. What the nurse was talking about was a sensational international event, which, as a brochure published by Old Parliament House in Canberra in 2004 put it, 'shook the political landscape'. Under suspicion by their own Embassy, the Petrovs were in the process of being flown home but, en route to Darwin, were persuaded by Australian Security officers and the air hostess to defect and were hustled off the plane. (Mrs Petrov famously lost her red shoe in the process.)

The Australian Security had got what they wanted. Unable to find any Soviet spies among Australian Communists, they had found them in the Soviet Embassy. Now they stepped up their surveillance of Canberra's Communists. Thanks to the Australian Archives Act (the equivalent of Freedom of Information Acts elsewhere), I have in front of me a copy of intensive security surveillance reports giving the number plates of the cars which visited our house (and the houses of all our friends), including the wife of my professor, who was bringing clothes for the baby. Since the car was registered in Siegfried Nadel's name, my professor went down on the list too.

But they weren't just making mistakes. They launched a massive smear campaign, a 'Royal Commission on Espionage', which dragged many of Australia's most distinguished figures onto the stand. Because of my visit to the Soviet Embassy only the week before, I expected to be arrested too.

In an epoch when the Prime Minister of Australia can rest his hand on the Queen's posterior, it now seems hard to credit that the Australian political class of the 1950s, including most of the Cabinet, whatever their military dependence on the US, still 'cringed' to Britain, that is, was culturally more anglophile than the English.

Paul Hasluck, the Minister for Territories (i.e. Colonial Office) was one of them. I have subsequently seen a copy of the file on me which he regarded as so sensitive that he kept it in a safe in his office. Another Anglophile was Michael Thwaites, a poet who had been a Rhodes Scholar at Oxford but switched to working for ASIO (Australia's equivalent of MI5) – and hence was dubbed 'the improbable spook' – who managed the Petrov affair. A third anglophile was Col. Spry, the Director General of ASIO, who masterminded the Royal Commission. The only Communist of note they found was Fred Rose, who had already been fired from the Public Service, and had gone farming on King Island, Tasmania. I saw him conduct himself with great dignity. Neither he nor I ever admitted to being Communists – firstly because it didn't seem a good idea for the person in front of a firing squad to hold a pistol to his own head; secondly, because the Chartists had not fought for decades for the secret ballot for their descendants to have their private political opinions forcibly proclaimed; nor was I willing to grovel and apologise for those opinions, as some of my colleagues advised me to. The Commission was unable to demonstrate that Fred was a Soviet spy (though he was called a 'most unsatisfactory witness'), and no charge was ever made against him, or, indeed, any of the other people they hauled before the Commission, who were mostly not Reds at all but good liberals like the writer Colin Simpson (who had written an excellent account of the National Geographic Anthropological Expedition to Arnhem Land, including a passage on Groote). But though the Royal Commission was a fiasco in terms of finding spies, it achieved what the Government wanted – the intimidation of opposition, especially in Canberra. And though it might have been a mark of distinction to be summoned, it was not one that the victims enjoyed.

The Aborigines, however, were my top priority, so I did no political work at all, but got on with my thesis and spent my scant leisure time protecting the baby's pram from the parakeets which flew down from the Snowy Mountains in the winter. Perhaps this is why I was spared the Royal Commission.

When I wrote an essay for a distinguished visiting US professor, he was so impressed that he urged me to send it to the *American Anthropologist*, then the most prestigious anthropological journal in the world, which I did. They accepted it for publication immediately,[32] which did my career no end of good.

With only a few weeks to go before my Studentship ran out, and a passage back to the UK already booked, I went down to Sydney to be examined by Nadel and the doyen of Aboriginal studies, A.P. Elkin, professor at Sydney. Elkin was a 100 % exponent of kinship algebra, so didn't like my analysis at all, but he wasn't able to refute the mass of material I was able to bring to bear, so I got my Ph.D.

The boat back to Europe was much more elegant than the old *Maloja*. We left Australia as the streamers fell into the sea at the quayside to the strains of the Aloha farewell. Even so, we were not spared the attentions of international security. When we landed at Colombo, carrying Deborah in a cot, two white-duck-attired Ceylonese men nodded to each other and proceeded to follow us all over the island. The irony was that I had been invited, via a friend from Canberra (a Trotskyist – for Ceylon and Bolivia were the only [unlikely] places in the world where Trotskyism had taken root on a large scale), to give a talk for the Ceylon Broadcasting Commission comparing the hunting and collecting Veddahs of Ceylon to the Australian Aborigines. The two detectives dutifully waited outside the whole time we were making the recording and followed us while we made a visit to a temple and a restaurant.

Deb was the youngest passenger on the ship. With her blonde hair and blue eyes, everyone adored her. I floated her in my arms in the swimming pool, and at night the Lascar stewards were particularly kind to her as I wandered the ship trying to get her to sleep in the heat.

At Marseilles we began to find out that parenthood wasn't all fun. We did see the Le Corbusier flats and the inner harbour but it was too rough to take a baby out to the Château d'If. We had also been looking forward to an elegant French meal for three years, and were nicely established in a restaurant in the Vieux Port, when Deborah made it clear that she wasn't as keen on bouillabaisse as we were. Since her protest could be heard two blocks away, we simply had to leave. We landed at Tilbury with a bucketful of dirty nappies.

Illustrations

1. Egypt: en route to Mombasa, 1944

2. Lieutenant, King's African Rifles, Nairobi, 1944

3. Abyssinia,1944

4. In forest near Nairobi, 1944

5. With African soldiers, 11th KAR battalion, Ranchi, Bihar, India, 1946

6. On leave, 1946

7. On leave at Dal Lake, Kashmir, 1946

8. With Maswili wa Ndhumba (driver), Mwanza wa Ngui, and Geoff: convoy taking soldiers on discharge to Songea, Tanganyika, 1946

9. 5th KAR battalion, Kenya, 1946

10. World Youth Festival, Prague, 1947

11. Doing intelligence tests with African, Ifunda, Tanganyika, 1948

12. With African Sub-Chief, Ifunda, 1948

13. Spearing fish in billabong, Groote Eylandt, Northern Australia, 1953 (photo taken by 12-year-old Aboriginal boy, Nakinyapa)

14. With bark-paintings, Canberra, 1954

15. At desk, Hull University, 1956

16. Speaking in Saskatoon at the first public meeting of the newly-founded CND, 1961

17. British Economic Mission, Tanzania, 1965

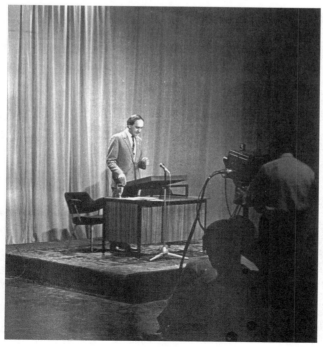

18. Lecture at Manchester University, 1968

19. Píllaro, Ecuador, 1977

20. Fiesta de Corpus Christi, Ecuador, 1977

21. Tepozotlán, Mexico, 1978

22. Anthropology Congress, Recife, Brazil, 1978

23. Wenner-Gren anthropology conference, Burg Wartenstein, Austria, 1978

24. Dean of Faculty of Economic and Social Studies, University of Manchester, 1975–77

25. West Head, Sydney, 1989

26. Lifting the Premiership Cup at Highbury, Arsenal's ground, 1991

CHAPTER 5

Out of Anthropology, into Sociology

Merseyside was a shocking sight. No longer were there sleek Atlantic vessels in the harbour; there were hardly any vessels at all. Even the ferries had been sadly reduced. Tate and Lyle's was closed; so were the thirteen miles of docks and the Overhead Railway which served them. The population had sunk from well over a million to eight hundred thousand.

We were lucky with employment. Sheila, with a young baby, couldn't do her work as an almoner, and when she did eventually start work again we always moved so she had to give up her job. Max, fortunately, had arranged a Research Assistantship for me, and we took over stewardship of Freddie Bailey's decrepit house in Victoria Park, Manchester, while he went to India.

The Department was going from strength to strength. Senior people like John Barnes and Clyde Mitchell returned from Africa and injected some much needed quantitative skills into the seminars, including seminal new ideas about network analysis. More and more visitors came from the US, plus an influx of postgraduates attracted by Max's reputation, including our first Brazilians, Alba Guimarães and Otávio Velho.

I had expected to start turning my doctoral thesis into a book and articles, but found myself increasingly diverted from publishing my Australian material. Firstly, Max pressed me to convert the MA thesis (a critique of Fortes' work on the Tallensi)[33] which I had done before I went to Australia into an essay for submission for the prestigious Curl Prize, awarded every year by the Royal Anthropological Institute. This involved cutting out half the thesis (which had drawn on the work of another Shanghai white Russian émigré, Shirikogoroff, on the kinship system of the Tungus [Evenki] reindeer breeders of Lake Baikal). I was duly awarded the prize in 1955 (jointly with another candidate), which was a feather in my cap.

Mau Mau

A different kind of diversion from my Australian research was the urgent need to confront the crisis that had emerged in Kenya, my old stamping ground. I had not been back there for five years, three of them ten thousand miles away in Australia, where people were not interested in Africa and where I was fighting to stop falling through the ice myself. So when the Mau Mau rebellion broke out in 1952 I was frustrated in the extreme at being unable to doing anything about it.

Like most people, I was completely taken by surprise when it happened. I thought I knew a good deal about Kenya and about Africans. I was perfectly aware of the massive theft of the land, particularly in Kikuyuland, in 1902–7, through the unbridled use of force to wipe out whole villages, whose inhabitants, even if they were as numerous as the Kikuyu, were quite incapable of offering resistance to rifles and machine guns. One officer, Francis Hall (for whom the town of Fort Hall was later named), declared that he would have been 'delighted' to wipe out the Kikuyu.

The population had already been decimated when 150,000 porters and 14,000 armed men had been recruited for the campaign in German East Africa (Tanganyika); the 50,000 who never came back and were never traced had mainly died from disease rather than German bullets. I was also more than usually informed about the years of smallpox, rinderpest, drought, famine and locusts which had killed off between a fifth and a half of the Kikuyu population and caused tens of thousands of others to quit the Reserves in search of food. The 1918 flu epidemic killed off another 120,000 Kikuyu.

Kenya was seized by Britain not because of the value of its resources but because the new Uganda railway from Mombasa to Lake Victoria was intended to secure territories which lay between two possessions crucial to the British Empire as a whole – the Nile Valley to the north, which controlled the Suez Canal and the route to India and, to the South, the minerals of South Africa. But building the railway had cost a fortune, which Britain wanted to recoup.

The successive depopulations of Kikuyuland were now used to argue that the country was underpopulated and underdeveloped. The colonialist solution was to bring in white immigrants. By 1905 there were already three thousand of them. Between 1905 and 1914 nearly four and a half million acres were alienated, mostly for very long periods on very low terms. In the 1920s, more prime land was sold off cheap to British minor aristocrats and ex-officers, and the whole area was designated the 'White Highlands'.

Very large areas went to a few companies and individuals: 320,000 acres to one company alone, and 100,000 acres to Lord Delamere, the leader of the settlers, who now formed themselves into a 'Convention of Associations'. They now organised themselves to seize political power as well – by planning a military uprising on Ulster lines, including the kidnapping of the Governor and the occupation of all strategic points. None of this was greeted by Government with the kind of hysteria that the rise of Mau Mau subsequently gave rise to. Instead, the 42,000 settlers were given fourteen members in the Legislative Council; the Asians six; and the six million Africans half a dozen *appointed* members.

The whites, however, had no intention of working the land themselves. That was for Africans to do. A labour force was created overnight by forcing Africans to pay a hut- tax and a poll tax which had to be paid in cash – which could only be obtained by working for the white man.

I knew all this but I had never experienced any of it as a victim. I had led the privileged life of a white man in a country where every single aspect of everyday life – even where you could sit or walk – was governed by the colour bar. I had been further sheltered by life in that most inclusive of total institutions, the Army, which provided food, pay, camaraderie – even the camaraderie of Africans. All this produced my own illusions, and I even tried to interest my father into moving his business to Nairobi, and nearly took up with a white woman who had moved to Kenya for the sake of her health.

But I had read, more than most, about Kikuyu resistance to Christian missions which had opposed female circumcision, and which gave rise to the setting up of independent Kikuyu schools, both strongly defended by Jomo Kenyatta.

Directly political secular organisations had long been far more sternly dealt with. In 1924, the year of my birth, Harry Thuku had established the Kikuyu Association. He was then arrested, and several people shot, after which Thuku became a moderate. A successor movement, the Kikuyu Central Association, was declared illegal in turn in 1940 and then went underground until in 1948 its secretary, George Ndegwa, was arraigned and sentenced.

The conscription of Africans to work on European farms during the Second World War generated massive new resentments which were harnessed by a new political movement, the Kenya African

Union (KAU), under the leadership of Jomo Kenyatta, who now returned after sixteen years in Britain to massive popular acclaim.

There were other kinds of opposition too, such as the militant trade union movement led by an Indian, Makhan Singh, who was duly deported; then ex-soldiers like Fred Kubai picked up the torch and led a new East African Trade Union Congress which conducted a whole series of strikes from 1948 to 1950, culminating in an eighteen-day general strike.

Then a quite new kind of resistance movement emerged – not a workers' movement or even an orthodox political party like the KAU, but a generation prepared to wage armed resistance. Some, like Stanley Mathenge, were ex-soldiers, but the great majority were peasants with no military experience whatsoever. Those who emerged as the military and political leaders of the people who had started to take to the forests of Mount Kenya and the Aberdare Mountains were quite unlike Kenyatta: only a handful of the new leadership, the most important of whom was Dedan Kimathi, had secondary school education.

This movement – which was now being called the Mau Mau (a name they didn't used themselves), like the earlier defence of female circumcision, drew upon ancient Kikuyu rituals in a new way – to create oaths of solidarity which bound those who took them to the movement. Though the Government's main aim was to smash Kenyatta's Kenya African Union, this recourse to Kikuyu cultural tradition on the part of the then not very significant Mau Mau was extremely convenient, for it allowed them to brand the new movement, and all Kikuyu opposition, as atavistic. When the Governor, Sir Philip Mitchell, retired to become a farming settler, his replacement, Sir Evelyn Baring, took only ten days to declare an 'Emergency'. Kenyatta and eighty-two others – teachers, trade unionists, businessmen and journalists – were arrested within a month, even though, as late as September, when the Emergency had already been declared, the Chief Native Commissioner affirmed that he 'did not know of any terrorism', only of 'a small subversive element … which should be controlled before it gets larger'.

The British had considerable experience, and success, in crushing the large revolutionary guerrilla movement led by Chinese Communists long resident in Malaya. More than half of those detained there were immediately deported to China. But the colonial authorities couldn't similarly deport Kikuyu from Kenya (the Governor too regretted that the Mau Mau were not Communists, because that made them more difficult to categorise and deal with).

But legalities, and international opinion, didn't stop them. Kenyatta was bundled into a plane (and thought he would be thrown out of it), taken to Kapenguria, a remote village near the settler town of Kitale, and immediately put on trial, together with Paul Ngei, Bildad Kaggia, Fred Kubai, Achieng Oneko and Kungu Karumba, in a school building hurriedly converted into a courthouse, before one Ransley Thacker, a colonial QC, now designated a judge, who was paid £20,000 out of special Emergency funds. He wasted no time in finding Kenyatta guilty of 'managing an unlawful society', and sentenced the Six to the maximum of seven years' imprisonment with hard labour, to be followed by a lifetime of restriction. During the trial, Thacker stayed at the settlers' Club in Kitale, while Rawson Macharia, the principal Kikuyu witness – who claimed to have seen Kenyatta administering oaths – was rewarded by being immediately flown to Britain for a university course.

Though Kenyatta had never supported Mau Mau's oathing or the guerrilla struggle, he was now being described by the right-wing British *Daily Telegraph* as 'a small-scale African Hitler'. He was to be kept cut off from the outside world, at Lokitaung – a 'lifeless place of sandstorms and hellish heat' in the remote north of the country; then at Lodwar, equally appalling, for over six years, until independence in April 1961. The effect was to make him, in Kaggia's words, increasingly 'on the side of the conservatives and the government'.

In Britain, criticism of colonial policy had historically been limited to mild criticism from the Fabian Colonial Bureau. Even the liberal *Manchester Guardian* had labelled Mau Mau oathing as 'barbarous' and 'filthy poison', while the socialist *New Statesman and Nation* called it 'mumbo jumbo' practised by people who had hacked settlers to death.

In Kenya itself, the defence of the 'Kapenguria Six' had, up to then, largely been left to three heroic Indian local lawyers. Now they were joined by the left-wing British lawyer, D.N. Pritt, QC; by a Nigerian lawyer; and by an MP from India who was a close friend of Jawaharlal Nehru. The colour bar meant that they couldn't stay together; Pritt stayed at the modest Kitale Hotel and with local Africans. All of them were subjected to police raids and restricted to ten minutes, contact with their clients before and after court.

A series of hammer-blows had overlapped with the trial. A white woman had already been stabbed to death by Mau Mau. Then, on the very first night of an adjournment, a settler family, the Rusks, was hacked to death. Photographs of the child's bloodstained teddy bear and trains in his bedroom were printed across the world.

It was significant that the main weapons used were *pangas* (machetes) since the Mau had little else. In the Imperial War Museum, later, I saw 'rifles' made out of gas piping with bolts actuated by bands of rubber or by springs, which could only fire one bullet at a time. (The display claimed that some of these Mau Mau weapons were made of solid wood, with no hollow barrel at all, and with bolts that used strips of rubber or metal springs; some were purely symbolic imitations of European guns.)

The rebels soon remedied that situation. Only two months later, in an attack on Naivasha Police station, a lot of European weapons were seized, and nearly two hundred prisoners liberated. Guns were also stolen from settler houses. Every settler, including women, now armed themselves and fortified their homes.

The new weapons were not only used against Europeans. On 9 September 1952, Senior Chief Waruhiu, a loyalist praised in the British Press as 'Africa's Churchill', who had tried to stop a Mau Mau oathing ritual only thirteen days earlier, was held up in his car and shot dead by men dressed as Kenyan police. To the poor and landless who were forced to work for the settlers or had to survive on subsistence farming, the death of someone like Waruhiu was an occasion of rejoicing and was celebrated, the Mau Mau General Karari Njama wrote later, 'with great applause and drinking parties'.

But many of those who owned land, or now came into possession of land taken from detainees, were only too ready to collaborate with the whites. A Home Guard was therefore readily recruited, despite being exposed to often ruthless reprisals from the Mau Mau. Only a few hours after the attack on Naivasha police station, ninety-seven people – men, women and children in the village of Lari, controlled by loyalist chief Luka, who had acquired 'vast' land concessions – were massacred and their bodies mutilated. Less often mentioned was the revenge reprisal in which nearly four hundred 'Mau Mau' were slaughtered by security forces in the village of Kiraura while listening to a young man who claimed to have visions about the end of colonial rule. For the massacre at Lari, three hundred people were tried and scores hanged; for Kiraura, no white or black member of the police force stood trial.

When I was in the KAR, the Kikuyu were regarded as a 'non-military' tribe, only recruited as clerks, drivers, batmen and the like. But these non-military people proved capable of taking on three British battalions plus four battalions of the King's African Rifles and the local Kenya Regiment; an artillery battery and an Armoured Car Division; a police force of 21,000 men equipped with their own planes; and an even larger 'tribal police' force, backed by RAF squadrons of Vampire jets and Lincoln heavy bombers (which, it was said, probably accomplished little more than to provide the forest fighters with game).

The coordination of these disparate forces was placed in the hands of General Erskine, specially imported because he had experience of colonial operations in Egypt and India. A personal friend of Winston Churchill, he was given carte blanche, including a letter authorising him to declare martial law and assume control of the government at any time. (He kept this crucial reserve power in the form of a slip of paper in his glasses case, which he would open and then snap shut whenever he felt that settlers or the government were getting too uppity.)

At the height of the campaign, some twenty thousand people were fighting in the dense forests of Mount Kenya and the Aberdare Mountains. Nevertheless, even a huge military sweep like 'Operation Hammer', in December 1954, when a division of troops was sent into the Aberdares, only resulted in 161 guerrillas being killed, captured or wounded.

Only two per cent of the huge British-controlled forces, however, were engaged in confronting the Mau Mau fighters in the forests directly. The rest were used to control the civilian population who supplied the men in the forests with food and bullets (often carried between the legs of babies carried on their mothers' backs). These supply lines were now cut off by cordoning off eight hundred villages in which a million Kikuyu were guarded behind barbed wire, gates and watchtowers. Strict curfews were imposed, and anyone entering the no-go areas cleared to separate the villages from the forest was shot on sight. The second clampdown on supply lines was the removal from Nairobi, in Operation Anvil, of 150,000 Kikuyu who were deported to the Reserves.

Anyone captured in the forest was put into the 'Pipeline', a gigantic series of detention (concentration) camps, of which there were eventually nearly a hundred. The huts of detainees were burned down; their lands and cattle sequestered or given to loyalists, who were also rewarded by being exempted from paying taxes, granted trading licences and having their children's school fees paid for them.

When I returned from Australia in 1954, it was very difficult indeed to unearth what was going on in the camps, though we knew it included tortures every bit as horrific as the atrocities which the British public were told was a monopoly of the Mau Mau – a white savagery flatly denied by the colonial Government and by the Colonial Secretary in the home government at Westminster.

The blanket control of the media was very effective: it was difficult in the extreme for the truth to leak out. One of the men I taught in an Extra-Mural class in Scarborough gave me photographs taken by his brother which showed an African having his arms sawn off. During the Malayan Emergency, the *Daily Worker* had printed photographs of British forces carrying heads taken from dead guerrillas in Malaya. I thought the same might be done with these Kenyan photographs, and sent them to Mervyn Jones at *Tribune*. He replied that they often received photographs of this kind, but that no one could prove who was doing the killing and torture, or prove who it was that was suffering, so they couldn't print them.

But by 1952 Michael Scott had founded the Africa Bureau, followed two years later by the establishment of the Movement for Colonial Freedom by Fenner Brockway, the Left Labour MP, while a group of exiles from Kenya living in the UK – headed by Peter Mbiyu Koinange, son of a detained former chief, and Joseph Murumbi – formed the Kenya Committee.

But it was not until September 1955 when more and more leaks, many from people who had played major roles in the camps themselves, became a flood. In 1957, Capt. Philip Meldon wrote about his experiences in the camps in *Reynolds News* and *Peace News*; Col. Arthur Young, brought in from London, where he had been Police Commissioner, to clean up the police force in Kenya, resigned after less than a year; his assistant, Duncan Macpherson, who had been in Japanese POW camps, said that those in Kenya were worse. Even two white criminals in jail provided their revelations about what had been going on, while missionaries appalled at what they knew forced the Christian Council of Kenya to speak out at last – only to be disowned by Archbishop Beecher.

By now, revelations about mass deportations and tortures such as the 'dilution technique' in which individual prisoners were set upon by gangs of camp guards, had become such public knowledge that the Labour Party itself – 'at last', as Barbara Castle put it – finally joined in the campaign. Even Enoch Powell condemned the killings in Hola Camp. Finally, Castle herself had to be given a carefully managed visit to some of the camps.

But half a century still had to elapse before two American scholars, Caroline Elkins and David Anderson, were able to document the details of the atrocities that had occurred in the camps on a huge scale[34] (by which time Tony Blair had to be persuaded to cut a line from a General Election speech in which he declared, 'I am proud of the British Empire' – a sentiment echoed by Gordon Brown soon afterwards on a visit to Africa). Reading Elkins' account caused me loss of sleep for many nights.

The first revelations about the camps, especially Hola Camp – the Guantánamo/Abu Ghraib of its day – came from people of undoubted probity, notably Eileen Fletcher, a Quaker missionary with whom I did meetings for the Movement for Colonial Freedom.

Eileen had resigned from her Government post in Britain during the Second World War, sacrificing her pension after ten years, work rather than advise companies how to increase their output of war materials, and then went on to serve for four years in Uganda. What she and others revealed about the camps was subsequently substantiated by a subsequent Colonial Office Inquiry.

Peace News then published a special issue on Kenya in which Eileen related what she had witnessed in Kenya, and I wrote an outline of the history of colonial Kenya.[35] Since it had made such an immense impact on the British public, I also tackled the question of Mau Mau oathing.[36]

The British public had been horrified by what they read in the Press every day about Mau Mau oathing practices, which were presented as what the settlers had always claimed: simply pure atavistic brutality aiming at intimidating the innocent. The settlers made maximum use of all this in their propaganda, even mounting exhibitions of photographs in the House of Commons. I tried to show how the oathing rituals were designed to create commitment and solidarity by using elements taken from traditional rites of passage such as passing through arches made of banana leaves and eating pieces of meat from slaughtered goats. The lowest grade of oath simply bound the oath-taker to helping the organisation, raising money, carrying out orders and observing meticulous security. But the higher levels, especially the *batuni* oath, bound the swearer to shelter rebels, to fight to the death and to kill any enemy – European, Asian or African – even, if necessary, to kill close relatives.

To induce people to do such things, the highest grade of oaths involved a crossing of the Rubicon: cutting oneself off from the normal behaviours of everyday life and breaking taboos which were strictly observed, even sacred, in everyday life. The most esoteric grade was said to even involve the drinking of menstrual blood and other acts which the Mau Mau General, Karari Njama, later described as 'horrible … though typically Kikuyu'.

The response to this mobilisation – practical and ritual – was the construction of the 'Pipeline'. Some of these camps were even privately run by settlers as mobile centres of torture which moved through the villages. Hundreds of thousands of people in the main camps were 'screened' by Africans who wore sacks over their heads with eye-holes, then pointed to different people whom they classified as 'white', 'grey' or 'black'. Terms like 'detention' and 'screening' did not mean just confinement and questioning. The detainees were there to be punished and to be 'cleansed' (brainwashed). If they confessed to having taken oaths, 'whites' might be reclassified as 'greys' and moved to a less vicious camp, where they would only be exposed to loudspeakers playing hymns and propaganda retailing news of Mau Mau defeats and about the civilised virtues of the British Empire and its monarchy. Many Christian missionaries, including the Anglican Archbishop of Mombasa, Leonard Beecher, seized the opportunity to try and convert prisoners to Christianity by bombarding them with hymns and propaganda through loudspeakers.

The 'greys' and the 'blacks' were subjected to far more brutal treatment; regular beatings with *kiboko* hippo-hide whips or rifle butts by camp 'loyalist' guards under white officers, many of them young settlers. Prisoners were hung upside down for hours, forced under water through cattle troughs, burned with cigarettes, had their testicles crushed with pliers, forced to wear shit-buckets on their heads (and to drink water from the same buckets), shackled and made to work with minimal food or water constructing agricultural ditches and even their own prisons.

At the very same time, a widely publicised programme of rehabilitation, which promised to provide jobs, education and housing for the more complaisant detainees, was set up, accompanied by an intellectual offensive. J.C. Carothers, an ethnopsychiatrist, produced a report which characterised Mau Mau thinking as 'pathological', and the settlers supplied the white soldiers with their ready-made images of Africans as savages. Even the eminent archaeologist Louis Leakey, who had grown up speaking fluent Kikuyu, gave evidence in court to back up Carothers, while the novelist, Elspeth Huxley, widely respected as a liberal in the West, declared that there could be 'no cleansing, no climbing back into the society of decent men'; Mau Mau 'irreconcilables' would be 'damned forever'. In the camps, many caved in under the appalling pressures, though enough of them kept up an organised resistance for Government to plan to keep them in camps for the rest of their lives.

In the forests, young Kikuyu- or Swahili-speaking settlers now led 'pseudo-gangs', who blackened their faces and tracked down Mau Mau fighters in the forests, helped by Mau Mau who had been captured and 'turned'. They were organised by Ian Henderson, his crowning achievement being the capture of Dedan Kimathi, who was immediately hanged, for which Henderson was awarded the George Medal. (At Independence he was deported by the new Government, whereupon the British Government despatched him to Bahrain where he spent the next thirty years running state security.)

At the end, the huge forces ranged against the guerrillas proved too much. Desperate shortages of food led to declining morale and discipline: some bands deteriorated into *komerera* gangs who took to preying on the villages. Gradually, the security forces gained the upper hand.

Estimates of the scale of the fighting and of the suffering in the camps vary enormously, mainly because official files, both in Nairobi and London, were thoroughly cleared out at the end of the Emergency.

Elkins partly overcame this problem by becoming an anthropologist: interviewing some three hundred ex-detainees and villagers. Even so, in the mayhem, records of every corpse were not kept, so that even her meticulous research reported wide ranges of variation in figures. Some twenty thousand Mau Mau fighters were killed, a thousand of whom had been hanged; between 160,000 and 320,000 people had passed through the camps. More precise were the losses on the other side: less than one hundred Europeans dead – thirty-two settlers and fifty British troops – plus some eighteen hundred loyalists. The financial cost was estimated as 55.5 million pounds.

In 1961, the dam finally burst when two non-Kikuyu, Tom Mboya and Oginga Odinga, were elected to the Legislative Council in the first colony-wide elections. independence now became unstoppable. On his release, Kenyatta told his followers to 'forgive and forget the past': Mau Mau was a 'disease', and those who still supported it were 'hooligans'. Anticipating Reagan's 'no free lunch', he announced that Africans would have to purchase land. Thirty thousand white settlers trusted him sufficiently to stay in the country; those who did not received £12.5 million pounds from the British Government for their land.

The new Government of independent Kenya exercised strict control over former Mau Mau, some of whom were imprisoned. Former detainees, whose lands had been taken from them, were now dependent on the charity of their relatives – isolated, stigmatised and scattered across the ridges of Kikuyuland; former Mau Mau Generals were left to fester in the slums of Nairobi.

By the time the Movement for Colonial Freedom mounted its campaign to explain and defend Mau Mau, Kenyatta was in exile, so Tom Mboya, who had inherited his mantle, was given, like so many colonial leaders, a year at university in England.

Max joined me on the platform once or twice with Mboya. But Max's most courageous act was to take on no less a personage than the Governor of Kenya himself both in the pages of the *Manchester Guardian* and in more academic analysis.[37] These highly public ripostes resulted in a visit to Manchester of James McGibbon, who wanted Max to expand his critique into a book about the Mau Mau. But Max wasn't a Kenyan specialist, so he suggested instead that MacGibbon publish the material I had collected about the Cargo cults, since – insofar as they involved what to Europeans seemed superstition of the most gross and savage kind – they resembled Mau Mau.

At this time, there was a growing interest in millenarian movements in all times and epochs, which resulted in one of the most stimulating weekend seminars I have ever experienced, when Max invited Eric Hobsbawm to speak on modern millenarian movements in Italy (which became his book, *Primitive Rebels*), while Norman Cohn talked on parallel movements in medieval Europe (which became his classic *The Pursuit of the Millennium*).

I contributed a paper, not on Mau Mau but on the Cargo cults, about which I had read a lot during my time at Canberra, and had envied Peter Lawrence and Kenelm Burridge the opportunity they had of studying two such cults, led by Yali and Mambu respectively, in the field.[38]

British anthropology then made overtures to sociology by agreeing to a joint meeting of the two disciplines, with papers from both. Vic Turner gave one on Kant. But the 'tribalism' of anthropologists was too deeply rooted to disappear easily. Going into the hall, Meyer Fortes took me by the arm and said, 'Now, Peter, we'll show them what a real social science looks like'. So much for togetherness and the unity of the social sciences. Similarly, Raymond Firth said he'd enjoyed my BBC broadcast on Cargo cults, but reproved me for having criticised the discipline of anthropology in public (I had remarked that anthropologists hadn't paid a lot of attention to the cults).

With a doctorate, I started on the treadmill which led to the crucial recognition as a professional anthropologist: acceptance into the Association of Social Anthropologists. This begins when one is invited to review books (not the important theoretical ones, which are given only to senior people to review) on areas where one has done fieldwork or is known to be knowledgeable about: in my case, East Africa and Australia, though I was too petrified to open my mouth in discussions dominated by such luminaries as Evans-Pritchard and Siegfried Nadel (who was perfectly prepared to put down even fellow-professors in debate, quite rudely). Then I was asked by Edmund Leach to join a deputation to the 'Old Guard' of the Royal Anthropological Institute, the historic organisation of anthropology headed by Lord Raglan, membership of which was open to anyone acceptable to those who ran it (and willing to pay the subscription). Our modest proposal was that we, the professional teachers of the subject, should take over the two journals controlled by the Institute, the *Journal of the Royal Anthropological Institute* and *Man* – and we won the battle.

Then followed a conference intended to heal the breach between American anthropology – focussed on the study of *culture* (an approach which our teachers had sometimes treated as if using that concept would result in softening of the brain, like masturbation) – and British 'social' anthropology, focussed on the study of social *structure*, by flying over a planeload of leading American anthropologists to Cambridge. The Americans came prepared with the latest technology for coping with a backward Europe, including adaptors for their electric shavers which would run off 240 volts. But they had not allowed for Jesus College, Cambridge, which had its own system, powered, I suspect, by a man on a bicycle, and they remained unshaven. For the first time, the two sides got to know each other and were surprised to be mutually impressed. One or two interventions I made (one involving Meyer Fortes) showed the Americans that the British theory was not a completely coherent united front. Numerous invitations resulted.

I now made another application to the Rhodes-Livingstone Institute. This time, Max informed me, I was indeed appointed. But MI5 stepped in to veto this. My anthropological achievements counted for nothing. After ten years studying the subject, and Africa, it was obvious that I would never be allowed to do fieldwork again in territories controlled by the Colonial Office. As individuals, anthropologists might sometimes (rather privately) be protective of 'their' tribes, but as a profession they never risked criticising colonial authorities, an avoidance based, I felt, on the fear that open objection to the exclusion of one person might result in a blanket exclusion of fieldworkers everywhere. So I was not surprised that I got no help from the ASA. Nor did the situation necessarily improve when new nationalist governments came to power. To some of them, anthropology had either been a direct instrument of colonial government – the 'child of imperialism' – or was still suspected of persisting *cultural* imperialism, the study of blacks by whites. Some, however, eventually developed a policy of licensing anthropologists by making them pay for the privilege of doing fieldwork.

Hell, Hull and Halifax

Max now said that I had little option but to move out of anthropology into sociology. I explored doing a very anthropological study of a mental patients' ward with Morris Carstairs at the Mawdsley Institute, but then applied for a post as Lecturer in Sociology at the University of Hull, where the incumbent, Francis Klingender, had died.

Hull has always had a bad press, embodied in the old saying at the head of this passage. It was actually a big city of three hundred thousand people, once so prosperous a port that it was proud enough to refuse Charles I entry into the Old Town, thereby starting the Civil War. But by now it was a poor city, with above average levels of unemployment. Its main industry, fishing, which had once sent out more than three hundred trawlers, was still declining when I got there, though still sizeable. Even so, an authority on Victorian working-class life could still be shocked at working-class life half a century later: 'I had never before seen such awfulness', John Saville wrote about Lister Street in 1963 (p. 148). The erosion of the fishing industry reinforced the stereotype of a city in decline. Nowadays, the docks in the city centre have been transformed into a yachting marina, and what has been described as the best museum in Europe, the 'Submarium' called 'The Deep', has been built nearby. Even so, as late as 2003, Hull was still designated number one 'Crap Town' in the UK.

To me, during the eight years I spent there, this was entirely unjustified. In personal terms, I started a new career in sociology, while, politically, two seismic international and national events took place at the same time: Suez, which led to the emergence of a new radicalism among the young, and eventually to the rise of the Campaign for Nuclear Disarmament; and the Hungarian Revolution, which led to the disintegration of the Communist Party, an upheaval in which Hull was to play a special part.

Due to its isolated geographical position (often described as 'forty miles down a siding'), Hull was a very inward looking city, with the fishing industry and the fishing community around Hessle Road still prominent. The loss of trawlers at sea for generation after generation had given it an unusual degree of self-consciousness and solidarity: in the Great Storm of 1883, 250 men had been lost in one night. But the most striking disaster is symbolised by the statue of the fisherman, George Smith, down on the Hessle Road in his oilskins commemorating the attack in 1904 on the small boats of the Hull fishing fleet by vessels of the Tsarist Navy (including the *Aurora*, which was to fire the first shots in the Revolution of 1917) on their way to fight the Japanese in the Far East. Paranoid because of rumours that torpedo-boats built for Japan in Scandinavia were lying in wait for them, the Russians fired several hundred shells at the little fishing boats while men held up fish in their hands to show that was all they were doing. This incident nearly provoked a war between Britain and Russia. But the trigger-happy Russians sailed on, provoking further incidents on the way. They got to the Sea of Japan just in time to participate in the battle of Tsushima, when the Japanese sank the flower of the Tsarist Navy – the first time an Asian power had defeated a European one.

Other industries had grown up in Hull, though – notably the large firm of Reckitt and Colman, which provided Hull University, one of a handful of new universities founded on the eve of the Second World War, with much of its finances (and its Chancellor) and its heraldic colours of mustard and blue – Colman's mustard, and Reckitt's blue (a dye used by every housewife to wash clothes whiter).

Hull was still a University College in the year I got there, its degrees awarded by the University of London. But straightaway it became an independent university, so we were able to award our own degrees and design our own courses, and the whole University grew rapidly.

There were still legacies of the past. When I wanted to consult Malinowski's *Sex and Repression in Savage Society*, I found that it was locked away in a Special Collections room behind an iron grille by the puritanical Ulster librarian. All that changed when Philip Larkin was appointed Librarian. Though we were miles apart in politics, he and I got on fine by using an anthropological mechanism – avoidance. We only talked about jazz – about which he was, naturally, reactionary too; a 'mouldye figge', as the nomenclature of the day had it, who had not moved beyond New Orleans jazz.

Had I been on the appointment committee for the sociology job, I would not have appointed Worsley, because there were five other good candidates, all with training in sociology (which I had not had) and all of whom became professors within a year or two. But as luck would have it the Committee must have been impressed by the radio talk on Cargo cults I had given only the week before on the very prestigious Third Programme.[39] I remember looking out into the Front Quadrangle and thinking, 'If they appoint me, I'll dedicate myself to developing a really strong department'. They did appoint me, and I did what I had promised myself. Then, in my first year in Hull, I published my very successful first book, *The Trumpet Shall Sound*.[40]

I actually wrote twice as much as was eventually published, thinking naively that I would cover all the millenarian movements that had ever occurred throughout history and across the entire world, a delusion which prompted my publisher, wisely, to cut out all the non-Melanesian material. But the book still had such an unusual and exotic subject – the expectation that the world was going to come to an end very soon – that it attracted readers not otherwise interested in anthropology, and was selected for a very favourable review in the *Observer* by the eminent anthropologist, Geoffrey Gorer. It then went into Italian, Russian, German and eventually, after ages, French.

On the teaching front, it wasn't difficult for the Department to grow, for there were only four other Sociology Departments in the whole country, and the discipline was growing fast. The greatest problem was that I didn't know much sociology, but by dint of very long hours burning the midnight oil, I managed to keep ahead of the students. We lived across the road from the university. Deb, less than two years old, was so upset at moving from Manchester that I had to sneak out, unobserved, to give my lectures in order to avoid floods of tears.

But there wasn't actually that much sociology to master. It is hard to realise now, but at that time it was possible to have read virtually everything that had been published in the subject – just as I possessed every single 'hot jazz' record that had been released in the UK (HMV and Parlophone each released one 10" record per month). Klingender, my predecessor, had been, by curious coincidence, a

Marxist, whose writings on the sociology of art were famous, particularly his *Art and the Industrial Revolution*. I even inherited notes he had left on sociological theory which I found invaluable. He had also started field research – firstly a study of small shopkeepers in Hull, and then into the fishing industry. Gordon Horobin, the research worker, soon involved me, which entailed a lot of daytime drinking in the fishermens' clubs on the Hessle Road.

Gordon, trained in sociology at Leicester, an excellent department, helped out so well with teaching that he became a lecturer, and the fishing research passed into the hands of Peter Duncan, my first graduate to finish with a first class degree. With my anthropological bent, we sent him off to Iceland. (Alas, Peter died young and was succeeded by Jeremy Tunstall, just down from Cambridge.)

Peter had been the first of a succession of excellent home-grown students, most of whom came straight from school, though a few were mature students from the handful of Colleges of Further Education – only three in the whole country. I made a point of trying to accept one applicant every year from this source.

I spent hours meticulously selecting and interviewing some three hundred applicants a year (photos of me at the time always showed me with a set of application files under my arm). The students I inherited had all had excellent training from Klingender. And young lecturers are only a few years older than their students, which gives them a particularly close rapport. Their numbers were small: only three in the first cohort I inherited for their final year (my first), so I could really concentrate on them. As a result, every year I had students who graduated with a First, which was exceptional for a new and tiny department. One of them, Tony (now Lord) Giddens, used to sit at the back, with faintly hooded eyes, and, I thought, a distinct air of *déjà entendu*; he became Professor of Sociology at Cambridge, and then Director of the London School of Economics, and was later kind enough to say that he had 'struck lucky' coming to such a good department, and that I had been 'very energetic and lively'.[41]

As with Canberra, there wasn't too much entertainment, but we hadn't enough money to go out a lot anyway – nor, with a baby and another on the way, could we get out much. My salary was £500 a year (I think it should have been more, with a Ph.D., but Hull was notorious for shaving off, some said, £800 from the salaries of its staff. Four cars were parked in the Front quadrangle – the Vice-Chancellor's, the Registrar's, the Bursar's and a Professor's. Nobody else had any cars. Today, you can't park for students' cars for blocks around.)

We got a mortgage for more than should have been allowed, and moved to Cottingham, where Julia was born. One of the few men in a hall of two thousand people, I had listened to Grantly Dick Read extolling the virtues of home delivery and painless childbirth. But his message did not register with the medical profession – today, most deliveries are done in hospital, not at home by the midwife. Julia was blue when she came out, and the first thing they did was to slap her to get her lungs going. They never failed her after that.

It was six years before we could afford to put any furniture at all in the front room so we used it to house our second-hand lawn mower; there was no heating in the bedrooms and no carpeting. Guests slept on a camp-bed in our box-room. We already knew people in the Labour movement in the town, splendid people who had devoted their lives to the defence of the living conditions of the workers: people like Don Major, Chairman of the Hull Trades Council, and Frank Swift, the full-time Communist Party organiser, whose first job was to try and raise a pathetic salary for his job. If he couldn't, then it was back to normal work for him. We now also met working-class neighbours outside politics, like 'Blackie' and Dora Brattan (still great friends), because Park Lane had privately-owned houses on one side and Council property on the other. Their children and ours could play in the large park right behind our house, disappearing for hours, perfectly safe, and returning covered in mud. After years of uncertainty, it was heaven, even if at the end of the month we sometimes had to borrow to pay the next electricity bill.

Then came the cataclysm of Krushchev's 'secret speech' at the Twentieth Congress of the Soviet Communist Party, when Stalin's reign of terror was officially revealed.

A fierce struggle now developed led by the historian, Edward Thompson, and another senior and respected historian, John Saville. Since John worked in Hull University, and Edward in Halifax, only hell was left, and for loyal Communists what followed was not far short of hellish. John and Edward first produced a cyclostyled journal called the *The Reasoner*, which was duly censured by the Communist Party leadership. But it was the beginning of the end for Stalinism, as the great majority of the Party's members quit. There then followed a fight to capture the hearts and minds of those who had defected on the part of a number of *groupuscules*, some built on pre-existing Trotskyist groups, others, like the New Left, with which I associated myself, quite new.

Such events are like civil war, and inevitably involve battles often with people who had been fine comrades. I am particularly ashamed of public recriminations I launched against Cliff Slaughter, once my best friend (and an excellent anthropologist),[42] and later, in Mexico City, against Nigel Harris, neither of whom merited such rudeness.

The Reasoner soon gave way to the New Reasoner, a properly printed journal, with Ralph Miliband, Mervyn Jones, myself and Michael Barratt-Brown now brought on to the Board.

The year 1956 produced a double crisis for the world – for the Soviet bloc, because of the Hungarian Revolution, and in the West, because the invasion of the Canal Zone aroused fierce opposition. In the universities it transformed politics. Throughout the post-war period, students had been notoriously passive and fairly conservative. Now people who had never been involved in politics at all marched in protest on the streets in thousands. New organisations therefore came onto the scene. The New Reasoner group did try, almost entirely thanks to Jim Roche, a skilled tailor from Leeds who had been a full-time worker for the CP, to put out a cyclostyled publication intended for workers, but it didn't get anywhere. Somewhat more successful, and bigger, was a campaign in Fife, Scotland, by Lawrence Daly, who had been Secretary of the National Union of Miners, and who now ran in a by-election.

But it was the newly-radicalised population of the universities that became specially involved in the new movements with which I identified myself – the New Reasoner and the new Campaign for Nuclear Disarmament (CND), which rapidly became a national movement far bigger than any of these small-scale developments on the Left.

Oxford University was the unlikely birthplace of Universities and Left Review, run by brilliant young graduates like Perry Anderson, Robin Blackburn and Stuart Hall. Our New Reasoner group then joined forces with them to form New Left Review, which quickly became more than a mere journal, but a movement, with a score of discussion groups across the country and an office in Soho, complete with coffee bar.

None of us had business skills, however, and fashionable as the New Left became (we even did film shows at the National Film Theatre), it soon went bust. For all this fashionableness, Stuart, the editor, lived on the proverbial smell of an oil-rag, and the journal only just escaped the fate of the coffee-house when money was put in which saved it. The take-over, however, changed the character of the journal into one of avant-garde, though very open-minded, Marxism. But as a movement the New Left disappeared.

In Hull, these developments brought academics into strong relationships with people in the town. Some were traditional Labour; some Quaker pacifists; others unconventional mavericks like Alec Horsley, ex-District Officer in Nigeria, ex-Labour councillor, late convert to Quakerism, and now a millionaire who financed much of CND's local activity out of Northern Dairies, the huge business he had built up. (His daughter, Val, is still trying to get Britain to abandon its commitment to nuclear weapons.) The majority of CND members, like Christine Jackson, were part of the newer youth generation.

As in all large-scale movements, these elements did not jell easily. Those who wanted to challenge nuclear policies more directly became impatient with marches and petitions, and joined Bertrand Russell's Committee of 100 in sit-down protests, and it wasn't the traditional Left, by any means, who were the most intransigent. Francis Deutsch, a Hull solicitor and refugee from Nazism, and a pacifist, was one of the first to be put in gaol for 'direct action'.

Many people have said to me that these were the happiest days of their lives, and remain in contact despite the fact that what bound us together was the terrible feeling that the world might end at any moment. The Cuba Missile crisis was the worst moment of all – I remember glancing up at the sky, thinking that there was surely a missile aimed at our city. The most unlikely bedfellows found themselves side by side, often for the first time. At a CND meeting in the City Hall, the Bishop of Hull, and Alec as an ex-Sheriff of the city, spoke alongside Stuart Hall, who spoke quite brilliantly.

March followed march, both national and local – Aldermaston every year; demonstrations at airbases (the missiles were all pointed eastwards). The militancy of the movement increased – 'sit-downs' were now the order of the day. At one demonstration near York, I wrote out cheques for Sheila to use while I was inside (having a joint account, with so little income, was too precarious), expecting a three months sentence. We went and sat in the mud, blocking the gate, and waited to be arrested. Along came the Chief Constable, who said, 'Well, if they want to get their bottoms mucky, just let 'em!'. Walking coast to coast, arguing with a Vegan (who, I think, got the better of the argument) was hard going. My ankles collapsed somewhere near Halifax.

My role on the *New Reasoner* had largely been confined to writing on colonial issues.[43] Despite ferocious brutality, France had been forced out of Vietnam, handing over the job of repression to the US, but clung desperately to Algeria. But the writing was on the wall both for France and, after Mau Mau, for the British Empire. Both now decided to throw in the towel; the 'wind of change' now blew across Africa, though bitter, armed struggles persisted in white settler territories like South Africa and Rhodesia and countries cursed with mineral wealth.

Anti-colonialism now meant looking backwards, not forwards. More than a dozen new countries had come into being in Africa alone, which began to hold Pan-African conferences and soon, together with major Asian ex-colonies, came together to constitute an even larger, worldwide grouping – the Afro-Asian Non-aligned movement – whose meeting at Bandung in 1955 even saw participation from China and Cuba.

The French demographer Jacques Sauvy (a Nobel laureate) therefore saw this as the beginning of the emergence of a new entity within what had been, since 1945, the bipolar world of the Cold War. He called it the 'Tiers Monde', a term which I picked up and introduced into Anglophone world as the 'Third World'. For one Aldermaston march, John Rex wrote a pamphlet which linked the nuclear issue to the emergence of this new grouping, entitled 'NATO or Neutralism?'

I was then able to see the beginnings of this new African grouping at first hand when newly independent Ghana hosted a Pan-African Conference in Accra to which they also invited representatives of US blacks and of allies from Europe, such as Michael Scott, who immediately went to the border to protest against French atom tests in Algeria. John Rex went from CND, and I went from NLR (*New Left Review*).

We were bowled over at the contribution from the Algerian Ambassador, a Martiniquais called Frantz Fanon, and went behind stage to talk to him afterwards. I was too embarrassed to offer him a copy of NLR, because it had a photo on the cover of Albert Camus, born in Algeria of modest white parentage, but by now an influential progressive intellectual in Europe. To the Algerians, however, he was simply a defender of the white *pieds noirs*. At a reception at the presidential palace, Flagstaff House, I arrived early and saw a tiny instance of Nkrumah's arrogance. Only Nkrumah was in the hall; then when the Party Secretary, Tawia Ademafio, descended the staircase Nkrumah snapped his fingers at him like a servant and told him to get a move on. Ademafio ended up in gaol not long afterwards. I also didn't think that the use of 'market mammys' as a claque who were turned on to ululate whenever the platform indicated they should, was a suitable role for women.

These were trivial indicators of the mobilisatory role of the Party in all the new states. All categories of the population – trade unionists, women, youth, and so on – were expected to promote the Party.

More serious was the reception I got at the Guinean Embassy when I went there to see what I could learn about the only ex-French colony that had stood up to France (when the French left, they had even torn out the telephones). I learned just how sensitive the Guineans still were. No one closed the doors in that heat, so when I saw a man sitting in one room behind a desk I went in and asked if I could get any literature about Guinea. His reply was to ask whether I normally entered someone's room without knocking, and eventually contemptuously flung over a couple of volumes of Sékou Touré's speeches to me.

I now began to try to situate these new developments against the background of what I had picked up from my years in Africa and Asia, and did a BBC broadcast on 'One-party Democracy in West Africa' (*Listener*, 4 August 1960) which eventually became the germ of a book, *The Third World*, which I worked on for the next two years.

* * * * *

The department in Hull grew steadily and developed a good reputation, and established scholars such as Lord Simey from Liverpool began to visit it. On the research front, I switched from writing about colonial issues in the *New Reasoner* to arguing that Britain was an 'unknown country',[44] sociologically speaking, and that sociology ought to pay more attention to the methods anthropologists used in studying other cultures. I pointed to the excellent new monographs which were beginning to appear from Michael Young's Institute of Community Studies, which focussed on close-up interviews with working-class people instead of relying exclusively on statistical literature; and – on the cultural side – to Richard Hoggart's *The Uses of Literacy*, based on his own life-experience in the north and on his immersion not only on the classical, 'authorial' English literature read by the highly educated, but his familiarity with the popular magazines and newspapers ordinary people used too.

Then, in a repeat performance of what had happened in anthropology: the 'young Turks' – the professional teachers and researchers – formed themselves into a 'Teachers' Section' within the British Sociological Association (BSA), creating stringent tests for membership via 'gates' designed to keep out non-professionals who had traditionally supplied the membership and the audience (and the financial support) for the BSA. The teachers now took over the Association, and launched a new journal, *Sociology*.[45] The outcome of this soon became apparent in the new kinds of issues that the BSA started paying attention to.

Sociology had also traditionally focussed on class, and especially on manual workers rather than non-manual workers, but John Goldthorpe's new team had been studying a new kind of manual workers, the 'affluent' workers in the car industry at Luton, while David Lockwood had focussed on white-collar workers. The three of us presented papers at an excellent colloquium of the British Sociological Association on industrial society,[46] and they helped us set up a study of white-collar workers in Hull, which went on for four years.

Publishers then started to press me to write a book on the British power elite, and it was becoming increasingly difficult for me to continue with my anthropology. In my special field, only a handful of people in the UK had done fieldwork among the Aborigines, and I knew none of them, so I got little encouragement to convert my thesis into a book. For a while I did continue to work through my notebooks: a small article on the Groote Eylandters;[47] an article for Max's *Journal of the Rhodes-Livingstone Institute*, drawing comparisons between African millenarian movements and those in Melanesia;[48] another, with Jean Guiart, of France, on the distribution of Cargo movements;[49] while an article on Cargo cults, solicited by the *Scientific American* and written for their popular audience, went on to sell in that huge market for decades.[50] A sarcastic review I did for *Science and Society* of Margaret Mead's study of a cult in the Admiralty Islands drew an enraged protest from her.

But keeping two disciplines on the go was a losing battle. My daily life, now, was teaching sociology. I only had time to keep up with the major theoretical books coming out all the time in anthropology, and began to decline invitations to participate in anthropological conferences I would have been glad to attend a few years before. Now I could only selectively go to those which seemed particularly important.

I began, too, to give up trying to publish anthropological papers, even papers already written up (such as my material on footprint tests, and on the cave-art of Groote), including the kernel of my Ph.D. thesis on Groote Eylandt kinship which I'd intended as a major book.

But I had one final fling. Working through my notebooks, I had become very impressed by the extraordinary extent of the Aborigines' knowledge of the natural environment – not just the sheer number of plants and animals they recognised but the way they had developed a *taxonomy*, a mode of classifying them. This grew into a paper about Claude Lévi-Strauss' study, *Le Totémisme Aujourd'hui* which Edmund Leach asked me to contribute to a volume about the work of this theorist whose writings were strongly influencing anthropology and, indeed, the general reading public everywhere – but not me.[51] When I went on later to develop my arguments against him further in my book, *Knowledges*, I was able to show that instead of the binary theoretical framework into which Lévi-Strauss had forced Aboriginal thinking, the Aborigines actually used no less than four modes of classification: a scientific one (which remarkably approximated the one Western scientists use); a classification of plants and animals as foods; a religious ('totemic') classification; and a linguistic one.

I further argued that whereas in the nineteenth century the Aborigines had been treated as vermin and poisoned or shot, in more recent decades – after whites had discovered the paintings of Albert Namatijira and the Hermansberg School – Aborigines had been recognised as capable of producing great art; now, it seemed to me, it was time to recognise that Aborigines had their own scientists too.

Then Max Gluckman invited me to participate in a panel at the World Congress of Sociology in Stresa, Italy. Unable to afford even a train ticket, I bought a second-hand Norton 125 cc motorbike, which just about got me up the Alps. The panel was very distinguished: Raymond Aron, who was said to write his lucid papers in a taxi en route to the Sorbonne; from the UK, Asa Briggs from the new University of Sussex; Max; and myself; plus the sociologist C. Wright Mills, whose *The Power Elite* had made a huge impression. Though my paper was invited by Max, and given under his Chairmanship, it contained criticism of his theoretical approach.[52]

The Congress made the kind of impact that an international gathering should. For the first time we met Russians and East Germans, but the delegation that made the greatest impact was the one from Poland, a country with a long tradition of outstanding social science, and where new shoots of independent thinking were emerging once more. I was particularly impressed by Zygmunt Bauman, and was able later to play an intermediary part in getting him to the UK when he was thrown out, firstly, from Poland, during a phase of anti-Semitism, but allowed to go to Israel. At Stresa, Jan

Sczepanski, a liberal senator and sociologist, gave a keynote address. In Montreal later he told me one of the by then innumerable anti-Soviet jokes: the Russians were building their gift to Warsaw – the ugly Academy of Sciences modelled on the one in Moscow. It was reported that there had been an accident; the Russians building it had had an accident on one of the top stories. 'How many died?', a passer-by asked. The answer was 'One'. 'Not enough', came the reply.

I had also written up my paper on Australian knowledge of plants and animals and deliberately published it in Hungary in order to foster links between anthropologists on both sides of the 'Iron Curtain'. I had intended to go on from Italy to Budapest to give it there but the Soviet invasion had occurred in the meantime, so I withdrew my participation by telegram, which was deeply appreciated by my Hungarian colleagues.

I had been greatly impressed by Mills, and began to put my best graduate students on to studies, for their MAs, of different sections of the British power elite – Chris Otley did his on British generals, and David Morgan on bishops of the Church of England. (I had thought the generals would resent approaches from young sociologists, especially one as hippy in style as Chris, but generals retire early and, as one said, nobody had taken much notice of him since!). Just as small football teams act as 'feeders' to big Premiership ones, I started to send people who'd finished their MA's to Max at Manchester to do their Ph.D.s. I also explored going to the US myself to work with Mills.

Canadian Interlude

In 1960, I did go to North America for the first time, not to one of the Ivy League Universities in the States but for a year in Canada, and to a most unlikely place – Saskatchewan in the Prairies. I had tried to disabuse four-year-old Julia of the notion that she would see lots of Indians, but after we had visited social scientists in Montreal, Toronto and Ottawa, the first person we saw at Saskatoon airport was a huge Indian, dressed in a full-size eagle-feather Sioux war-bonnet (to welcome a business convention of dentists). 'See!!' she triumphed.

The Prairies had been colonised by pioneers who had endured terrible privations when they first opened up the land for wheat farming by dispossessing the Indians. In the grim winters, some had to live in dwellings made of turf, even in holes dug out of the riverbanks. Willa Cather's early novels about farming life in Nebraska, *My Antonia* and *O Pioneers!* are the finest literary evocations of the life of the people who had opened up the Plains on the US side of the border. The astounding flatness of the landscape was a shock – it was like living on a vast billiard table. On a 400-mile trip to Winnipeg, we cheered, crossing the border, because there was a hill about fifty feet high. Even the flatness was used to advantage by ingenious road builders who raised the roads high enough for the wind constantly to blow the snow away.

Canadians had learned how to cope with appalling winters, with clothing often derived from traditional Indian models. The Chipewyan Indians lived in tents throughout the sub-zero winter, warmed by Hudson Bay's wood-burning stoves with metal chimneys stuck through holes cut in the canvas roof – which not infrequently caused them to be burned to death. In more modern terms, heating plugs running from power-sockets inside the house replaced one of the bolts in the cylinder-head of the car's engine-block so that it would start first time in the morning, while the snow was efficiently removed from city streets by huge machines. Doing door-to-door interviews in the north, winter started at four o'clock one afternoon, and I suddenly felt that my feet, in thin English shoes, would turn to ice, so had to seek refuge in a house.

Nature was not the only enemy. Canada had its due share of urban class struggle, notably the very violent General Strike in Winnipeg in 1919. But the reactions of Prairie farmers were not the same as those of urban workers. Many were not just pioneers but also immigrants from many different European countries. Whole districts were populated entirely by English people, or Germans, or Norwegians. But nationality was not the only cultural bond which people could draw on in adversity. There were even large communities of Hutterites and Mennonites, who ran their lives on the basis of religious beliefs, though these could be very different. For some it meant a communal sharing of worldly goods, for others the rejection of the nuclear family household. In British Columbia, the Doukhobors had refused military service, just as they had refused the Tsars, and refused, too, to send their children to godless State schools. Their naked protest marches profoundly embarrassed both the Federal and the Provincial Governments; at one time in the 1930s, there were more Royal Canadian Mounted Police in the Okanagan Valley of British Columbia than any other part of Canada.

Religion seemed more important for most people too. We were greeted by 'Welcome Wagons' from different dinominations which hoped to recruit us. Much social provision, such as parks, which would have been provided by local government in Britain, was supplied by churches, charities or voluntary associations. And when women found out I was an atheist, they thought I must be 'promiscuous'. More than that, how could I have any morality at all, if I wasn't religious?

I am always grateful that I entered North America via the Prairies of Canada and the Plains of the US, which are not only the physical heartland of the continent that is the centre of world capitalism, but precisely because of this have also been the heartland of radical 'populism', predominantly among wheat farmers in the West and cotton farmers in the southern states of the US, and among miners who wanted 'free silver'.

This kind of populism had nothing to do with the famous populism of the Russian Narodniks; even less with the loose use of the term to mean any political movement which has widespread popular support. Since all mass parties in parliamentary democracies have to develop such support, even Mrs Thatcher or President Reagan have been called 'populist', as were the new parties (radical but not socialist) which were emerging in the Third World in the 1960s.

By European standards, farms in the Prairies are huge, measured in 'sections' of 640 acres, and a farm of four sections was barely economically viable, so farmers had long resented the power of the banks 'down East', which determined the price they got for their crops, and the railroads and the owners of the elevators which charged them high prices for storing the grain and shipping it. These small farmers were not peasants working pocket-handkerchief plots; they were landowners. Nor did they wish to overthrow the State, which had given them cheap land and built the railroads which took their grain to the world market, but used the State to further their own interests. In the words of the leading historian authority, Richard Hofstadter, they were 'cash-conscious commercial farmers'. These movements did not fit into the traditional European models of class society, which led me to two new fields of interest – populism in general, and rural sociology, particularly contemporary peasant society.[53]

As long ago as the 1890s, populist candidates for the Presidency of the US were getting nearly ten per cent of the votes, largely in the West. But radical populism was still very much alive. In Alberta, 'free silver' tradition had morphed into the 'funny money' policies of Social Credit, which had sixty out of the sixty-four seats, the rest split between four parties.

In Saskatchewan, the much more radical Cooperative Commonwealth Federation, the CCF, ran the provincial Government. The farmers had at first developed a strong regional network of cooperatives; then a political party, the Cooperative Commonwealth Federation, with some links to urban Labour. In 1944, the CCF came to power in the Province, but quickly went far beyond purely agricultural issues. The provincial bus system, life insurance, car insurance, even garages and large retail stores, were all run on cooperative or publicly-owned lines. Now T.C. ('Tommy' to everyone) Douglas' Government was planning to introduce a Provincial Health Service, the first in North America, an irony since there were quite a number of British doctors who had fled the NHS for private practice in Canada, and had landed up in Saskatchewan. The province was already very advanced in medical services – unlike the UK, nurses had degrees, and the Professor of Nursing was a woman who had served with the Republicans in the Spanish Civil War. There was also a sizeable population of radical Americans who had fled from McCarthyism, including my boss, Arthur Davis, who was rightly proud that he, the son of a Vermont farmer, had succeeded in making his way to Harvard (and had a ceremonial chair to prove it), and had become one of a team that worked with Talcott Parsons in developing his early theory. Arthur, however, turned Marxist.

I was to study the situation of the Indians and the Métis, who lived in the poverty-stricken north of the province. The Métis, descendants of mixed Indian/white parentage, had originally been nomadic hunters of the huge herds of buffalo, and suppliers of beaver fur for the hats of the gentry of Europe. Regina, the capital of the Province, had originally been called 'Pile of Bones' – until the hunters finally killed off virtually all the buffalo, and thereby the livelihood of the buffalo hunters.

The world knows, if only from Hollywood, about the genocide practised across the US border on the Indians, and something about Indian resistance too. Less commonly known is the sizeable Métis population, described by a nineteenth-century priest as 'one-and-a-half men'[54] – 'half Indian, half white, half devil' – who tried twice (in 1869–70 and in 1885), with arms in their hands, to establish their own government, but were defeated by the Canadian central government. Louis Riel, who led the second Rebellion with Gabriel Dumont, was hanged. Now they were reduced to subsistence hunting, trapping and fishing, plus Provincial Welfare payments.

I was then taken straight away to Prince Albert, the jumping-off city for the north, and there met two of the most remarkable men one could meet anywhere, both Métis – Jim Brady and Malcolm Norris. By an ironic coincidence they were both Marxists. Both had done every kind of job you can think of – Malcolm in the police, then the law, and in the provincial administration. Jim was much more proletarian; he had been a 'smoke jumper' parachuting into the forest to put out fires, then a geologist, and any other employment that gave him a living, including sheer subsistence. He had also fought from D-Day right through to the end in Germany, and told me that Canadian troops had walked up the beaches in Normandy with slogans on their backs saying 'Vote CCF!' He was also an amazing scholar. His log cabin in La Ronge was crammed with books. Jim had made considerable progress with translating Giraud's *Le Métis Canadien*, published in Paris and three inches thick (which must have cost him a fortune), into English. (In Canadian accounts of the Métis today, which rely almost entirely on English-language literature, this work seems to be ignored.) Jim mysteriously disappeared into the bush in which he had spent so much of his life. Rumour had it that he had gone to Cuba to join Guevara.

My research had been designed by sociologists, who did not work as anthropologists do by immersing themselves in the lives of very small-scale local communities. I was supposed to live in the university city, Saskatoon, with my family and where the children went to school, and study miniscule communities hundreds of miles away. Only once did I get a few continuous weeks in the largest of the northern communities, La Ronge. Research, under these conditions, was frustrating.

It was a post-colonial situation I was used to from northern Australia. Most of the villages had only a few hundred people, with the men away hunting and trapping much of the time, and, socially, were under the spiritual control of the Roman Catholic priest, and the economic control of the Hudson Bay's Company, which sold them their staples of everyday life and bought their fur pelts. Some settlements were only accessible by air.

In the first village I went to I was greeted by Robbie Fontaine. I remarked that it was famed as a very Catholic community. 'Yes', he said, 'but we also like the Devil!' Father Mathieu was very hospitable. He took me on my only dog-sled trip when we went fishing like Inuit through holes in the ice, but he could not credit that I could have lost my faith after having been brought up by his

Order. We argued in circles until 1.30 in the morning, when we decided to call it a day (and night!).

So the only things I wrote were not based on close-grained fieldwork: an account of the history of the Métis in the Province,[55] another, after I had left, for a Festschrift for C. Wright Mills when he died. The latter was not about Indians or Métis but about the white bureaucracy[56] – the officials of the Department of Natural Resources, who were not only responsible for subsidising hunting and fishing activities in the north, and the marketing of fish and furs (to try and break control of the market by private wholesalers), but were also all-purpose administrators and, most crucially, gave out welfare payments. I drew a sample from hospital records and went into the Indian reservation to interview people. I had already found that I needed to fend off the Indian girls, but the opposite obtained here. I thought that people had looked at me askance, because, it turned out, the first person on my list was a well-known prostitute.

Back in Saskatoon, two more fulfilling activities emerged. My radical friends were very keen to repeat in Saskatchewan what had already been done in the UK, so we sent for the hymn sheets of CND songs like 'Can You Hear the H-Bomb's Thunder?' and learned them off by heart for our first march across the city.

Then we marched on the capital, Regina. It is a measure of CCF radicalism that Tommy Douglas issued a three-line whip to his Cabinet, telling them they would all be on the platform to receive us. In his speech, at a time when Britain had permitted US nuclear listening-posts to be built at Fylingdales, just north of us in Yorkshire, the Premier forthrightly called for Canadian withdrawal from the NORAD joint US-Canadian radar system, the DEW (Distant Early Warning) Line, designed to pick up incoming Soviet missiles and planes across the Arctic (at the time, the world's biggest construction project).

A second Line – the Pinetree Line – ran across Northern Saskatchewan. I understood Tommy Douglas' doubts about the reliability of this system when Earl Dodds, the pilot on one of my northern trips from Prince Albert, suddenly cursed after take-off. He had forgotten to inform Air Traffic Control that he would be crossing the Line. 'Oh hell', he said, 'I'll just go under it.' So we dipped just above the trees. I asked whether if he could go under it the Russians couldn't too. 'Sure!' was his only reply.

The invasion at the Bay of Pigs in Cuba provoked great opposition in the circles I moved in. At a more local level, we also decided to go up to Batoche and Duck Lake, to commemorate for the first time the battles of the Métis resistance. In those days, only the 'Pionera' of the white colonisers was celebrated as the province's heritage, with its own museum and annual festival. Our meeting, however, was well covered in the *Saskatoon Star-Phoenix*; since then, the two Métis Rebellions have not only been recognised as part of the Province's heritage but the sites of the battles have become major tourist attractions.

We had been able to buy a second-hand Morris Minor, which enabled us to spend a holiday visiting the Rockies, during which we saw the Calgary Stampede and the staggering beauty of Banff and Lake Louise. Julia, aged four, went off on her own hunting for bears. In Vancouver, we stayed with Cyril Belshaw, our colleague from Canberra days. We entered the US for the first time, not as most Brits do via New York, Chicago, or LA, but by ferry from Victoria on Vancouver Island to Port Angeles in Washington State. We had been assured by the British High Commission in Toronto that we would be allowed in, having been living in Canada, but I fully expected to be sent back by the next ferry. But we weren't, and got to see the Grand Coulee.

It wasn't all pleasure, however. The children were eaten alive by blackflies and the appalling corrugated road over the Rockies proved too much for our ancient car. After having it repaired twice (and having to borrow the money to pay for it), we had to be towed into Jasper by a Cadillac, and were finally obliged to sell the car for $80, the price of our train tickets back to Saskatoon.

Then it was time to go home to the UK. Once more, coming from Canada, we were allowed in to New York. The children loved Coney Island; in the appalling heat of a New York summer, we stripped them down to their knickers and let them play in the fountains in Washington Square. The parents' reward was that Miles Davis was playing at the Village Vanguard, the high-point of my jazz days. Then we got the biggest ship in the world, the *USS United States*, back home.

*****

Once back in Hull, I had no time whatsoever to undertake what had been my main intention – to convert my Ph.D. material on Groote Eylandt kinship into a book – and I have never been able to to this day.[57] But it now seemed much more urgent to work on a book on a new phenomenon – the Third World. My involvement in Third World issues was not confined to academic reading but drew heavily on my wartime experiences, and the new ferment of the transition from colonialism to independence involved me with students like the Ghanaian, George Acquah, with whom I started an Afro-Asian Society. People were surprised to find out that the Emperor Septimius Severus had died while visiting the remote outskirts of the Roman Empire, in York (of a cold). Despite the lack of interest of the language departments in the University in the arguments we made for studying non-European languages, we were able to fill a thousand-seater hall in town for a concert of African and Asian music and dance. George was a very lively and amusing person (he warned people that he could 'magic' them with a special carved African stick he had, right across the front quad). He changed from law to sociology and then wrote a history of his own people, the Fantse.[58] After graduating, he sailed into the same front quad in a chauffeur-driven Rolls-Royce as Ghana's Ambassador to Somalia, leaving behind a photograph of himself bearing a message addressed to the staff at Hull, telling those of them that had looked down on Africans that they should now think again. Alas, he was to serve time in one of Nkrumah's jails.

But one of the biggest anti-colonial struggles had not concerned an African or an Asian country at all, because it was not just a legacy of colonialism but of the disintegration of an enormous empire that had been a dominant power when Britain was just an island off the coast of Europe, just beginning to make a bid for a bit of the trade of Asia.

The British authorities were worried about Cypriot students going to the notorious 'Red Base' of the London School of Economics, a reputation it had acquired because of the presence of one or two eminent teachers, notably Harold Laski. In fact, it never was until the student revolution after 1968. But those in charge of scholarships for colonials nevertheless decided to send them to a safe provincial university – Hull – where they arrived just in time for the convulsions of 1956, and we got to know them well.

They were left-wingers, and the Communist Party in Cyprus was a powerful mass party. But the revolt which had broken out in 1955 had not been led by the Left, but by a Greek officer, George Grivas, who wanted *enosis* with Greece. It took 30,000 British servicemen, 104 of whom died, to suppress a revolt in which the main street in Nicosia became known as 'Murder Mile'. When it ended, in 1960, Cyprus became independent, with Archbishop Makarios as President.

But Makarios rejected union with Greece, so when, in 1967, a fascistic junta of 'the Colonels' seized power back in Athens it was the green light for a second EOKA (the National Organisation of Cypriot Fighters), which Grivas launched in 1971. He was able to overthrow the island's government within three years. Nikos Sampson, one of the first EOKA terrorists to have killed British soldiers (and many Turks), became President. Now there was mass butchery on both sides. The first thing I saw at Kyrenia airport (renamed Girne) in the late 1980s was a poster with the names of missing Turkish villagers. The Greeks countered by recording the butchery committed in the villages of the north after three brigades of Turkish troops plus forty tanks had landed there in 1974.

It was not the Turkish military, noted for their repression of the Kurds, who invaded Cyprus, but one who had opposed them for decades, the left-wing President Bülent Ecevit.

The Left and the liberals in the UK knew Greek Cypriots personally, but didn't know any Turks. Greece, too, was the cradle of Western civilisation; Turkey had been an alien civilisation and the main enemy of Western Europe for centuries. So there was a knee-jerk reaction, even on the Left, to support Greek Cyprus against an illegal invasion, even though it had been an invasion to stop fascist Greece taking over an island with nearly half a million Turks in it. Their numbers increased when lands, including the rich Mesaoria, were handed over to Turkish immigrants (many from ethnic minorities); conversely, hundreds of thousands of Greeks fled to the South. One consequence of this population exchange was the singularly sad sight of the once elegant middle-class town of Varosha on the edge of Famagusta, now an empty buffer zone with grass growing in the streets.

One of the heroes of the invasion had been Takis Konis, a former Hull student and now a very senior official in the field of social welfare after his gargantuan efforts to cope with the mass exodus from the north. In his natal village we saw the new Cyprus, when his mother's old earth oven for baking bread was being dismantled and replaced by a modern oven. We men went to the coffee shop, from where we saw a blonde Englishwoman – an ex-Hull student who had married a man who came from that community – amongst the black-clad women. They didn't dare enter that male preserve; nor did Marion, who was walking in the street with the other women.

Because of the invasion, and the international support of overseas Greeks, especially in the US, Greek Cyprus soon recovered – firstly, benefiting from wars in the Levant which had opened up a new market for Cyprus' agriculture, which had lost its best lands in the Mesaoria in the north. Far more importantly, a new tourist industry was brought into being, catering for hundreds of thousands of Western Europeans who reported the pleasures of life in the sun. By contrast, the north was only propped up by Turkey, though there were bizarre innovations such as the six new universities which attracted not only the sons of the Turkish rich to the eastern Mediterranean, but even other foreigners who enjoyed the privileges of big cars with special, free licence plates.

Our former students had organised a conference on the future of small states, and succeeded in attracting even Edward Said.[59] But there was only one Turk who had dared come – Ali Sirmen, a journalist from the very liberal newspaper, *Cumhuriyet* (a kind of Istanbul *Le Monde*), who not only kept us in tucks with his sophisticated Turkish political jokes but took me with him to cross the frontier with the north, taboo to Greeks, where we dined with the Rauf Denktash, President of the Turkish Republic of Northern Cyprus, recognised by no one except Turkey. (Years later, in Istanbul, Ali took me to Prinkipo, the island famous to us because Trotsky had been in exile there.)

Kyrenia, with its historic Castle museum (which showed a Turk being broken on a wheel by the Franks), Saint Hilarion Castle, and Lawrence Durrell's Bella Vista, were so exquisite that I determined to come back when things got better – and did so as a tourist more than a decade later. On this holiday in Istanbul, Turkey was under military rule, but when we went to an upmarket restaurant we hadn't expected the squad of six-foot Anatolian paratroopers which burst in. But it was near the politically suspect students' quarter: the waiters' hands shook as they poured us unnecessary water. Then we were all lined up against the wall. Then, thank God, they left.

A handful of Brits left over from the Durrell epoch were still there living in comfort but there were virtually no tourists.

Like Korea, that other division which has preoccupied us since the 1950s, Cyprus remains divided, despite a referendum in which the majority of Turks in the north, ironically, voted in favour of reuniting the island (and thereby hopefully gaining entry to the EU), but the majority of Greek Cypriots voted against.

CHAPTER 6

Manchester University: Upheaval

Back in the 1950s in Hull, where this interest in Cyprus had begun, I had been moving steadily up the promotion ladder, without making any special effort, because I was very happy with my position. To a young teacher, it was a cycle of new people and new ideas – not a treadmill – with a constant flood of talks, visits to other universities, the very hard grind of examining, sometimes, excitingly, abroad. Then suddenly out of the blue I got an invitation to come for an interview for the new Chair of Sociology at the University of Manchester. I had just agreed to stand as an Independent Nuclear Disarmament candidate in North Hull, but had to hand that job over to Richard Gott, of the *Manchester Guardian*, who got the couple of hundred votes that I would have got.

I'd always rather enjoyed examinations, so found being interviewed by twenty professors quite interesting. Tom Burns, of Edinburgh, was the other candidate. In the end I heard from Max by phone that they had decided not to appoint either of us. This quite suited me since I was more than happy where I was. But after nearly a year's silence – by which time I'd forgotten about it – I received a letter saying that I had been appointed!

It was, though, an offer you couldn't refuse. Working in a joint department with Max seemed ideal. (And Hull had been a football desert. When the Munich disaster happened, Max rallied the troops, including me, to go to down to London for the next United match – away at Highbury – to back the team. It was a very sad occasion.)

I had finished the manuscript of my book on *The Third World*[60] just before moving to Manchester, but had to spend the first week re-compiling the index, which had got lost in the post. It was a job I always loathed, and had to be done by oneself, because professional indexers always include unimportant things and leave out things an author thinks important. The book was very well received by reviewers, for the most part – even by Edward Shils, a leading intellectual anti-communist from the Congress for Cultural Freedom (and a good sociologist). But enthusiasm for an emerging 'Third World' which might undermine the hegemony of the superpowers attracted a much wider audience than that of academics. The term therefore soon became common currency. (It still is, though by now connotes little more than the poor of the world.)

The Western powers wasted no time in bringing the new, would-be independent African and Asian governments to heel. Armed revolutions from the Dutch East Indies and Vietnam to Algeria and Kenya continued, especially where settlers and important mining interests were involved. In Africa, the Belgian mining corporations – which produced sixty per cent of the world's uranium and eighty per cent of its industrial diamonds in the Congo – took the lead on behalf of the Western world. When the Congo became independent in 1960, white mercenaries were sent in to protect Belgian citizens and to wrest back political control of the Congo from the new Government, using Moise Tshombe and then the Army's Col. Mobutu to sponsor a breakaway state in Katanga, the main mining area. The charismatic leader of the Congo, Patrice Lumumba, was murdered and his body put into a refrigerator, whilst no less a personage than Dag Hammarskjold, Secretary-General of the United Nations, was mysteriously killed in an air-crash. At a more lowly level, my colleague, Valdo Pons, who had been teaching in the Congo, was lucky to survive when rebels stormed the hotel he was in and put all the blacks up against the wall. He escaped by hiding in the air-conditioning system in the ceiling of his room.

The costs to the imperial powers were becoming ever heavier, though, so, during the 'wind of change', rather than risk protracted resistance, power was increasingly handed over to reliable nationalist governments, even in countries such as Malaya and Kenya, once armed resistance movements had been crushed. The contribution of those who had fought as guerrillas often went completely unrecognised, and a new class of fat cat politicians replaced them.

The governments which emerged were extremely weak. Dependent on selling primary commodities like cocoa on the world market, the new states were unable to resist Western pressures to conform. If they did offer resistance, direct military-political intervention of the Congo type was one option, but economic destabilisation was much easier and 'cleaner'. Radical governments were quickly subverted and pro-Western conservatives installed. Typically, Nkrumah's government was overthrown while he was out of the country. The sad, nigh-universal response to these pressures was to convert the nationalist claim forged during the struggle for independence that there were no class or cultural differences at all in the new states into the assertion that if there were there shouldn't be. Ethnic political parties were now denounced as 'tribalism' or 'separatism'. Where feeble class-based movements existed, they were repressed too. The 'one-party state' had triumphed, whilst as an international movement, the Third World became merely a forum for rhetoric. Africa, above all, became a continent where any change to colonial boundaries established by foreign powers less than a century ago became absolutely taboo. The Third World, as an effective force, had not lasted long.

One country, Tanzania, adjoining both Kenya and the Congo, had escaped direct Western military intervention because it was not economically important. Sisal was the main export, and it had few white settlers. Originally taken from the Germans during the First World War, it had become a UN 'Trust Territory', though still effectively a British colony, and then independent Tanganyika. But when a small, bizarre and complicated army mutiny broke out off the coast in Zanzibar, near the capital, Dar es Salaam – with a strong anti-Arab content, partly led by a Kenyan Luo ex-corporal and partly by a Marxist-leaning Zanzibari, Sheikh Abeid Karume – it soon threatened to involve the whole of the new country in the Cold War, so the new President, Julius Nyerere, immediately asked for British military assistance. Tanzanian troops then ensured that the mainland and the Zanzibari offshore islands were fused into a new entity – 'Tanzania'. The leading Marxist Cabinet Minister on the mainland, Babu, was also imprisoned.

The government's ideology, 'Ujamaa' ('family-ness'), was an Africanist variant of one-party ideology, opposed to class-based Marxism, but was relatively mild, harking back to the cultural roots of the Bantu population. So Swahili, not English (as in Kenya), became the national language. (Nyerere had translated *The Merchant of Venice* and *Julius Caesar* into Swahili.) Class was declared to be a divisive and irrelevant force, threatening Tanzania's newfound independence; what differences there were, Ujamaa held, could be settled in the traditional way, by discussing them under the village tree. Nyerere also drew on their common negative experience of life as colonial subjects of Britain. So Tanzania was still regarded, both on the Right and the Left, as offering an alternative to Western imperialism.

In the first summer vacation back at Manchester, because of my knowledge of the country, I was asked to join an Economic Mission of the British Government to Tanzania to explore the possibility of giving that country aid. This involved leaving my family, new to Manchester, for six weeks on their own.

Absolutely characteristic of Nyerere's decisiveness was the reception he gave us in the splendid presidential palace at Dar, built for the German colonial Governor. The leader of our Mission, a former Secretary to the Cabinet, said that there were two imponderables, and that whatever policies Tanzania adopted would massively affect anything we might recommend. These were the Village Resettlement policy – which, in an overwhelmingly agricultural economy, would affect the whole country – and whether Tanzania would take the decision to invest in a new Railway from the coast to Zambia, which would be immensely expensive. Nyerere laughed. 'We've consulted the Canadians [then considered almost neutralist, unlike the US]. They've advised us not to do it. So have the Russians', he said. 'Both of them have said we shouldn't do it – so we probably will'! And they did, in the end (a very unacceptable decision for Western-bloc powers), with gigantic financial aid from China and the manual labour of thousands of Chinese labourers who lived in camps secluded from the local population. They did the job in record time, making the entire Southern Province a new potential region for commercial agriculture by linking it not only to Tanzania's existing railway line but to the countries which had been the 'Rhodesias' to the south, especially the Copper Belt.

Nyerere also provided camps where Liberation movements from southern Africa could train their guerrillas. Decades later, it transpired that terrible things had happened in these camps when different factions started to struggle, not against apartheid but for power over their own movement, even to the use of torture. As usual, such factions adopted one or other of the 'Marxist' identities on offer, because foreign Communist governments could provide arms and political support. (In the guerrilla camps where the Zimbabweans trained in exile, Mugabe even wiped out the entire 'Chinese' opposition to his leadership.) So when I once remonstrated with Ray Alexander, a leading South African communist, about their notoriously unswerving support for the USSR, long after other Communist Parties had become openly critical of the Soviets, she simply retorted 'And where do you think we would get our arms from?'

My role in the British Mission was to look at the Village Resettlement Agency, for which we were given total access to the government files we needed in the magnificent old German offices on the waterfront. An illiterate taxi-driver professed incredulity when I, who didn't know the city, used a town plan to guide him to the place I wanted. 'You're a clever lot, you Europeans!' he exclaimed. On one afternoon off we went out to the reef by trimaran; even better was going there by outrigger canoe (originally brought by colonists from across the Indian Ocean many centuries ago) from one of the coastal villages. I was also thrilled to see dhows which had just come in from the Gulf, blown by the monsoon, using, it was said, centuries-old charts; and ancient tombs with Persian and Arabic inscriptions, and even Chinese plates, inserted into the stonework. The Chinese had, indeed, visited the East African coast, notably in the great voyage of the Ming period under Cheng Ho, and the 'auspicious giraffe' was brought to the zoo in Peking to prove it.

When I visited the first experimental villages they seemed so badly run that years' more development would be needed. The existing twenty-five settlements needed 'urgent re-organisation'; 'not a single one [was] "likely to ... produce sufficient cash income to enable settlers to earn increased incomes and begin to repay their loans at a rate anything like that originally envisaged if at all." Only one of eight new Pilot schemes showed any promise whatsoever'.[61]

I nearly didn't get home, however, when the Kiwi pilot of the little Cessna which was to take me to an island in Lake Victoria was so hung over that he couldn't get the plane to start on the button, so got out, groaning and clutching his forehead, to try and start the plane by swinging the prop. He was only too successful. After several misfires the engine fired up and the plane headed for the Lake a few hundred yards away, but without him. I, on the other hand, was inside, strapped in. Fortunately, he was able to clamber back through the open plane door.

Despite my misgivings, after we left, Nyerere was to radically up the ante, introducing a far more radical reorganisation, not of a few experimental settlements but of the whole of agriculture, on a colossal scale, moving hundreds of thousands of people overnight into new, centralised 'Ujamaa villages', where water, electricity and medical services could be provided. I think this shows the difference between an academic and a politician, because Nyerere simply did it. The one radical economist on our team also argued that it didn't matter if things were inefficient – we should give them the money, even if most of it got wasted; at least they would be learning how to do things their way. Nevertheless, the villagisation programme, as

Nyerere eventually carried it out, was severely to disrupt Tanzania's mainly agricultural economy for years.

Nyerere's decisiveness was once more in evidence – for the good, this time, when Idi Amin invaded northern Tanzania, burning villages and murdering their inhabitants. In no time at all, the Tanzanian Army hit back and took Kampala.

When we went to a village near Iringa there was, for me, a moving encounter when one of the workers on the Scheme there asked me if I hadn't been at Ifunda. It was Aaron, my old friend Mamfugale's son, whom I'd known as a teenager. We had to be at the airport, so I was only able to spend three minutes with him. I asked after Mamfugale. 'He passed away', said Aaron. Tears welled in my eyes at the passing of man who had been like a father to me. Nor was I able to visit Ifunda, my old home for nearly a year, only twenty miles away.

At the end of our work, we were taken to Ngorongoro crater, where 25,000 animals were crammed into the largest volcanic caldera in the world. On the plane back to the UK, I ran into Joe Murumbi, my old comrade from Movement for Colonial Freedom days in London, now Foreign Minister of Kenya.

* * * * *

Back in Manchester, the overwhelming priority was to build a sociology department, and everything was in our favour. Sociology was growing not only across the country but across the world and Manchester had optimal resources. In those days, every new professor got a 'honeymoon' appointment of one or two additional lecturers, and we got more every year.

The first job in building the new department-within-a-department was to recruit staff. Given the very recent development of the subject, there were only a handful of trained sociologists in the whole country, and as a result of the equally recent development of a dozen new universities that sprang up with the publication of the 'Robbins Report', we were desperately pressed to find teachers. I even had to ring Chicago to try and recruit teachers, and was myself offered several Chairs at new universities within a few weeks.

With the spread of guerrilla warfare in Central Africa, researchers were beginning to be deported or banned. Police had invaded the campus at the University of Rhodesia, so white colleagues gradually started to trickle back to the UK. Max had the bright idea of bringing Clyde Mitchell, then Vice-Chancellor of the

University in Salisbury, as a second Professor of Sociology, which solved the problem of my innumeracy.

Clyde was a rarity: a working-class white South African who had come up via the University of South Africa, which taught people by correspondence. Like most of our early people, he then trained in anthropology and had produced a good book on the Yao. But he had also flown round the Mediterranean navigating a bomber with sociology books propped in front of him. He was a delightful human being, with whom I never had a cross word in eight years. He was also a splendid and principled liberal who didn't like doing politics, but would do so whenever his conscience made him, and was influenced, like Max, by his rich Communist wife, who had been exiled from the country to Ghana (though allowed access to her money), then to Mozambique, and finally to Rhodesia with her new husband.

In Manchester, students were pouring into Sociology. We certainly didn't hand-pick them, as in Hull; they were admitted (or not) entirely on A-level results. Whereas I had inherited three Final-Year students in my first year at Hull, at Manchester there were 450 in my first-year lectures, so these tended to be theatrical occasions.

The anthropologists wanted to send one young woman in the audience to the Sudan to study witchcraft. Instead, Anna Ford went on to become the first female President of the Student Union, then the best known news presenter on the BBC, and eventually Chancellor of the University.

We tried various artificial devices to balance out the two sides of the Department. Before they made any choice of specialism, the Faculty exposed students to three basic subjects: economics, government and anthropology/sociology, in which latter subjects, however, they only got a one-hour lecture a week – first anthropology, then sociology. So, in a month, we were supposed to teach them sociology on the basis of two hours of lectures. At the end of this most inadequate first year, students who wanted to go on with sociology/anthropology had then also to choose which of the two they would then continue with.

As at Cambridge, there was a stupid convention that lectures were almost private property. Only one member of staff ever attended one of mine. So tutors, some pure anthropologists, had to teach students on lectures which they hadn't heard, and for which there existed no printed materials. We then tried lecturing for one term in anthropology, and one in sociology: equally unsatisfactory.

Most of our sociology teachers had been trained as anthropologists, so could tutor either subject well, but for others it wasn't so easy. Just how ludicrous all this was became apparent in our post-graduate/staff seminars. One week, Lester Hiatt, Professor at Sydney, spoke on 'Why Do Australian Aborigines Throw Spears at their Mothers-in-law?' The following week, we had Peter Nettl, political scientist from Leeds, on Rosa Luxemburg.

All this might seem to be parochial problems within one particular department; in fact, it was part of a worldwide rise of sociology, which had fateful consequence for a department which had an international reputation for its anthropology, but which was now threatened by the rising tide of sociology. The only solution was to split the Department, which we eventually did. Max, naturally, fought tooth and nail to stop this happening, since it might have reduced anthropology to a rump. I argued that anthropology would have to move away from its traditional focus upon 'tribal' societies and begin to tackle problems of development in the Third World, particularly new forms of rural organisation and urban life. If it didn't, the subject would simply wither away. This naturally infuriated Max and the anthropologists, and when I followed this up by giving a paper at the Evian World Congress of Sociology entitled 'The End of Anthropology?', his fury knew no bounds.[62] (I was wrong – it didn't die at all.)

Added to the problem with anthropology, we looked like having a faculty that would be half sociology, and half everything else, which was ridiculous. Even the historic Economics Department, founded by Stanley Jevons, was threatened. Left-wing friends in economics opposed our splitting the department in two on the intellectual grounds of preserving the 'unity of the social sciences' (not the preservation of their historic dominance!). To stem the flood into sociology, I was quite relieved to put a ceiling on the numbers of students who would be allowed to enter our department for their second year.

Servicing sociology was difficult because it was a new subject in most universities, and there wasn't even a really good textbook. So one of the youngest members of our staff suggested writing our own, entirely for our own use, which we did, each taking a chapter. When Penguin then came along and asked us to write a sociology textbook, we were able to reply 'We've just written one'. We then rewrote it, and tried it out both in the University and at various colleges in the Manchester area.

We'd intended no more than a course-book for our own students, but *Introducing Sociology*[63] was an amazing success, adopted by dozens of universities and colleages. We also produced two companion books, one of introductory readings, the other on social 'problems'. When the textbook was adopted by the new Open University, which already had a huge student population, it was national news, reported on the front page of the *Guardian*. By the time we completely revised it as *The New Introducing Sociology*, seventeen years later, it carried on its cover something I'd never bothered to work out – that we had sold over half a million copies. It also went into Swedish, Portuguese, Spanish and Icelandic. Though the right-wing press continued to inveigh against sociology, we probably even helped introduce new ways of thinking about society outside academia too – 'role-models' and the 'extended family' are now part of everyday speech. The US was uninterested in our book, however, because a textbook there has to be about US society, and cover every conceivable aspect of that society. Ideally, it should also weigh about two pounds. So I never became well known as a sociologist in the US. I was always an anthropologist, known for my other books.

Given my anthropological background, much of the research we initiated at Manchester was fieldwork-based. I sent one very cosmopolitan upper class/caste Indian to continue the cultural studies tradition for his Ph.D. to a big holiday camp at Blackpool, where he did hard manual jobs to pay for his fieldwork costs, one behind the bar. He was taken aback by the vast quantities of beer that were consumed by British teenagers; even more by their sexual strategies: the first day was spent surveying the 'talent'; on the second, a direct approach to the chosen target was made; the rest of the week was devoted to sleeping with him/her.

When I asked the manager if he lived in Blackpool, he responded: 'I do not; I *reside* in Lytham St. Annes' (the posh suburb next door).

Champions!

We had great success on the football front. I had been in Hull at the time of the Munich air disaster, on 5 February 1958, in which seven of the 'Busby Babes' were killed. But I got back to Manchester just in time for the run in which we ended not only as First Division Champions, but Champions of Europe.

Much of the credit went to the great trio – Denis Law, George Best and Bobby Charlton – but the importance of support from myself and my daughters at the corner of the Stretford End should not be underestimated. Four of us went down to London for the penultimate decisive match, without tickets, and couldn't get into the ground. Then West Ham supporters started leaving. 'Law's scored again!', one said and handed us two tickets. We got another two tickets after another goal, and ended up as League Champions with a 6-1 victory. Passing a pet shop on the way back to the station we bought a tortoise and named him 'Nobby'.

Then came the greatest triumph of all. Celtic had won the European Cup, but no English team had. We were in the Final now with Benfica. In those days you didn't have to be a celebrity or a millionaire, as at Stamford Bridge or Arsenal today, to get into Old Trafford. Manchester United was very democratic, and regular supporters, not just season-ticket holders, could cut out tokens from their match programmes and get tickets to Cup matches and European ties, which eventually won us regular seats in the new Cantilever Stand, where I encountered six other Manchester University professors. One, Brian Cox, whom I had known at Hull when he was in CND, was now the editor of the 'Black Papers' attacking progressive trends in education. Even his writing a piece about a wonder goal by Stuart Pearson in the weekly 'Don's Diary' in the *Times Higher Education Supplement* didn't compensate for his reactionary views on education in my eyes, though. Another professorial denizen of the Cantilever Stand was Tom Kilburn, co-inventor of the pioneer computer memory, who couldn't raise the capital in the UK to put it into production; a medium-sized, then relatively unknown, American corporation called IBM came to visit him, and they did.

When we got to the Benfica Final, I only had two tickets, one for myself and one for one daughter. I needed two more; one for a friend. This was one of those rare occasions when sociology came in useful in my personal life. I asked myself, in true interactionist style, what kinds of people met lots of people in the course of their daily life? I thought of barmen; then of milkmen, so I asked our milkman if he knew of anyone who might have any spare tickets. Not only had he heard of one; he turned out to have been the former butler of Louis Edwards, the boss of Manchester United. So we got our tickets.

I had an ex-Salvation Army bugle with which I used to sound the charge. At Wembley we were all standing in a sea of bodies, which surged in waves in those pre-Hillsborough days. When Bobby Charlton scored the first goal (a rare header) the bugle was smashed out of my grasp. I never did find the mouthpiece, but I still have the abbreviated bugle. Then, for the last goal, I had my glasses swept off, lost somewhere beneath trampling feet and flying bodies. When I got them back one lens was badly splintered, but I still had the other one. It was worth everything, though I was completely hoarse. But it was revolution time, and I had to give a lecture next morning, the first of three: one on Frantz Fanon,[64] the second on Che Guevara,[65] and the third on the Mau Mau. (I was even flown across the Atlantic to give a talk in Michigan on the revolutionary party.[66])

When I finally collected the girls, who were in a seated part of the ground, Deb was still gazing at the crowd, which was still cheering but beginning to leave, and when I suggested that we too moved to get our very late-night sleeper back to Manchester, she said, 'I just want to see a bit more. I may never see anything like this again!'

Then United began to falter, ending with the sad scene of my hero Denis Law, by then playing for Manchester City, back-heeling us into the Second Division and walking off in tears. I met him later in the gents at Euston Station wearing his City team suit, when we occupied adjacent stalls. I'd just come from a conference and was wearing Scottish plaid trousers. 'I like your trews, Peter', he said. Astonished, I blurted out, 'But we've never met. How did you know my name?' 'From that name badge on your lapel', he replied – an anecdote which was printed in the Newsletter of the British Sociological Association, and became celebrated in sociological circles.

United spent the next year at the top of the Second Division, scarcely losing a match. We were back where we belonged.

The Student Revolution

The football successes went hand in hand with the growth of the Department and the success of our textbook. But there was a cloud on the horizon no bigger than a man's hand. The academic successes were merely the domestic experience of something far bigger, and by no means simply academic, fuelled by forces that transcended what was going on in any particular university or, indeed, any particular country. In the UK, the rapid growth in the number of new universities and the expansion of the older ones had brought into all the universities a new cohort of students, including large numbers of women, who had quite un-traditional attitudes and agendas. It was the beginning of the 'student revolution'.

Student protest was eminently understandable in the US, because of the war in Vietnam. Though the government in France, after the political crisis of the Algerian War, was also seriously threatened by the *evènements* on the streets of Paris in 1968, the US was the only

Western country where military force was used to stop student protest (at Kent State University, in Ohio), and then not on a great scale, since the state troopers only killed four students and wounded nine.

Further, the protests in Paris had different consequences for Europe because, being French, they had an ideological not just a political content – a root-and-branch questioning of the assumptions underlying all disciplines, especially the social sciences, and much more widely, orthodox society as a whole. I soon found myself defending students who were mainly focussing their attacks not on capitalism or war but on a soft target, sociology.

We had dedicated the first edition of our textbook 'To our students'. This was no rhetoric, for we had, indeed, written it for them. But it was no protection whatsoever against the new storm that now broke on our heads.

I had aligned myself with the new Council for Academic Freedom and Democracy (CAFD), an offshoot of the National Council for Civil Liberties, which involved me in helping to expose instances of scandalous abuses of power, especially professorial power, in other universities and colleges. I was a member of two CAFD inquiries, one in Bolton College of Technology and another in Lancaster University. So chaotic were those times that I don't even have a copy of either report we did.

But then the attack was turned onto our own University, and finally upon my Department.

A temporary lecturer in the Philosophy Department, Anthony Arblaster, who had been teaching for a year or two and was nominated by his colleagues as the strongest candidate for an available post, was turned down by his professor. Professors could do that sort of thing in those days, so CAFD took up his case, sending John Saville and Professor John Griffith from the LSE Department of Law to report on the case. Being a member of the Manchester staff, I could not, of course, be involved myself.

Some of the staff went ballistic. I was 'cut' in the street by the Dean of Arts (who later apologised), while in the Senate and among the lecturing staff generally heads disappeared behind parapets – virtually everybody except the handful of non-professorial staff, and Clyde Mitchell, plus the odd student representative, was totally opposed to the students. One member of Senate told me that they quite looked forward to a spectacle which they saw as a kind of entertainment – bear-baiting the house radical. I did not find this amusing at all.

The students reacted by using radically new tactics – huge mass meetings, the occupation of buildings, and breaking into the administration offices and copying files which revealed that thoroughly indefensible things had been going on.

In the event, the Professor of Philosophy was not only protected but rewarded. Nor did Arblaster get the job. Nevertheless, the inquiry conducted by CAFD did prove to be a turning point. From then on, non-professorial staff were gradually given the right to be consulted on the kind of post that was to be filled and allowed to participate in drawing up lists of suitable candidates – hardly revolutionary matters, though in defending them in the Senate I had to argue that I was not being anti-professorial. Indeed, I said, (echoing the old wry comment about anti-Semites), some of my best friends were professors and one had to remember that many non-professors might soon prove to be worthy of appointment as professors.

Very sadly, one of the people most hostile to the students was Max Gluckman. He had been very bitter about the revelations in the Soviet Union (feeling, I think, that he had been made a fool of) and his South African upbringing had imbued him with a post-colonial reverence for British academia, especially Oxbridge. (The only time he ever suffered for his Jewishness in England was when a Cheadle golf club refused him membership.) He did not lose his anti-colonialism or his social egalitarianism, but these events took him quite a way on the all too familiar, tiresome journey from left-winger to reactionary. At the height of student protest, he had to be virtually physically restrained when militant students tried to stop him and anyone else going through the door of the Senate which they were picketing.

Though I relate things as if they happened in blocks – here the student revolt, there work abroad, there writing books and teaching – things were not neatly separated from each other or sequential at all. They overlapped. Any one of them was demanding enough; taken together, the load was sometimes near intolerable. Nor did one's non-academic commitments cease in the slightest, notably the revival of CND in 1980/1 when Pershing and Cruise missiles were installed in Europe by the US, though that revival didn't last long, consigning self-sacrificing full-time workers like Dick Nettleton in Manchester North-West CND once more to penury. And somewhere amongst all this one had to try to find time for one's personal life.

Everyone has a research disaster somewhere that doesn't get highlighted in their CV. Max, for example, had been able to get money from Sidney Bernstein of Granada to bring over several researchers well trained at the Hebrew University by Eisenstadt, which resulted in several good monographs. But another project to study the mining and cotton town of Leigh misfired, and virtually nothing got published.

My disaster was the Edinburgh/Manchester Study. In the middle of the student turmoil, Tom Burns, Professor of Sociology at Edinburgh, approached me proposing that we jointly study our two universities. I would do Edinburgh and he would do Manchester. The Social Science Research Council, under Michael Young, was under pressure to do something about research in this highly public area, so we got money from them very quickly and began.

Designing the research and recruiting staff in no time at all, the weekly travelling between Edinburgh and Manchester, plus constant interviewing, was demanding (apart from running a department). The two universities had formally endorsed the research but many of the staff were anything but well disposed towards it, especially in the Science departments.

The data once collected and printed out, there 'only' remained the writing up, which turned out to be the worst problem of all, for we had not budgeted for the time we would need *after* the research was completed (which funding agencies aren't keen to finance). Once the largely junior research team had been disbanded none of them were available. I didn't even have a copy of the printout.

The report never got written. We were pilloried as an instance of 'late reporting', which should never be allowed to happen again, and controls were tightened up – too late – by the SSRC. I of course felt very guilty.

I am not now convinced, however, that this kind of intensive and localised research was what was called for. I have read much of the torrent of ink spilt on the events of the time which told us what was happening, but hardly any of it explained much. It was empirical description, not theoretical analysis.

Firstly, it was obvious that the phenomenon of student protest was a global one, not peculiar to any one country or even continent, and certainly not peculiar to any one university. Each country, of course, has its special features, as we saw for the US and France.

It was, however, primarily a *cultural* revolution rather than a political or economic one. To understand it, a much more historical perspective, which looks at changing generational consciousness, is called for, which I do not think the dominant social science methods – whether the sociological 'meat-grinder' survey or the more close-grained anthropological study, or any other kind of snapshot at one point in time – can begin to grasp.

Women, for instance, had been arriving at university at a time when the women's movement had already become both large and militant in society at large, and was by no means restricted to institutions of higher education. This new student population, female and male, brought their intelligence to bear not just on their formal academic studies, 'out there', or on politics alone, but used it to think about their own situation. As we saw, students had been politically inert (or conservative) from the end of the Second World War up to the twin crises of Suez and Hungary. The next generation, effectively my generation, was the first politicised one. But it also left a much broader legacy – that of questioning *everything*. By the mid-1960s, an even newer generation brought up on this kind of across-the-board radicalism was arriving in the universities. It was a population not only suffused with intellectual and political energy but charged too with the sexual energy of the young ('Make Love, Not War'). It was a changing world, not just of students but of the young.

'Youth culture', like the women's movement, had emerged long before student political radicalism, and I had written about it in an article entitled 'Authority and the Young',[67] long before one part of it had become the organised student radical movement. Sociologists generally didn't write much about culture in those days; their focus was on social structure. But I was intrigued by a variety of cultural topics: the plurality of cultures,[68] the spread of jazz across the world,[69] and was even persuaded by a friend to address the Annual Conference of the Library Association on the subject of libraries,[70] which reduced senior officers of the Association to apoplexy because it began by mentioning Karl Marx as an eminent user of British libraries. It drew enough attention, however, to be picked up by the *Guardian* and was even reprinted in the US and Italy.

To use the term 'student revolution' might seem fatuous when one compares the cataclysms which overthrew state and society in Tsarist Russia or China with what now erupted in the universities of the West, but the forms and methods, and the techniques they used, departed massively from traditional forms of student criticality such as Oxford Union 'debates'. Now, picketing and occupations were normal, plus demands for interminable meetings to discuss whatever the students wanted to discuss.

A revolution, as Mao Tse-Tung classically remarked, is not a dinner-party. But earlier in his career he had also observed that dinner-parties were not unimportant. Long before they turned to guns and organisations, the peasants had begun to break social ties that had never been questioned before. Social structure (class) and culture had reinforced each other for millennia. Now, peasants were starting a cultural revolution, turning their backs on traditional customs – boozing, fireworks, feasts – shared by peasants and landlords alike.

Traditional relations inside the university were similarly turned upside down. Deference had long disappeared. But cordial human relationships and trust soon went as well. When, despite the uneasiness of the Dean, we took on Dick Atkinson, who had been victimised at Birmingham, as a temporary lecturer, my fellow Professors in the Faculty insisted that that I get the approval of the Vice-Chancellor (which I was able to get), Atkinson expressed his gratitude but also had the honesty to say that he wouldn't refrain from agitating against anything he didn't approve of in the Department. He certainly didn't. After a very few weeks he launched a series of lengthy articles in the student newspaper, *The Independent*, attacking the entire university system. I was soon being threatened, too, by virtually the only member of staff (a member of my Department) who, hitherto totally apolitical, now came out strongly in support of the students, and was now sent bearing the message that if I didn't vote the way the radical students wanted me to in Senate I would be denounced as a 'fink'. (I was going to vote that way anyhow.) Finally, there was a strong contingent of highly intelligent people, whom I can only call 'barrack-room lawyers', who exploited every opportunity to query everything on every possible occasion, and to call a whole succession of interminable meetings. The pages of documents about all this would be impossible (and extremely boring) even to summarise.

The attack now turned on an easy target, the Sociology Department. We had changed the Departmental Committee from being entirely a committee drawn from the lecturing staff to virtually equal numbers of staff and students (twelve student representatives, ten permanent and five temporary members of staff). Tutorial assistants, who did a very small amount of teaching, also came sometimes. The upshot was that the lecturing staff could get outvoted, something I now think of as quite misguidedly idealistic. There was no question of rational debate – under charismatic leadership, the students simply voted as a bloc.

I had opened up the idea of reforming the syllabus to be debated, with position papers, and so on. But the most radical of the student representatives wanted the revolution yesterday, not today, and anyone who counselled any delay was a traitor. So they then immediately called for massive reforms to the entire syllabus. I was certainly not prepared to accept such changes, which didn't just affect the Department but had huge work-load implications for the teaching staff (not the students), and further affected the whole Faculty. And, at the end of the day, since I had the legal (and moral) responsibility for running the Department, I wasn't prepared anyhow to accept that the views of people – some of whom had studied the subject for less than a year – were equal in significance to the views of those who'd spent a lifetime at it. This was of course interpreted as gross authoritarianism.

Tedious as it may sound, issues like this were the substance of the student revolution. But they involved unending negotiations, and much ill will, week after week, and for months on end. In the event, the rest of the Faculty did back me up, but allowed us to add a new course (Theory) in the second year.

Having failed on the syllabus front, a quite new issue was now suddenly seized on – how to continue five posts held by temporary members of staff hitherto paid for out of savings from the salaries of three members of staff on leave. The following year we would only have enough money to finance two, at best three. This was immediately denounced as an attempt to fire malcontents (who were far from it).

The student newspaper duly splashed this new treachery across the front page. Though a pack of lies and distortions, it was clever and devious and, like all smears of this kind, left some people, especially naïve and idealistic students, confused or persuaded, and took vast amounts of effort to counter. All senior left-wingers on university staff everywhere suffered similar experiences. Few of us could afford financially to do what Edward Thompson did – simply resign his post in protest and ambiguously label the upheaval a movement of 'revolting students'. But long-standing friends and colleagues were also confused. Few of the people in our department were hostile to the student movement, but most of them solved the problem of conscience by keeping well out of trouble, and left it to those who had to take responsibility anyhow. The buck stopped with idiots like me. Worse, one sometimes found oneself backed by people so reactionary that they would even support me against the radical students. In the end, it took a wretched law case to bring a 'full and complete withdrawal and apology' from the student newspaper. I got my retraction – any suggestion, they now said, that

I had delayed proposals for course reform and was reluctant to devolve power were 'totally unfounded': 'In fact, it was Professor Worsley himself who had initiated discussion of the proposed reforms and carried the agreed proposals through three meetings at Faculty level in three days'. I who had written, duplicated and circulated them, and got the approval of the Staff-Student Committee within two days. They also 'disclaimed any imputation' that I had opposed student representation on the Staff-Student Committee. The opposite, they said, was the case – that it had been I and Clyde Mitchell who had initiated student representation. But, to my despair, this was a Pyrrhic victory – clearing my name caused the paper legal costs that brought about its financial collapse.

There were plenty of attacks also from university staff. One classic instance came from a Dean at Birmingham who had phoned me asking about Dick Atkinson's politics. I told him that I had found Atkinson to be a competent teacher of sociology. That wasn't what he wanted to hear, however. Wasn't Atkinson 'disruptive'? I replied that as a Professor of Sociology I couldn't comment on a person's political beliefs and activities. He subsequently wrote a letter to the *Guardian* (17 June 1970), accusing me of having declared that 'under no circumstances' was it appropriate for an academic referee to comment on anything other than a person's teaching or research record. What I had said was that non-academic matters might affect a person's ability to teach – if, say, they suffered from some personality disorder – but that there was no evidence that anything like this pertained in Atkinson's case. Rather, his colleagues at Birmingham had expressed their confidence in him and sympathy for his ordeal at that university. I myself by no means always agreed with Atkinson's ideas, but I could say the same about other colleagues (and, no doubt, they about me). Many people had very strong opinions about academic reform, but could not be described as 'disruptive'.

There was support for this kind of underhandedness, however, in the august columns of the *Guardian*. One philosopher produced a classic instance of exactly what the radical students had been arguing – that illegitimate, behind-the-scenes, 'discreet' and 'private' political inquiries between 'colleagues' were part and parcel of the way control was illegitimately exercised over both students and staff. In a reply in the same paper (23 June 1970), I said that some people frankly acknowledged their opposition to student radicals on political grounds; others called their objections to them 'academic in the widest sense' – or what I labelled 'some other mealy-mouthed circumlocution':

I prefer to call a witch-hunt a witch-hunt, not a 'concern with balance'. If we do not resist in this case, the way will be open ... to raise irrelevances about freedom of speech and fascism that have nothing to do with Mr Atkinson's case except as smear by free association. I would remind her that not only sociology, but nuclear physics is 'everybody's business'. So is philosophy, and the major targets of the Nazis – the spectre she, Professor Beloff, and others so frequently raise – were the Left and 'difficult' independent thinker, not the compliant and orthodox.

There was no reply to this. The whole event, I heard, caused the Dean at Birmingham very deep distress. All this had been very painful and exhausting to me too. Yet when the revolution subsided, I felt that it had been worth it. The gains might not have seemed very great but never again could a professor appoint just whom he liked. Even with persisting power to affect the careers of his staff, he would have had to argue a case and persuade them (and one or two student representatives) as to what kind of need there was in the Department for a teacher in this area or that. Then he and the other committee members would have to draw up as list of suitable candidates and interview them. Even this was a 'revolution'.

These restraints upon carte blanche victimisation, too, probably wouldn't have got anywhere had it not been for the use of quite illegal methods by the students – occupations, and so forth. Whatever my ideological politics, brought up in a political culture that eschewed violence and preached the rational resolution of differences, I found these radical methods difficult to accept, though I never condemned them. The same dilemma occurred when anarchist youth trashed Trafalgar Square over the poll tax, a tactic I found hard to take (the shopkeepers whose windows were smashed had nothing to do with imposing the tax). But the riot did bring down Margaret Thatcher, who otherwise would have continued with her ruthless policies.

The student revolution gradually subsided. In my own university, I now continued the familiar routine of publishing, teaching, lecturing and examining, and giving talks or the punishing job of external examining in other universities in the UK, with occasional visits to universities abroad, mostly nearby in northern Europe – Bergen, Oslo, Tromsø, Copenhagen and Amsterdam.

I also continued with dozens of book reviews, especially for the *Guardian*, which can be very demanding, since literary editors like to lump together several books at once and get you to do the review in three or four days. After sweating blood to reduce a particularly difficult volume by Lévi-Strauss to some kind of comprehensibility for the non-specialist reader, I was rung up and asked if I couldn't make it simpler!

There was a growing amount of activity, too, in the field of development studies. I had done a radio broadcast on Kenneth Alsop's show, *Twenty-four Hours*, and had been put in the hospitality room with Claudia Cardinale and a man who I thought might be a Cape Coloured from South Africa. It was not surprising that strong men were falling off camera booms while Claudia was being interviewed; more remarkable that the quiet man was Malcolm X. A few weeks later he came to Manchester and had asked that I be on the platform. The audience, I felt, was not well disposed to him at first, but he silenced them by beginning 'I'd like to start with a few *suras* from the Koran'. That forced them to respect a world, religion. By the time he'd finished, if he'd handed out membership forms for Black Power, he'd have recruited a lot of people. We talked a lot afterwards, but there were one or two issues I wasn't happy about. When I said there was a real danger that not only could the First and Second Worlds be destroyed by nuclear weapons but the Third World too, he replied, 'It would be better than going on as we are doing', which horrified me. Later, he sent me a postcard of the Statue of Liberty from New York with a message on the back: 'They give us the symbol, but not the substance'.

Decline and Fall

Being so close to Liverpool, I had been able to visit my parents regularly. Pam, my sister, lived with both of them in the upper-floor flat of a house divided into two flats. I was the unwitting cause of a disaster for her. Trained as a secretary, she had worked at the Ritz, the new, leading cinema in Birkenhead, and had also used her talents as a singer on the prestigious opening night. (There is a film of this.) Soon, she easily got a job in New York because English girls were much in demand as 'trophy' secretaries in those days.

I had met a very lively Marxist American economist at Manchester and put Pam in touch with him. In no time they were in love and engaged. But he had decided to improve her politics, and sent her to evening classes at the Communist-led Jefferson School. When she came home on holiday she was refused a re-entry visa. She then tried to get in via Canada, to no avail. Terrified as so many people were during the McCarthy period, my mother then got my sister's Jesuit uncle (my father's brother) to inform the US Consulate of her Communist associations. After that, her mental health deteriorated steadily. She ended up back in the arms not of her lover but of the

Catholic Church, prone to periodic paranoid fantasies that a Jesuit priest was pursuing her. She did eventually bounce back, trained as a nurse at the Radcliffe Infirmary, Oxford, where she graduated as the number one nurse of the year. But her life was ruined. I was ten thousand miles away in Australia, having my own rather different encounter with McCarthyism, and knew nothing of all this until I got home three years later. I was deeply reminded of it on reading of Stuart Hall's parallel experience when his sister in Jamaica made the fatal mistake of falling in love with a black man, when the family's aim in life was to move upwards in the colour and class hierarchy. She was given electric shock treatment from which she never recovered, and spent her days washing her hands, into her seventies. 'She looked after our father and mother', Stuart wrote, 'till they died, then my brother George, who went blind, till he died. She never left home, and never had another relationship'.[71]

For my mother, the world was divided into 'nice' people, who had money, and others. She had never been able to stomach anything 'nasty', like serious illness, and abandoned the friend who was a business colleague of my father's – whom she had greatly admired because she belonged to a superior social class – once that friend was consigned to a nursing home. Then she abandoned her brother, whom she'd been delighted to rediscover after decades, when he became unable to walk properly. When my father deteriorated, Pam and my mother at first put him into a home; then parked him in the downstairs flat, like a leper. He resorted to soiling himself to attract sympathy and attention, and died, mystified as to why he couldn't be upstairs with them.

This harsh treatment did not insure them against equally sad fates. Pam died three years before our mother, who dragged on an isolated existence in a comfortable nursing home near her last house in the Wirral, where she had lived all her life. I could use Pam's flat nearby and saw my mother every day. We watched lots of snooker on TV. She was always scrupulously polite to her fellow residents, but never associated with any of them because they were 'common' – apart from a gentleman who had been the manager of the most prestigious hotel in Chester and was therefore acceptable. She yearned for the days of Sunday morning gin parties with rich neighbours and important civic figures in Prenton, many of them people whose stupidity was only exceeded by their vulgarity. Then she died and never saw the newborn grandchildren we brought to her funeral and wake.

As a transatlantic port, Liverpool's fate had been foredoomed as early as 1919, when the Cunard Line shifted its express passenger New York service to Southampton. Despite a massive renewal during the Second World War, when Liverpool became the main port for the Atlantic Western Approaches, and over a million American troops disembarked there, it never recovered. I felt that my family, which had lived on Merseyside their whole lives, had gone the same way.

* * * * *

Because of my Canadian experience, I was invited to teach Summer School twice in Montreal, at Sir George Williams University (later Concordia), and was able to take the family. Sir George was an excellent university, which, rather like Birkbeck in London, catered for part-time mature students. It was as different from northern Saskatchewan as could be imagined, being located in downtown Montreal and surrounded by department stores, restaurants and go-go establishments. The department was headed by two Chicago graduates: Kurt Johnasson, a refugee from Germany, and Hubert Guindon, from whom (and from other Chicago graduates who taught alongside me) I learned a lot about symbolic interactionism. (One, Ray Mack, was Chicagoan in another sense, as he played drums.) Between them, Kurt and Hubert tried hard to bridge the huge cultural/political gap between the Anglophone and Francophone communities. In the Chicago tradition, they had their feet on the ground too. After a weekend visit to the shrine of St Anne de Beaupré, I reported that the statistics there showed a huge increase in the number of pilgrims in the early 1950s. 'Had there been a religious revival at the time?' I asked. 'No', Kurt replied, people had got automobiles, so could more easily do the two hundred mile journey.

Later Canadian visits took me to Newfoundland and Halifax in the Maritimes, the University of Alberta at Edmonton, the University of British Columbia (Vancouver) and Victoria in Western Canada, and back to Montreal. Considerable changes had taken place in Quebec since my earliest visit to Canada due to the rise of Quebec nationalism. In 1966, none of my Anglophone colleagues spoke French; only five years later they all did, and if you asked for something in a department store in English, you were met with a stony stare.

In those days, US universities had lots of money, and started to invite people from other parts of the world. A number of us foreign academics were flown in just for a couple of days (and paid well), and I was even able to take the family once more to North America, to Brandeis in Boston. I only had to give a few lectures, and rented a beautiful suburban house, where our nearest neighbour was a delightful 80-year-old 'Boston Brahmin' who gave me 'smashed eggs' for breakfast in return for clearing her snow. When she heard I was an academic, she asked whether I was at 'the College' (Harvard) or 'the Tech' (M.I.T.)! (Brandeis was not within her frame of reference.) So we were able to visit Cape Cod, the Plymouth Plantation, New Hampshire and Maine, as well as the historic sights of Boston.

I still had to get the wretched waiver of Congress for every visit, however. This was nothing at all compared to the hassle serious immigrants from countries unpopular in the US had to go through (I was to see appalling insults hurled at Mexicans trying to cross that border by US Customs officials – who didn't allow them in), but it was tiresome enough having to go specially to the US Consulate in Liverpool or even down to London for the next twenty years.

You had to present a written list of every organisation you'd ever belonged to – quite a task – and I thought that it was important to present exactly the *same* list every time, lest you be accused of omissions or alterations, so the first time I went I had to scribble down hastily a copy of what I'd just put on the form. And at the height of the Vietnam war, I had to bite my tongue when the Consul told me that in the US they resolved political differences via the ballot-box. He didn't seem to have heard of napalm.

At the airport, I was always vetted in the huge black book in which they keep the names of political suspects. (I don't think the McCarran legislation has been formally done away with, but lawyers and politicians can always find a way of 'fiddling' inconvenient laws, and I always got my visa.) However, en route once via JFK to Mexico, even though I wasn't visiting the US, merely being in transit counted as 'entering' the country (i.e. the airport), so I was handed over to a black police sergeant for the couple of hours before my connection was due. Eventually he said, 'Bud, could you take care of yourself? I've got to get back to my wife'.

It was a great pleasure, at Brandeis, to meet up again with Vic Turner, even though he had by that time been converted to the Catholic Church by a Stockport Jesuit. Now he was a member of the grandiloquently named 'Committee on Human Thought' at the

University of Chicago (together with Saul Bellow). There was additional intellectual stimulus at Harvard and Brown and the American University in Washington. At Brandeis the revolution was still in full swing – '88 Or Bust' was the black students' demand (88 paid scholarships for black students only). One sophomore who'd spent a year at a girls' secondary school in Stockport, and made to wear school uniform, told me that she didn't think it had done her any permanent damage!

An alarming incident occurred after we had arrived home. It was impossible to have any peace in the office, and I needed to finish some writing, so I was working at home. Then I smelt smoke and tracked it to the boiler room where our central heating system was located. The installation of central heating was becoming common at that time, so many 'cowboys' were attracted into the business of servicing the boilers. We had an oil-fired system, with the boiler and a tank containing four hundred gallons of oil in a tiny utility room. When I opened the door, the boiler was on fire. They had left a sharp-edged door off the machine on top of an electric cable. I managed to get the fire out, and called them in to repair the damage.

A short time afterwards, I was again at home, and again smelt fire. This time I couldn't put it out, and had to retreat across the hallway to get to the phone before the flames would have made it impossible to do so. It was a very modern house, with thick glass windows and internal walls everywhere. The glass now started to explode with very loud bangs, like field artillery, but I managed to get out of the house, and was out in the street, which was covered with fire hoses, just as my daughter, Deb, was turning the corner on her way home from school. Smoke was still pouring out of the ground floor. She burst into tears.

The Fire Brigade was quite magnificent. Efficient and courageous, they were round and had it all put out in five minutes. When I eventually got back into the kitchen, the telephone had melted, and the plastic clock on the wall hung down like a Dalí painting. I don't' know why – because there are dozens of fires like this every day in any large city – but the *Guardian* saw fit to put the incident on their front page.

Into China

Hong Kong was still a Colony, so not only the economic and political but also the cultural connections of empire still had plenty of life in them. Though the US was already attracting more and more teachers for their postgraduate training, the more senior teachers were still either expatriates or had all been trained in Britain, and External Examiners were still usually appointed from British universities. I was now asked to do that job for the Sociology Department.

Hong Kong in itself was fascinating enough. But it seemed crazy to be on the doorstep of China and not to try and get in, so I applied for a visa. At that time, virtually no one went to China. Most China-watchers, lifetime experts on the country like John Gittings of the *Guardian*, watched that country from a distance. They had never been allowed in. So when people wanted to find out about communism in China in 1972, they still turned to Edgar Snow's *Red Star over China*, written thirty-five years earlier.

I furiously read everything I could manage for months, but though used to learning exotic languages, Chinese is a different matter. The tones are bad enough but the insuperable problem is the written language – the ten thousand characters you need even to read the newspaper. In Hong Kong I carefully copied down two (difficult enough) which I thought were essential: the characters for 'Gents' Lavatory'.

Knowing that Beatrice Webb, H.G. Wells and Bernard Shaw had each given the USSR a clean bill of health in the Stalin era, I tried to specify what I wanted to see – major kinds of institution from primary and secondary schools and universities, to communes, light and heavy industry, and the major cities – Beijing, Nanjing, Canton – plus the Wall and the West Lake.

This did not protect me, however, from having the wool pulled over my eyes in no mean fashion. China only let me in because the visit of Nixon in a couple of months earlier had been a major international rapprochement. On an infinitely smaller scale, I was considered friendly, 'progressive' (and gullible) enough to be given a conducted tour.

I got my tour exactly as I'd requested. On my return to Britain I was received as if I'd just come back from Mars (which was exactly how I felt). I told people that there were now two types of China-experts – 'two-week experts' and 'three-week experts'. I was a three-week expert. But they wanted to hear about Utopia (as I did), so the book I rushed out in six months[72] got enthusiastic reviews. I kept very close to what I had actually seen, though I was also very explicit in denouncing what was only too evident – the denigration of even such a major figure in the Revolution as Chou En-Lai, and the all too evident ruthless internal struggle for power which ended with the flight of Lin Piao. But I said nothing about the genocidal starvation of millions of peasants, not so long before my arrival, because I simply knew nothing about it, and saw nothing at all of that on the two communes I was taken to – just as we British troops saw nothing of the Bengal Famine in which $1\frac{1}{2}$ to 3 millions had starved only the year before we arrived in India.

The story of post-revolutionary China, particularly of what happened in the countryside, only seeped out gradually, and the full horror only reached me as it reached most people – when Jung Chang published *Wild Swans* nearly twenty years after my visit.

* * * * *

In the summer vacation of 1973, my Canadian experience resulted in my joining a team which had to visit and report on the teaching of sociology in several of the thirteen universities in Ontario, in two two-week stints. I had to do Toronto, the University of Western Ontario, Hamilton, Windsor and Guelph. It was gruelling but fascinating. It was also well paid. We had had two or three holidays on the English canals, which we loved, and now, at the end of the year, were able to purchase a second-hand narrow boat. I had to learn how to maintain the engine, and spent hard hours in the winter pumping out freezing water, and getting her ready every spring, and there were the inevitable near-disasters. But it was worth the hard work. Since there are over two thousand miles of canal to use, it was to play a big part in our lives, helping maintain my mental equilibrium during the bad times. We went practically everywhere over the next twenty-five years, bit by bit, from Ripon to the Thames.

The girls decided that the boat must have a Marx Brothers name, so we chose 'Otis B. Driftwood', because that sounded apt. (I ran across a coffee shop in New York called the 'Rufus Q. Firefly'.) When I sent a photograph to Groucho, simply addressed 'Groucho Marx, Hollywood, California, US', it not only got there, but he sent back a card 'To Pete and Sheila', signed in a very shaky hand, as he was into his nineties.

At the beginning of the 1970s, Clyde Mitchell, who suffered from diabetes (his poor secretary frequently found him sliding into a coma), left for a less stressful job, and one more congenial to a quantitative scholar, at Nuffield College, Oxford.

Three years later, his wife Hilary died. Clyde remarried and set out to show his new wife, Jean, his own country, South Africa, on a vessel of the Flotto Lauro. Had I known I could have warned him, for we had been told that when Lauro was Mayor of Naples he had solved the problem of passenger complaints at being moored within sight of the teeming waterfront slums of that city by building a wall so that the tourists couldn't see them. Next, an Australian friend of ours, Tom Kaiser, had travelled to Europe on the same vessel (the *Achille Lauro*), when the captain had refused to put in to port to take an injured passenger to hospital. The *Achille Lauro* was a vessel of doom once more when Palestinian guerrillas boarded her and killed an American passenger, Leon Klinghoffer, by tipping him overboard in his wheelchair. But this floating albatross reached its apogee when, rounding the Horn of Africa, the boat sank in the middle of the night. Clyde and Jean were separated in the dark and ended up in different life-boats, he without his diabetes medicine. He was taken to Djibouti, and they were eventually reunited in South Africa.

His successor at Manchester was a very different kind of man. I had met Teodor Shanin at a conference organised by Ronald Dore at Sussex on peasant cooperatives. Knowing of my recent experience with the Village Resettlement Scheme in Tanzania, Dore had included me in the conference, and I ended up editing the volume of papers that resulted.[73] Since most of the major movements of resistance in the world were based on peasants rather than workers, as orthodox Marxist theory insisted they should be, I was becoming increasingly interested in the nature of the peasantry. But when Shanin wrote from Sheffield suggesting he come over to discuss peasants, I was reluctant, thinking that this was perhaps some kind of professional anti-Soviet person who, to use an Australianism, wanted to blow down my ear about the horrors of collectivisation, which sadly I knew only too much about already. So I tried to put him off. But you don't put Teodor off. A large figure filled the doorframe of my room. (It actually felt as if the door had been taken off its hinges.) But in the next hour and a half I learned more about peasants than I had learned in the whole of my life.

When he later applied for the vacant Professorship left by Clyde Mitchell, he had a lot going against him because the dominant school of thought at the time was symbolic interactionism – first developed in Chicago before the Second World War, whose theoretical emphasis was not upon whole societies. It had spawned a whole generation who had produced marvellous research into the dynamics of how people coped with the problems of their everyday lives, including quite unorthodox communities and categories, from taxi-hall dancers to marijuana users. We were all so impressed with this long-established American research that it now took off in Britain in the form of the new 'Deviancy' school. Laurie Taylor studied long-term prisons, Stan Cohen the clashes between Mods and Rockers at Brighton, while he and Laurie Taylor did research on maximum-security prisons, plus a plethora of other research by people like Jock Young. We felt privileged to be able to invite such *galácticos* as Erving Goffman and Howard Becker to Manchester.

Everyone has to make some kind of sense of the world, of the welter of facts and experiences which impinge on us all, and they have to evaluate this too, with ready-made frameworks of analysis which purport to explain everything and which are commonly enforced on them. But professional intellectuals have a further special, and difficult, obligation – to try to develop analytical frameworks of their own which are acceptable to their intellectual compeers. So even in Britain those who specialise in theory, and who aim to do more than mere fact-grubbing, are in the end recognised as the very exemplars of scientific endeavour.

When I began, anthropology was dominated by functionalist theory, developed by Malinowski and Radcliffe-Brown. For them, society was not a mere random assemblage of social practices but constituted a system made up of sub-systems built around institutions. The family, for instance, was one such institution, and any sub-system such as the economy or the ways in which the young were educated fitted together, not in random ways, but so as to form a coherent whole.

For many of us, this was far too systematic. Patently, new ideologies and new social formations have come into existence over time, even where power lies in the hands of very few and where the individual is not allowed to challenge entrenched belief-systems. But systems of social control can never be perfect, and in the end too even the most entrenched paradigms do get overthrown, even if it takes centuries.

The major alternative to Establishment thought, at the time, was Marxism. Most of my contemporaries who came to challenge the functionalist orthodoxy which dominated anthropology from the 1930s through to the 1950s were by no means Marxists, though they might be attracted by one aspect or another of that mode of thought. The great majority of those who did become Marxists came to it primarily because they were engaged in politics in the class struggles of the 1930s against fascism, which was spreading throughout the world, not because they were attracted by arcane (and dubious) theories about primitive communism.

Anthropologists were also often drawn to other cognate theoretical approaches, such as that of Max Gluckman, who saw conflict as a normal dimension of social and natural life, in both class and classless societies. Marx's own view of class struggle was actually only part of a much wider vision, because to challenge the dominant paradigms of his day he had to try to identify just what it was that gave rise to social, including theoretical, change.

For him (more accurately, for his co-theorist, Engels), contradiction was even built into Nature. Few have followed Engels along that path, but when it came to human society, the crucial contradiction they identified seemed to be much more convincing and relevant to generations of those who came after them: it was institutionalised social inequality – the contradiction between the ways in which people worked together to produce what they needed to live, but where much of the surplus they produced was appropriated by a minority.

This had not always been so, Marx and Engels thought. There had been a long period in human society ('primitive communism') when class inequalities had not existed, and there would be a future society – 'socialism' – in which classes would disappear again. This was a utopian dream which appealed to millions who were unconcerned about contradictions in Nature but very concerned about class inequalities in the societies in which they lived.

After the Second World War, the conception of a world composed of nicely functioning societies necessarily began to crumble, and new theoretical schools began to take the place of functionalism. Marxism, though, was a European ideology, whereas the schools of critical sociology that emerged in the United States drew upon a singularly American school of philosophy, the pragmatism of John Dewey. Even Texas, of all unlikely places, produced C. Wright Mills, a sociologist strongly influenced by pragmatism. But the major centre for sociology was Chicago, which drew upon the ideas of the social psychologist G.H. Mead, further elaborated by Herbert Blumer, with a final flowering in the work of Erving Goffman.

In the UK, young Turks influenced by US symbolic interactionism founded the National Deviancy Symposium. Bright young university teachers and their students wanted to hear people like Goffman, Howard Becker, Anselm Strauss and others, so we invited them all to Manchester, where they were very popular and stimulating.

Into the middle of all of this came Teodor Shanin. His own intellectual formation could not have been more remote from Chicago and its works. It belonged to an utterly different cultural, political and personal background, in an intellectual line of succession that began with the great debate of the nineteenth century in Russia between Slavophils and Westerners, and gave rise to the amazing school of 'Zemtsvo statisticians', quantitative statistics about what was happening in the countryside – which meant most of Russia. Teodor's own classic work was right in the centre of this tradition: a study of the Russian peasantry, *The Awkward Class* ('awkward' because peasant economy and mode of life didn't fit into current economic theories, whether those of bourgeois economics or of Marxism; 'awkward' too because peasants stubbornly pursued their own interests).

The Tsar had rigged up constitutional machinery for the countryside, the 'Zemstvo' councils, under the control of the landlords, to try and head off revolution. But there were enough liberal landlords and bureaucrats to use this opening to kick off an enormous amount of statistical research. The Slavophils had put their money on the traditional communal tenure system of the *mir*. Lenin joined in the debate, arguing that capitalism was *already* established in the countryside and that the *mir* would go under. The peasants would lose whatever land they had and become proletarians, either in the countryside itself or in the fast-growing cities. (In the event, the *mir* remained the dominant mode of peasant production in economic terms, and of village life – and therefore of Russian life – until well after the Revolution of 1917.) Whatever all these theorists might argue, the main concern of the peasants was to hang on to their land rights, and the village communes were actually growing in importance when the Revolution began.

Teodor had grown up in the 1930s in Vilnius. He could not have chosen a worse place or a worse time. His father was a Jew who owned a very Eastern European-type factory (making galoshes) and had been born there when it was part of Russia. When his mother had been born in the same city, it had become part of Germany; it is now the capital of Lithuania. Teodor grew up speaking Polish and matriculated a year ahead of his age cohort.

Then, in 1941, the Soviets occupied the Baltic states, and ten-year-old Teodor, as the son of a capitalist, was deported to Central Asia. His sister stayed behind and was killed, along with all the other Jews, when the Nazis arrived. In Uzbekistan he was put to work on cotton plantations and experienced the life not of the small peasantry but of *kolkhozniks* under Soviet collectivisation. But he soon learned from the peasants how to evade even the ruthless controls of the collective system by going into business on his own account. For two years he stole bread and re-sold it.

He somehow acquired an education, made his way to France, and from there to Palestine, where he lied about his age (seventeen) in order to join a special unit fighting to establish the state of Israel. Today he is regarded as one of the heroes of the struggle for independence, even though he has always resisted the blandishments of Zionism.

He then became a social worker working amongst the very poor and started to study sociology part-time, though restricted to what was available in Russian (mainly the Zemstvo statisticians) and Polish, both of which had their own formidable sociological tradition, and Hebrew, which did not.

None of these, though, were on the radar-screen of the Manchester staff. Instead, they backed an excellent British theorist, who had, however, published extremely little, which told against him with the Appointment Committee. So Teodor got the job, to the very deep, and continuing dissatisfaction of the staff.

After a few weeks, Teodor realised that they hated him, a response which I felt to be devoid both of human empathy and sociological imagination on the part of people whose collective contribution to sociology was (and remained) quite exiguous. With a history like his, Teodor was no shrinking violet, so they resented his personality too.

I could usually get away from Manchester a couple of times a year – to Denmark or Norway, and once had to be summoned from a beach in Algiers where Ernest Gellner and I were swimming, with a taxi waiting, to give an opening paper (impromptu, in French!) at a conference. I was even called to Singapore to interview candidates for a job, where a singularly tough university administrator informed one candidate that Singapore was a 'disciplined' society, not a congenial climate for people with liberal ideas about deviancy.

I was also hauled in to deal with an internal fracas at the University of the South Pacific in Fiji, exacerbated by personal ambitions and ethnic tensions. On my day off, I decided to visit a former postgraduate student on Vanua Levu, the second big island, and walked several miles down the beach to find him. He was amazed. 'If a white man had done that just a few decades ago, Peter', he said, 'you'd have been seen as an ancestor returning from the Land of the Dead' (my book on Cargo cults, indeed, had started with precisely one such Fijian cult from as long ago as 1877).

We spent the afternoon drinking *kava*, famous as a narcotic, in the traditional ritual manner, but as a drug it didn't seem to do much for me. Even less did I enjoy yams or the famed breadfruit which had been the cause of the mutiny on the Bounty because the raison d'être for Captain Bligh's voyage to the Pacific had been to bring back breadfruit plants in order to feed the slaves in the Caribbean cheaply. (At first, they wouldn't eat it.)

What was wildly exciting was the scent of frangipani when women students from the Cook Islands performed their *kula* dance (yes, the same thing), the most erotic spectacle I have ever seen. It was unbelievable that the human pelvis could vibrate so quickly. I was far too embarrassed to join them on stage when invited. One could understand why the going rate the girls in Tahiti asked for from Captain Cook's sex-starved crew was thirteen nails.

Some time later I had to review a book by an anthropologist which argued that stories of cannibalism were just myths. I remembered that up in the mountains of the main island my friend had shown me a gap in the hills through which the great potentate, Cakombau, had brought a large army to invade the mainland from his small offshore island fastness, on a fleet said by Marshall Sahlins to be the greatest ever assembled until the Second World War. 'And there', he said, pointing to another gap in the hills, 'is where we ate them'.

But the main source of friction in modern Fiji had been brought about when the white plantation owners imported tens of thousands of indentured labourers from India, and thereby created a society divided in two by race. When the Fijian military finally staged a nationalist uprising to settle the matter, my postgraduate sided with them, and became Fiji's representative in Sydney (but died soon afterwards).

CHAPTER 7

Latin America

After fourteen years of departmental work, I was finally punished with an absolutely unavoidable sentence – two years as Dean – a relief from routine departmental admin and internecine theoretical squabbles, but with its own new miseries, reflected in the 'Don's Diary' I wrote for the *Times Higher Educational Supplement* a few months later: a litany of complaints about the books, articles, essays and theses which 'descended like hail, and the piles of unread offprints and unanswered letters that inched heavenwards'; brief hours interrupted by having to break off to attend a meeting, by phone calls ad nauseam, or by student sit-ins, all of which resulted in my annual visit to the doctor, every November, who diagnosed 'stress' and prescribed Valium. Even Sundays had to be devoted to reading Ph.D.s, newly-published books and articles, essays and theses; to preparing future lectures and exams, which, I explained to the bus-drivers at the hairdresser's, meant that I wasn't really 'on holiday', but overwhelmed – but their faces betrayed total disbelief.

My publisher had told me that my book, *The Third World*, was a very 'passionate' book, and that it would take me round the world. I thought this was a wild and surprising idea, but he proved to be right. Chicago quickly published it, where it became their number one academic best-seller. France, resistant to Anglophone culture, never did (perhaps because I'd pinched the term 'Tiers Monde' from them). But it was the Spanish-language edition which had the greatest success, not in the Peninsula but in Mexico, where Siglo XXI sold five editions across the continent in a decade.

These interests, combined with Teodor's, naturally gave a big impetus to development studies, especially among the Latin American students, who now came in increasing numbers, in part because of the interest in radical ideas inspired by the Cuban Revolution.

Ecuador

When our children left home we were rattling around in our large Victorian house, so started using the spare rooms for, largely, South American postgrads, who were usually short of money. By now, I was very keen to fill in the huge gap in my knowledge of the Third World – Latin America. But where? One postgrad suggested his country, Ecuador. In 1997, we decided to go there, because it still had an Indian population as large as the mestizo population descended from the intermixture of Indians and Spaniards. We planned to go on to Mexico and Brazil, where I had contacts. Beforehand, as a tyro, I attended a conference of Latin Americanists at Cambridge held in the very same lecture room where I had started my English course thirty-five years earlier, and heard impressive luminaries like Fernando Henrique Cardoso, later President of Brazil, and Miguel Murmis, whom I was to come to know in Quito.

One consideration I had raised was 'Does the sun shine?' It did indeed. Quito was extraordinarily beautiful, situated at the foot of Pichincha, the mountain where the Spaniards had been definitively defeated by the revolutionary army in the war of independence under General Sucre. I came to love the olivey-green vegetation and the orange flowers all year round of the *lantana*. From the Panecillo (Bread Roll) Hill you could see five snow-covered volcanoes. Twenty miles away was the Equator, *Mitad del Mundo* – the middle of the earth (not, as one cynical friend called it, *Fin* del Mundo, the '*end* of the earth', because it produced the worst wine he had ever tasted – proudly named *Vino Nuestro*, but which tasted like the syrup of figs forced down me as a child). It was there that Condamine, the French explorer, had done his historic work on the location of the equator and the shape of the earth which had given the country its name as long ago as 1739. Even more impressive than this trace of Enlightenment science were the buildings we found throughout the region of one 'Casa de Humboldt' after another, where the great polymath, battling appalling conditions from the Amazon to the Andes, had passed through a century and a half earlier.

On the very first morning, I woke up with the mother of all headaches and stomach-aches. 'Oh', said my hostess, 'It's the *soroche*' (mountain sickness). It was, but it passed quickly. If you were a pregnant woman, however, it could be very serious indeed. You were advised not to fly in to this city, situated at nine thousand feet, but to travel up the Andes slowly by land. Later, in Mexico, another mountainous city, a friend of ours who was out to tea at a posh hotel with Sheila suddenly started pouring blood from her nose. Despite attention from US-trained gynaecologists, in both Ecuador and Mexico City, in exceedingly expensive hospitals for foreigners, the twins in her womb were not noticed, and were stillborn when she got back to the UK.

We got our first taste of Latin American bureaucracy when we had to get our visas endorsed (using special stamped legal paper). It took us three visits, twenty miles each way every time, but some poor people there had been coming for ages from much further to the desperately overcrowded office, which dealt with everything down to planning permission. Over the weeks we got to know a poor nun who was applying for a school extension – and was still at it when we'd finished. But it was nothing compared to the anxiety felt by penniless immigrants to the UK facing deportation and possible torture once more.

We had arranged to stay on the colonial-epoch cattle hacienda owned by the family of one of our students, and study it. I thought that it would be full of cowboys in chaps, breaking in mustangs and wrestling steers. It turned out in fact to be a Cheshire dairy farm (even the cows were black and white Friesians), though it was situated beneath Cayambe volcano, and the labour force was drawn from nearby Indian villages.

Walls along the roads, made of rammed earth, had been there since colonial times, and the hacienda buildings were painted a cerulean blue, the colour the Spaniards had designated for the Audiencia of Quito, a division of the Spanish Empire (in adjoining Colombia, such buildings were a deep green). It was one of the quietest places on earth. A few hundreds yards into the woods and you could hear a pin drop; at night, it got a lot quieter. There were some interesting things going on, like the artificial insemination of cattle, but we couldn't even talk to the Indians as our Spanish was very limited, and in any case they spoke Quichua, not Spanish. Quichua looked as bad as the other Indian language I'd run across in Saskatchewan, Cree, and we only had less than a year.

After a few days we woke up in the middle of the pitch-black night and started laughing, eventually uncontrollably. 'What on earth are we doing here?' we asked each other. Next day, we were back in Quito.

By extraordinary luck, there was a course in Spanish for foreigners beginning at the Catholic University, every morning for six weeks, so we instantly signed up. It was brilliantly taught by total immersion, and we walked out able to manage our lives and to read. Sheila, new to the language, started at Level I and got 97%; with my rudimentary Spanish, I was put into Level II and got 96%. As with Swahili, Spanish opened up the whole continent (except Brazil). And we used a US textbook, using American English – much more useful than one using BBC English and castellano.

Though Quito had been part of the Inca Empire, its distant capital had been hundreds of miles away, at Cuzco, in modern Peru, and this northern region had only been fully conquered a couple of centuries before the Conquistadors arrived from Spain, so there was only one Inca ruin to be seen in the city.

Not long before the Conquest, two brothers, Atahualpa and Huascar, had fought for the throne in Cuzco and then compromised by dividing the empire between them, half of it (the northern part) into what is now Ecuador. Both rivals in the end were killed by the Spaniards, leaving resistance now in the hands of the general Rumiñahui, who carried on a guerrilla campaign in the north until he too was captured and tortured to death for information about the treasure of Atahualpa which the Spaniards believed had fallen into his hands. Today, therefore, Rumiñahui is widely regarded as the father of Ecuadorean nationalism.

These divisions, harking back to the incorporation of diverse peoples over vast distances into an Inca Empire of fairly recent formation, continued to shape Ecuador's future. As the northern segment of the former Inca Empire, it remained a separate Audiencia of the new Spanish Empire, and when that empire came to an end, became an independent state. So despite Bolívar's dream of a united Latin America, the boundaries established by the conquerors remained, just as the colonial boundaries established in colonial times when Africa was carved up – and not Pan-Africanist dreams of a united Africa – are sacrosanct today.

The new state identities – Ecuadorean, Peruvian and Bolivian – were in any case only modern political/national divisions imposed on top of a much wider and older cultural identity, that of the Quechua-speaking peoples, still one of the largest Indian cultural/ linguistic zones in South America. Yet once the Inca Empire disintegrated, no political coherence between these Quechua fragments assimilated into the Inca Empire remained, and splits between different Quechua-speaking communities conquered at different times (such as the Cañari who sided with the Spaniards against Rumiñahui), opened up. Indeed, smaller, even village-level units reasserted their identity, and the Sierra reverted into the small components which Eric Wolf has classically called 'closed corporate communities'.

One such community was the market town of Otavalo, where people spoke not the local version of Quechua but – according to a Soviet linguist – the dialect spoken in distant Cuzco, because (as in Northern Ireland) they had been 'planted' there to strengthen the frontier population by the Inca conquerors. They continued to maintain their distinctiveness by converting themselves into producers of vividly-coloured tunics and chunky sweaters which they sell to the tourists who flock there. Otavaleño peddlers can even be seen, together with carpet sellers from North Africa and black Africans, selling carvings on the streets of Amsterdam and Paris.

Quito was an extraordinary blend of colonial beauty, incipient Americanisation, and dirt. There were the eighty-six churches, built out of the sweat of generations of Indians and filled with gold-leaf statues; the grand houses, ancient and new, of the bourgeoisie; the tourist Centro (where the merry market women laughed and called me 'Four Eyes', because I had dark shades which flipped upwards from my glasses); and the slums where the ever-increasing influx of tens of thousands of Indians lived in conditions little better than the rural hovels they had left.

The houses of the rich were equipped with rather archaic American equipment worked by *muchachas* who lived in a tiny box-room, and got a day off per month. The justification given by their employers was always the same – 'The wages they get keeps a whole family going back in their village'. To the upper classes, Miami was the centre of civilisation, as Paris had been for us; they went there for their honeymoons, not to New York; and sent their children to learn English as au pairs with middle-class families in middle-sized US cities.

The class war was being fought by pit-bull terriers and Alsatians on the one side and Indians on the other, not against demonstrators, but to control the workers building the new house next door. When one building worker was bitten he swore he would poison the dog the next day – and duly did. Walking past bourgeois mansions at night, you were startled out of your wits by huge patrol dogs which hurled themselves at the wire fences as you passed. I swore that when we left I would join with the building-workers and throw poisoned meat into these elegant gardens.

The Central Bank had a magnificent display of archaeological treasures, and the city also had more modern attractions – *peña* clubs where you could listen to Highland music on the tortoise-shell ukulele-like *charanga* and drink *chicha* beer; and good cinemas. Stepping past the beggars, we regularly enjoyed the Sucre Theatre, with its opera-house decor of cream, red and gold, where the Symphony Orchestra performed, and where foreign touring companies competed for the hearts and minds of Ecuadoreans – the Russians with their circus, the Canadians with their Dixieland band. But we were also exposed to a wide variety of Latin American cultures – great films like *El Condor Pasa* from Bolivia; the music of Inti Illimani; an excellent Ecuadorean play about Manuelita Sáenz, Bolívar's lover, who, faced with a political rival who saw her just as a woman, sweeps open her military cloak, revealing not just her female shape but the medals she had won as a Colonel during the struggle for independence. (When she and Bolívar parted, she supported herself by weaving and embroidering, and refused the fortune left by her husband.)

In the beautiful plazas of the central city, wealthy German tourists were arriving on luxurious Brazilian coaches, on which they slept at night in coffin-like niches. For some of them, however, their appetite for yet another cathedral was steadily diminishing, and one of them was relieved to find an Englishman whom he could regale with stories of how he had sunk forty thousand tons of British merchant vessels in the Second World War.

Quito has since been designated a World Heritage City, and has therefore undergone a tremendous face-lift, with better roads, cleaner streets, and the refurbishment of buildings on the lovely central plazas with floors made in traditional style out of the backbones of animals or polished river pebbles.

But this tourist influx has brought about a huge distortion in the world's image of Ecuador, since it has now become a stopping-off point en route to the Galapagos Islands. But the Galapagos are a thousand kilometres away, and Ecuador has always had an entirely different image of itself as a country oriented to the jungle, to the East, not to the Pacific Ocean. It was from Quito that Orellana, the Spanish conquistador immortalised in Herzog's film, *Aguirre, Wrath of God*, had succeeded in his crazy project of battling his way down nearly two thousand miles to the mouth of the Amazon, in modern Brazil, even building ships en route. This historic pride in Orellana's achievement was massively reinforced during successive wars with Peru over the Amazon, common to both countries, culminating in the war of 1941 which was only settled when the United States imposed the 'Rio Protocol' on the warring parties, resulting in the loss of a third of Ecuador's territory. As well as appealing to this long-standing hostility to Peru, the discovery of oil in the Amazon was now bringing a new dimension to the conflict; another, very high-tech war was fought just after we left. That is why a huge slogan, dominating the city, proclaims defiantly to the world (and especially to Peruvians) that Ecuador has always been, still is and will continue to be an Amazonian country.

Near the university, the Shuar Indians from the Amazon had a museum devoted to their culture. A fatuous upper-class Brazilian tourist asked if they still shrank human heads. 'Señora', he replied, 'You bring us the heads; we'll shrink them for you.'

In the modern flat we ended up in, it took us some time to get used to living at three kilometres above sea level – twenty minutes to boil a kettle for tea, while cooking meals took hours. The porter and his family lived in their one-room lodge, where they were woken up by the tenants imperiously blowing their horns at two o'clock at night to get them to come and open the gates. I asked the porter how they liked this life. 'Wonderful', they said, it was so *tranquilo* – a response I regularly got. 'You should see the village we came from in the mountains', they said.

Our hosts had got me attached to the Anthropology Department in the very traditional Catholic University. Socially, we were surrounded by Christian Democrats, and members of the reactionary Catholic organisation, Opus Dei, who were very influential in the media and in government, and everybody seemed to be related to everybody else. So on the first weekend we missed the Ecuadorean equivalent of May Day since our hosts didn't think to mention it, and went to a very boring football match instead. Nor did we ever get to know people at the other major university, the Central, which was regarded as a Red base.

It is difficult to get to understand another culture, and their political culture is one of the most difficult things of all, because understanding it depends upon knowing not just about institutions and organisations, which can be quite different from those of Europe, but knowing a great deal about the individuals, personalities, the social background and the activities of those who have made up the leadership of this political culture over decades. (Aside from political parties, the Cardinal intervened in politics with pastoral letters, while military commanders constantly threatened to take action.)

The conservatives and the communists were recognisable, but Ecuador had a long and complex legacy of mass movements in between these extremes, usually described as 'populism'. As we had learned in Canada, this label doesn't tell us very much because all parties, Left and Right, try to build mass support. 'Populism', then, tends to be simply a residual category in between naked conservatism at one end of the spectrum and egalitarian, redistributive ideologies such as socialism or communism at the other.

Ecuadorean populism had two strands: one was nationalist, reflecting pride in Orellana's achievement. The more modern component was social. Everyone in Europe knows about Perón (and sometimes about Vargas in Brazil) because these are very large countries with developed industry, huge cities and massive military clout. But the outstanding populist President in Latin America was in some ways Ecuador's Dr José María Velasco Ibarra. Velasco was able to harness nationalist resentment over the disaster in the Amazon with demagogic appeals to the new city population which was flooding into the cities from the countryside.

Ecuador had had modernising dictators in the past, like García Moreno, who, though a religious conservative, had promoted science and education, so was cut down on the steps of the Government Palace in 1875. (Some say that his supporters were so fearful at losing him that they propped up his body on a throne outside the Palace.) But Velasco was something new. Described by his CIA opponent, Philip Agee, as 'the stormy petrel of Ecuadorean politics', he was 'a spellbinding orator who allied himself with the impoverished masses in violent tirades against the ruling oligarchies who, he claimed, were behind the candidates of the Liberal and Conservative parties'. Some of the flavour of that rhetoric can be seen in his classic demagogic claim to unite everybody – 'conservatives and reds', 'the monk and the soldier', 'men and women, academics and workers', all of whom, he said, he would lead on a voyage across 'the infinite sea of all that is noble, to fundamental justice and ultimate humanity'.[74]

The new urban poor flooding in from the poverty-stricken villages to Quito and to the city of Guayaquil on the coast loved to hear Velasco's Ministers taking the mickey out of traditional politicians – one Minister, only five feet tall and with a Van Dyke beard, rode a decrepit old nag to the Legislative Palace, claiming that his orthodox predecessor had sold the animal to the last Government for an outrageous sum. Spectators in the Legislature hurled spit, orange peel, banana skins and abuse, howling down Ministers from the public galleries of the Congress. To Velasco's opponents, they were simply the 'city mob'. To him, they were his beloved *chusma* (mob), who, for the first time in history, would have their due place in Ecuador's political life. So they elected him President no less than five times between 1933 and 1968, against resistance so uncompromising that he finally tried to break it by assuming dictatorial powers. This was all bad enough for Ecuador's traditional ruling class, but he now did something which the CIA would not permit. He had long drawn upon historic anti-American sentiment over the Rio Protocol. Now he began to flirt with Castro's Cuba. In the 1970s, there had even been one or two coups, both in Ecuador and in Peru, led by left-wing generals, but these were soon dealt with by their right-wing enemies, backed by the CIA. The inevitable now happened once more when Velasco had been overthrown, the year before we arrived, in a right-wing military coup.

Yet what everyone called 'populism' did not die out entirely, and I found that a new progressive movement had grown up, quite unlike Velasco's, among the new population of the so-called 'marginals' in Quito, for if many in the rural areas were not even part of the money economy, these new city-dwellers still earned less than $100 a year.

But Ecuador was overwhelmingly still an agrarian country, the second poorest in South America, with the highest density of population, because one thousand rich families owned the best land (and most business and commerce), while three million out of Ecuador's 6.5 million people lived in poverty; two-thirds of the population on a family income of $10 a month. This explained why Indians had scratched out patches of land all the way up the almost vertical sides of Pichincha, though a medical consultant we met attributed it simply to their stupidity. In fact, they were being highly entrepreneurial, trying to escape the myriad ways through which landlords had extracted rents for centuries: *arrendatarios* had to pay in cash; *huasipungeros* in unpaid labour; *precaristas* had to hand over part of their crop.

The next phase in Ecuador's history came when the traditional landed elite in the Sierra was forced to share power with a new economic force on the coast – the giant US corporations which had moved their plantations to Ecuador from Central America. Some said they did this because the seizure of power in the 1950s by the radical government of Arbenz in Guatemala had frightened them; others, that disease had struck the trees in Central America. And now Ecuador was entering another phase: it was becoming an oil country.

Given all this, the country had long been a notorious example of South American political instability (70 presidents in 130 years), and was still very unstable. The biggest social upheaval of the century, however, had occurred even longer ago, in the form of the Civil War of 1895. It had been no mere coup, a seizure of power by a military faction, but a real social revolution under the Liberals led by Eloy Alfaro, based not on the Sierra but on the coast around the growing commercial city of Guayaquil. It ended with his being hanged and his body burnt in a public park in Quito. When I remarked to a leading Christian Democrat political scientist that the Liberal Revolution seemed to resemble the alignment of class forces in the English Civil War, I was strongly rebuked: it had not been a class war, he said, but a war over religion – the same kind of ideological controversy that divides historians of the English Revolution.

The upheavals of the Velasco period were well over when we arrived. The Parliament building might be closed, and we were living under a right-wing dictatorship, but the country was quiet. And although General Videla, the butcher of Argentina, came to visit his buddies, the rule of the Ecuadorean military government was very different from the murderous regimes in Argentina and Chile, and political activity, even on the part of the Communist Party, was tolerated.

Forces far more sinister than the Christian Democrats had been at work in Ecuador, however. One of the most sensational political documents of the age, Philip Agee's *Inside the Company*, had been written by a CIA agent who had worked in Ecuador and then defected.[75] It revealed an astounding, carefully documented story ranging from the international connections of the CIA and its internal structure as an organisation dealing in uninhibited and systematic secret espionage, subversion and large-scale bribery, to the lesser details of their training in the tricks of the trade. These included forgery, the use of codes, the writing of invisible messages, phone-tapping, opening mail, bugging hotel rooms and the uninhibited use of indigenous sources of information such as the Ecuadorean Customs – the agencies which issued identity cards and were responsible for passports; plus, whenever it suited, resorting to violence. Most of the bombs planted at the entrances of churches, Agee says, were put there by Social Christian squads who then blamed it on the Communists. The 'Company' was thus able to penetrate every area of public life from trade unions to sports clubs and student organisations, from the church to Cabinet meetings, and was effectively independent of the US Embassy.

Nearly three-quarters of a million dollars a year were being spent to rein in a Communist Party of only one thousand members, though with a strong following in trade union, student and youth circles. But Agee and the CIA were living through a period of real fear that what had happened in Cuba in 1956 – when eighty-two guerrillas had landed on the yacht, the *Granma*, and had taken over the entire country, followed, despite CIA support, by total failure to remove Castro in the invasion at the Bay of Pigs five years later – could happen again in another country.

In Ecuador, though, things turned out much better for the US. Velasco was once more forced into exile. Then came the ominous news that Ecuadoreans were being trained as guerrillas in Cuba, and finally, a year after the Bay of Pigs, an actual guerrilla force was reported near Santo Domingo de los Colorados inside Ecuador. All of them, however, were rounded up within a week. Ecuador then broke off diplomatic relations with Cuba, Czechoslovakia and Poland; Velasco's successor was removed by a military junta; and the leaders of the guerrillas were expelled by their own Party for 'adventurism'. It had been a most successful CIA operation. A leading Professor of Law [sic] told me that bombing churches might be regrettable, but in the struggle against communism anything might be justified.

* * * * *

By 1977 there was no sign of the bombings of churches, of sabotage, of shoot-outs in Congress (there wasn't any Congress) or of violent street demonstrations. My colleague, Eduardo Archetti, took me to see tear-gas being used on the Catholic University students (a routine experience when Eduardo had been an undergraduate in Buenos Aires), over some quite internal domestic university issue, but it never happened again.

In the university I shared a room with three postgraduates, one exiled from Argentina, another from Chile. The latter had escaped because his father worked at Santiago airport and had bundled him onto a plane. More senior people were more fortunate – they had appointments with FLACSO, the pan-Latin American organisation for the social sciences which had campuses in several capital cities. Two of the most brilliant, Miguel Murmis and Eduardo Archetti, were Argentinians, as was the scholarly Atílio Borón, who I met later at FLACSO, Mexico, where he wrote a brilliant analysis of the difference between 'southern cone' dictatorships and the European fascisms of the 1930s.

National libraries in Quito were poor, and huge depositories of valuable colonial records in decrepit Jesuit monasteries went unclassified. The best library was provided as an aid project by the German Social Democrats. But we did have first-class Ecuadorean colleagues, one of whom had used the historic records in the Spanish colonial archives, the Casa de las Indias, in Seville (mining, he said, only the tiniest bit of that huge collection) to write a study which showed that movements of revolt (often millenarian) had never ceased in one part or another of the Spanish Empire, culminating in the eruption of the great Rebellion in Peru in 1780, led by a descendant of the Inca royal family, Túpac Amaru.

Given this paucity of resources, it is not surprising that the best single study of Indian society and culture, a study of the city of Riobamba, had been done by a foreigner, the Mexican, Hugo Burgos, one of the brilliant *indigenista* school of anthropology which that country had developed.[76] Again, it was unavailable in English because only infrequently were good studies of Ecuador published within the country; usually they appeared in English, written by Americans, in the States. In the market at Riobamba, Burgos showed, Indians were sold cloth using a *vara de indios* which measured less than the measuring-stick used for selling cloth to whites. Water was a luxury not easily available on tap in the villages, but Burgos provided an insight into the equally unsanitary lives Indians were forced to lead, because in the market they had to pay per sheet for lavatory paper and so generally couldn't afford it.

A new generation was coming up in the universities, and I got an opportunity to join senior students on a field trip organised by their teacher, a nun who was an authority on Indian religious festivals, to a large Indian community which even had its own municipal brass band that made LPs. (She seemed to consider Durkheim 'insufficiently materialist'!)

The Indians, with pitiful incomes, were generous in the extreme, offering bottle after bottle of rum and constantly firing off expensive rockets to the accompaniment of the brass band.

High in the mountains we needed thick woollen jumpers, but towards dawn I found myself in a circle of around thirty people, and was suddenly asked an ominous question – not 'Was I a communist?', but (coming from England) 'Was I a Protestant?' I had read the penny pamphlets sold in the churches about the horrors of Protestantism and one heard stories that Peace Corps volunteers had been beaten up. Agee reports one incident in which a doctor and social worker from a medical team of the Andean Mission, believed to be communists, were killed with the connivance of the local priest (pp. 253–54).

When I was asked this question it suddenly seemed to have grown distinctly colder than it had been a few minutes earlier. So I flannelled some response to the effect that people everywhere usually had a (different) conception of God (or gods) – and that England was a Christian country.

I wondered if I was being paranoid until, a few weeks later, I was invited by an American anthropologist to a San Juan fiesta in another village together with my colleague, Alan Middleton, to see a fascinating performance about the encounter between the Inca king and a Spanish Conquistador, during which a man sidled up to our hostess and indicated, delicately, that it might be advisable for us to move on since there were people who thought it improper that there should be two men with one woman and we might get beaten up. We didn't wait to argue.

We visited markets in towns like Ambato and Latacunga, and thought it quaint that men were crying *polvo de pungas* (flea-powder), until our daughter, Julia, who had joined us, acquired her own fleas, so we had to go back to the market to get her some powder. We did several trips by bus to beaches on the coast (Julia could never get used to men hawking and spitting, however accurately and politely, across her face through the open window), passing through several ecological zones, down to Montecristi, where the so-called Panama hats really come from. There we paid homage to Eloy Alfaro's home, crossing miles of banana plantations. At Atacames, a singularly dirty village with a superb beach, we rented the cheapest possible cabin (water from a 44-gallon drum), but after listening through the thin partition-wall to our neighbours telling scabrous stories about nuns and priests until one o'clock in the morning, we decided to pay a bit more to get some sleep. The *alcatraz* pelicans did a stately patrol along the shore looking for fish. When he heard we were English, the fisherman who took us for a row racked his brains to make polite conversation. 'So, in England, do you live on the coast or in the Sierra?' he asked. (We were also asked if England was near Australia – after all, they spoke the same language.)

'When I was but 13 or so,' Walter Redfern Turner wrote, in his nineteenth century poem, 'Romance', 'I went into a golden land/Chimborazo, Cotopaxi/Took me by the hand ...'. Reaching the snow-line on Cotopaxi, it stole our hearts away too.

But the big expedition, intended as a family holiday by bus to Macchu Picchu in distant Peru, involved a series of disasters. I had advised Deborah and her partner to buy money-belts to go underneath their clothes. They did, but Deborah's partner left his on the coffee bar at Charles De Gaulle airport, with his passport, money and return ticket in it. So, with breaking hearts, we had to leave them behind to follow later. Then a section of the Pan-American Highway between the capital and Ecuador's second city, Cuenca, had fallen into the valley, so we had to wait for a bulldozer to make a new stretch of road.

At Incapirca, the 'Inca's throne' had been tumbled down the hillside (probably during the chaos of the Spanish invasion when factional struggles broke out between different Quechua communities). But hostility towards outsiders was still not dead: a party of extremely drunken Indians made threatening gestures to us *gringos*.

Across the border, we shared the beach at Tumbes – which had been the launching pad for the Spanish Conquest of Peru – with the local pigs.

Northern Peru turned out to be pure desert. By the time we reached Trujillo there were still over five hundred kilometres to go to Lima. We were so exhausted that we had to have some sleep, which we did for hours, which enabled us to visit the spectacular archaeological site of Chan Chan nearby. Here we discovered that the famed empire of the Incas was only the latest (and quite recent) of a series of earlier cultures: twenty-eight square kilometres of nine great citadels surrounded by nine-metre-high walls, and a part of the great Chimú civilisation which had once stretched a thousand kilometres along the coast as far as Guayaquil in present-day Ecuador. Royal burial sites, as well as row upon row of storerooms and wells, were all preserved in the dry climate. The Chimú had only been conquered by the Incas around 1450 AD. The Incas, though they borrowed much from the Chimú, did not despoil the site of its gold and silver statuettes and ornaments. The Spaniards, who arrived only a century later, did. The man selling replicas of the Mochica pottery solved one mystery – why the male figures had such huge erect penises. 'Those', he replied, in an anachronistic joke, 'were the cannons our people used against the Ecuadoreans', he answered.

After Quito, we were like country hicks in the huge city of three million people, with a spectacular Gold Museum. Much of the sacred Inca city of Pachacámac, twenty kilometres away, had been destroyed immediately by Hernando Pizarro, but much was preserved by the climate, for it does not rain on that awful coast for much of the year, until the dismal *garúa* Scotch mist takes over. Up at cockcrow, we took the train up the Andes, rightly called 'one of the wonders of Latin America', which climbs up via twenty-two zigzags, one set of which went back and forth eight times. Eventually, you glance out of the window at a notice which tells you that you are now higher than the peak of Mont Blanc in Switzerland. A man with a big bag of oxygen went round the train sticking the nozzle up the noses of those who were passing out.

Oroya was the stop for Peru's biggest mine and smelter, where the miners, deep underground, like their congeners in Bolivia, had their shrines not only to the Virgin but to the pre-Christian Earth deities. The anthropologist Michael Sallnow has shown how the very rocks outside the mine, too, the high peaks of the Andes, were objects of veneration on the part of thousands of pilgrims.

Then followed a bone-shattering 261-kilometre ride in a battered taxi to Ayacucho where the last rays of the sun illuminated the battlefield where the sun had also once gone down on the Spanish Empire. On the road, we were at last on the true altiplano, with flocks of llamas – not branded, like cattle, but with pretty ribbons in their ears to denote ownership – outlined against snow-covered mountains. (At the Sacsahuamán ruins at Cuzco I even got to cuddle a tame one.) The Indian population expressed contempt for the architecture of the Spaniards compared to their own staggering achievements, for, as with the Egyptian pyramids, you cannot get a razor blade between the blocks of stone.

In the cathedral, a large painting of the Last Supper hung over the High Altar. There were Christ and the Apostles. There were the bread and wine; but the centre of this holy communion was a plate of guinea-pigs. The explanation for this nagged at me until, years later, Eduardo Archetti sent me the fruit of years of his research, in his book on guinea-pigs.[77]

The Conquistadors had witnessed impressive feasts when the Inca Emperor had received his notables, during which thousands of guinea-pigs were consumed as the main dish. They were also consumed on religious occasions: on one occasion, more than a thousand guinea-pigs and hundreds of llamas were slaughtered and offered to the gods to influence the forthcoming harvest. The guinea-pig, Archetti showed, thus occupied a special place in Inca culture, and still does to their Quechua descendants.

Guinea-pigs are destined, eventually, to be eaten, and may be exchanged; but how and when they are eaten is determined by cultural values and practices. It is always an occasion of special social significance – a public festival like Easter or the Day of the Dead, or as part of cults of the Virgin or of the family saints, or even as part of quite secular public rituals, such as celebrating a civic holiday or the opening of a new road, or when peasants participate in mutual aid work on each others' fields. Other occasions for enjoying consuming guinea-pigs (Archetti provides the recipes), are quite private, domestic rites de passage within the family, like birthdays or weddings. But they are not eaten as everyday part of the everyday diet, and the special social status of the animal is further indicated by the fact that it is the women, not the men, who rear them. Finally, guinea-pigs are important not merely as food, but are widely used in curing many kinds of illness.

Foreign agronomists, however, now proposed to rear them as 'protein', using modern, hygienic methods which involved moving the animals out of the home into hutches outside. Yet the millions of dollars spent by the development biologists failed to persuade the Indians to eat these animals as regular items of everyday diet, because that was precisely what they were not.

This lack of appreciation of the symbolic and social significance of guinea-pigs was shared by the Archbishop's Secretary at the cathedral. When Eduardo phoned him to ask permission to reproduce the altarpiece painting on the cover of his book, there was an explosion at the other end of the line: 'A book on guinea-pigs!' he shouted, 'No, no, no!!!'

We went on to Macchu Picchu, stopping at the stupendous fortifications at Ollantaytambo, built of masonry on top of terraces where the Incas had repulsed the Spaniards. Yet when Cuzco did fall to the Spaniards in 1538, and the Inca Emperor was executed, that was not the end, for a new capital was established at Macchu Picchu, then abandoned – never to be found by the Spaniards and only rediscovered by an American archaeologist, Hiram Bingham, in 1911. Nor was Macchu Picchu the last Inca capital of the Incas, who moved even further into the interior. Thirty-six years after the fall of Cuzco, the very last capital, Vilcabamba, was founded by Manco Inca, who had escaped with 55,000 men, but it was found by the Spaniards who destroyed and depopulated it, after which it was swallowed up by the jungle until modern expeditions located its ruins.

We were overwhelmed with the sight of Macchu Picchu – and the sound, for the site is like an echo chamber. There were not half a million tourists per annum then, as there are now, so I could hear every word from the American girl several hundred yards away, patiently explaining to her companion 'But I told you before we came here that I didn't love you!' At the end of the main site, I saw a party of energetic German senior-citizen *alpinistas* and followed them to see where they were going. Richard Gott had written an article in the *Guardian* describing how difficult it was to climb the adjoining, virtually vertical peak Huayna Picchu, so I had determined not to even try it. The Germans, though, I soon found, were steadily moving ever upwards so, sheep-like, I followed them. No climber, I was on my way up Huayna Picchu after all, clinging on to loose wires here and there. Some 10,500 tourists had arrived in the Andes from France alone, so I found myself helping a beautiful blonde Parisienne up the last few hundreds yards. Near the top we saw what we took to be a rescue stretcher. Next day, the local paper reported that it was not a stretcher but a hang-glider used by an intrepid Italian, René Ghilini, in a descent to the Vilcanota river in the valley bottom below, which took over ten minutes. The much slower bus back to the station was raced down its zigzag route by a boy on foot, who must have done it many times a day.

Puno, on Lake Titicaca, was the end of our journey. There you could make a choice between Inca and pre-Inca civilisations, such as the massive ruins of Tiahuanaco or the impressive remains at Sillustani. Living today on floating islands of *totora* reeds (which they also eat), old ladies paddling reed canoes on the Lake imperiously (and reasonably) demanded money for taking their photos.

Deborah had followed her partner by losing her passport, money and return ticket in the hot springs at Aguas Calientes, so we had to leave her in a dreary *pensión* in Lima while she got a new passport (a committed feminist, she was forced to resort to traditionally feminine tears at the unsympathetic British Embassy). Julia flew back home for a wedding, while for her mother and father it was the bus back across the Ecuadorean border.

Guayaquil, Ecuador's main port and commercial city, was famous as the place where the two victorious leaders of the war against Spain, Bolívar and San Martín – the latter fresh from liberating Peru – met in 1822. They had joined together to create a pan-South American confederation. What happened at that meeting remains a mystery to this day, but the outcome was clear – San Martín went into exile in France.

We checked in at a hotel, where we saw a note at the desk for Brian Moser, whom I knew because he worked for Granada TV in Manchester on the wonderful *Disappearing World* series. Next day, he and I clung on to the back of a vehicle bound for the rubbish dump miles outside the city, on the edges of a creek which was flooded daily by the tide. Hundreds of people lived there: as in Mayhew's London, some specialised in rags, others in metal, others in collecting bottles, others in paper and cardboard. Flocks of gulls lived on the decaying food, and the place was swarming with flies. But when I asked people about their lives, they came up with the usual response: 'You should see the village we came from in the Sierra'. A social worker said the place had improved markedly from last year, and that we should come back next year, when a road was going to be put in.

Brian went on to make films about the cocaine trade in Colombia, the main source for the US market, going down-river in canoes heavily loaded with petrol which was used not just for the engine, but to prepare the drug from the coca leaves. The only available accommodation was the local brothel. When he woke in the morning he had a pistol in his ear. What was he doing there? they asked. But when he pleaded that he said he wanted to see his children again, they let him go.

In Quito, we were reunited with the girls for a few days, then had to part once more.

¡Qué Viva México!

All this exploration, albeit on a shoestring, plus the costs of getting two daughters to Quito and Peru, and their embarking on university careers, had been financially hard, so I had to go back to work – in Mexico.

We stopped off at Bogotá to see our postgraduate León Zamoscz, who had finished his excellent study of peasant movements in a country which had been the site of a most ghastly civil war, the aptly named *violencia*, the rationale of which is incomprehensible to me to this day. People had not only killed each other on a massive scale for a decade but had done so with singular viciousness. Cutting the throat became an art form: in the *corbata*, the tongue fell forward out of the mouth, like a tie. León introduced us to his liberal Senator father-in-law, who had fought for the Republicans in Spain, was put up against a wall, and then released. He also took us to see the places where Bolívar had lived, and the superb Gold Museum with its ten thousand pieces of Precolombian gold-work.

Then we flew through an electric storm which illuminated most of Central America and landed just in time for Mexico's Independence Day, celebrating the *Grito de Dolores* call to arms of 1810 issued by the revolutionary priest, Hidalgo – duly executed by the Spaniards, as was his successor in the leadership, another parish priest, Morelos.

I had been in Mexico before and had been able to visit Oaxaca and see the ruins, not of Aztec cities but of the Zapotec capital at Monte Albán and Mitla. So I knew that though the outside world thinks of history in Mexico as beginning with the arrival of Cortés and his 508 men, and the sixteen horses they brought with them (which were so important, like modern tanks, that the chronicler of the invasion, Bernal Díaz, lists the names of each one), he would never have conquered the huge Aztec Empire had he not been skilled enough as a diplomat to enlist as allies tens of thousands of other ethnic groups who were sworn enemies of the Aztecs.

Mexico City, though built on the ruins of the capital of the defeated Aztecs, Tenochtitlán, was neither Zapotec nor Aztec, but a creation of Spanish colonialism. But the Indians had not disappeared. From its beginnings, Mexican society was both multi-ethnic and born of revolution, for the wars of independence had involved alliances between *criollos* – people of Spanish descent but born in the colonies (and therefore despised and discriminated against by 'Peninsulares' born in Spain, even poor ones), mixed-race *mestizos* (of whom Morelos was one), and Indians. Out of this cauldron, a new nationality – 'Mexican' – had emerged.

Independence (as in the US) had ushered in a lengthy period of turmoil – rule by a self-styled Mexican Emperor, Iturbide, then by the flamboyant dictator, Santa Anna. The territory between the Canadian border and New Orleans had already been lost by the Louisiana Purchase of 1803, when Napoleon, forced out of Haiti by the revolt of the slaves, had tried to rebuild his empire in the New World by selling much of the country he had taken over from Spain to the US for $15 million.

Mexico now suffered the further indignity of having Texas wrested from it, not by the power of the dollar but by military power, in the war of 1847. US armies took Vera Cruz and finally Mexico City, where the military cadets known today as the *Niños Héroes* fought to the end, while even more Mexican territory was sold to the US, which now stretched to the Pacific Ocean. Conflict with the US on the border was endemic; the final irony came when gold was discovered in California, which had been lost to the US.

Even after the loss of so much territory, Mexico was still the third largest country in Latin America. But no sooner had the Indian President Juárez embarked on a period of liberal reform than he had to face down a traumatic invasion in 1864 by a new imperialist power, France, which installed a puppet Habsburg Emperor, Maximilian. At great cost, the French were driven out, only for the country to fall into the hands of the modernising dictator, Porfírio Díaz, who ruled with an iron hand until he was forced into exile in the Europe he admired so much. Then, a whole century after independence, came the great social Revolution of 1910 under Zapata (an Indian) and Villa.

Not for nothing, then, was the street claimed to be the longest in the world called 'Insurgentes'. Where London names one of its major stations and tube interchanges after a king, Mexico's parallel to King's Cross is called 'Revolución'. Many of the other stations bore Aztec names. And the Party which had stayed in power ever since the days of Villa and Zapata was still called the 'Party of the Institutionalised Revolution' (PRI).

Mexico City was far larger even than Lima, and was now the third largest city in the world, spread out under the smog between the snow-covered volcanoes of Popocatépetl and Ixtaccíhuatl where Cortés had first looked down on Tenochtitlán. But it is the persisting legacy of Aztec history that explains why the Museum of Anthropology has such a special place at the heart of the City, and why the school which emerged as Mexico's distinctive school of theoretical anthropology – *indigenismo* – paid special attention to the country's Indian cultures, as did political leaders who, after the revolution of 1910, began to take Indian pre-colonial names like 'Cuauhtémoc' (the Aztec Emperor who succeeded Moctezuma). (The place where Cortés is buried, on the other hand, is only marked by a brass plaque in a church.)

The magnificent Colégio de México, to which I was attached, again reflected the Indian legacy in its pyramid-like architecture. I could meet (and read the works of) its doyen, Aguirre Beltrán. There were outstanding next-generation scholars like Rodolfo Stavenhagen, and visitors came from all over the globe, especially Latin America, just as scholars of the Pacific had come to Canberra.

It was the best possible place from which to study what had been happening to the millions who had been flocking to the city for decades (2,500 of them a day by the mid-1970s), for my arrival coincided with the publication of an outstanding study of the city by Colégio staff under Humberto Muñoz. A very different, but equally illuminating, study was carried out by the anthropologist Larissa Lomnitz, who only started her academic career after bringing up a family, and used classic microscopic techniques of network analysis to trace the social ties among the poor people who lived near her home.

Both kinds of study – the wide-scale sociological survey, and the fine-grained anthropological kind – were needed, for there had been more theories than research on the ground. But facts do not dictate theory. Even when anthropologists like Oscar Lewis did do detailed US-style field research, he came to the conclusion that the poor lived in ways which were incompatible with modern capitalist values, not just in terms of their attitudes to work but in terms of their attitudes to everything. They lived in matricentral families from which fathers were absent, where privacy was minimal, where sexual activity began too young, and where they were cut off by authoritarian kin from the institutions of the wider society. So they grew up with no experience of a rich associational life. All this jelled into a generalised 'culture of poverty', a set of dysfunctional values rooted in and communicated via the family.

To South American theorists like José Nun and Aníbal Quijano, however, these attitudes derived not from the family but from their structural position in society as a whole – these people were not part of the working class, but 'marginal' to an underdeveloped capitalism. Whole generations of Marxists in Europe, from the nineteenth century onwards, had been led astray by Marx and Engels, for whom the nineteenth-century European forerunners of Mexico's urban immigrants were a scandal – 'lumpenproletarians', 'rubbish', ragamuffins, not proper class-conscious proletarians. To Marx, they were 'scum, offal, refuse'; to Engels, a 'dangerous … passively rotting mass … a tool of reactionary intrigue … the worst of all possible allies … absolutely venal and absolutely brazen'. To W.W. Rostow, the architect of US policy in Vietnam a century later, on the other hand, they were simply a phase in the development of capitalism and, in his rosy-eyed view, destined eventually to disappear. To all these kinds of grand theorists, though, in one way or another, the poor were 'marginal' to capitalism.

The reality, in Mexico, was that capitalism, in a city as smog-ridden as LA, penetrated everything, even our lungs. Even refuse collectors sold what they sorted to firms which specialised in buying and selling rubbish, and what Sol Tax had called 'penny capitalism' was nevertheless a part of capitalism. A third of the so-called 'marginals' in fact worked in manufacturing industries, doing the lousy jobs (labourers, porters, cleaners, etc.) because they didn't receive the minimum wage when employers would have to pay social security contributions for them. Skilled workers, on the other hand, earned five and six times the minimum wage, especially in the state sector, where social security provision was even better, and not just in terms of wages. As insured employees in a national institution, we could buy Christmas presents ranging from household appliances to cars for forty per cent below market prices.

But even in industry the 'marginals' were the first to be laid off. Women and children who worked in the home sewing materials supplied by big companies, or who cooked the food which other members of the family sold on the street, were also invisible. Three-quarters of the two hundred thousand women who worked as servants were hidden in other people's houses. And there were uncountable beggars and unemployed people, criminals and deviants, notably prostitutes.

The label 'marginal', then, covered many different kinds of work. Researchers who looked at work in the home only, or who looked at sweatshops only, or at street-vendors only, therefore came to very different conclusions as to how many 'marginals' there were. The label 'unemployed', too, simply meant 'not counted by government officials as working more than forty hours a week'. The reality was that they were all certainly workers, working at anything, all the hours God sent.

So they couldn't afford to wait for the meagre help the government or anyone else provided; had they done so, they would have starved. Wages apart, for 4.5 million of them the state provided no piped water or sewage disposal. So they helped themselves, firstly by occupying land illegally and calling in the TV, the radio, and the Press and local politicians to expose official efforts to expel them. As time went on, they ploughed anything they could save into improving their shanties, using the labour of their families and neighbours (after a week's work). When the Dean of my Faculty, frustrated by months of waiting for the state to supply him with electricity, turned to his poor neighbours, they immediately plugged him in to the *teleraña*, the 'spider's web' of illegal connections they used themselves (for free). Hardly any of them wanted to go back to the countryside once they had acquired TV sets and gas cookers, and they saw a positive future ahead too: half of them thought that their children would be middle class; two out of three that their children would get to university (understandable enough, since the Autonomous University alone was probably the biggest university in the world catering for adult part-time students).

Given such a variety of occupations, it would have been surprising to find any consistent outlook or common action amongst the poor. They used politics when it helped, and voted, but otherwise kept their heads down, for the authorities who controlled politics defined the boundaries of what was permissible. Only today, thirty-six years after the event, have tentative inquiries begun into what happened to the hundreds of students (many from impeccable upper-class backgrounds) killed in the notorious Tlatlelolco massacre (and now described as 'Mexico's Tiananmen Square' or 'Kent State') in the run-up to the Olympic Games of 1968 – for which the Communists, Cuba and the USSR were duly blamed.

Studying poverty from luxury of Polanco and the Colégio was all too comfortable. I was also teaching, though trying to convey the latest vogues in US theory wasn't at all easy given vastly different conceptions of what even constituted sociology. Did it really include Erving Goffman's illustration of a 'with' – the situation where you encounter a couple walking towards you on the pavement but do not dare walk between them because *you* recognise that they are *together*?

The heart of the city was the Zócalo square with its gigantic Mexican flag; the cathedral on one side; the large Monte de Piedad pawnshop on another; and, opposite, the National Palace where the young Frida Kahlo had sexually stalked Rivera while he was painting the murals that are still there. The city was full of what to us was exotic entertainment: the Frontón México, where we could bet on the ninety-miles-an-hour *jai alai*; the mariachi bands in the Plaza Garibaldi who played whatever tune you wanted for a handful of pesos (my favourite was 'Guadalajara'); and outside the city, the floating gardens of Xochimilco, the last remnants of the lakes that had once been there when the city was Tenochtitlán, now the working-class' favourite place for a day out, hiring a boat, and buying food and music from other boats. Not all of it was so fascinating. As an Anglo-Saxon, I found the one-sided bull-fighting revolting. And there was all the life of a world city, especially one bordering on the US ('Poor Mexico, so near to the United States; so far from God', as the saying has it). Sarah Vaughan could easily fly down to give a concert. The Cineteca was an excellent national film theatre, while at the Auditorio, on Chapultepec Park nearby, we could see Nadia Comaneci, and the bare-breasted Guinean dancers who induced frenzy in the audience. But when we drove to see *Star Wars*, I lost the plot – and Sheila. The cinema was on a huge four-lane highway, on with its back wall, not the front. A man shouted '*a la vuelta*' (round the back), so she went off to get tickets while I parked. When I eventually got there, the cinema was full, so I spent the next two and a half hours hunting for my wife. She wasn't in the adjoining supermarket, nor could I raise any interest in the two police stations I visited, who finally suggested I go to the Bureau for Missing Persons, miles away. I joined the queue. The official asked how long she had been missing. 'Three hours', I said. 'Well, if she's not come back in two months' time, come back and we'll help you', he kindly replied. Sheila had taken my wallet, and I was running out of petrol. I got home in time to see her arrive in a taxi. 'Did you enjoyed the film, sweetie?' she asked – at which I collapsed. Being a rich foreigner, they had let her stand at the back for free.

The very first weekend, we were invited to a villa at Acapulco which not only had its own pool but even a private beach. At the end of the next promontory was a Greek temple which, rumour had it (and rumour was right, so it turned out, nearly thirty years later) belonged to the Chief of Police of Mexico City. The big tourist hotels and the forty-metre dives of boys between narrow rocks were interesting enough, but, at the risk of sounding academic, I found the fortress in the harbour more interesting, because it had been the sole official terminus on the Pacific coast for the historic trade with China via Manila, which had introduced blue and white ceramics, and much else, to the Spanish Empire.

Next, we struck out on our own to Cuernavaca. The decayed Borda Gardens beloved of Maximilian and Carlotta were now overrun with vegetation. But the legacy of the Revolution was preserved – at the foot of the stairs in the hotel was a photograph of Zapata standing at the foot of those very stairs in his huge antique sombrero. The post-revolutionary epoch was embodied in the mariachi Mass instituted by the liberal cardinal in the restored golden cathedral.

We think of Europe as a continent full of history; England as the land of the Tudors or the Normans. But the huge civilisations in Mexico went back before the Normans and were far bigger. And when we think of Mexico we think of the Aztecs. But the huge brooding statues of the Olmecs at Jalapa went back to 600 BC; the two miles of pyramids in the Avenue of the Dead at Teotihuacán, near Mexico City (the largest as big as that of Cheops in Egypt), nearly a thousand years before the Spanish Conquest; and the Toltec statues at Tula preceded the Conquest by half a millennium. When the Spaniards took the holy Aztec city of Cholula, which had once had one hundred thousand inhabitants, the streets had run with blood. It is said that 365 chapels were then built on top of the seventy temples they found there, though some of the eight kilometres of tunnels which ran through the pyramid temple sacred to Quetzalcóatl were still accessible. Though the Indians did eventually become Christians, the frescoes in the church there and the statuary and paintings at Tonanzintla and Acatepec nearby show that what emerged was a mixture of Spanish baroque and Indian art. And just before Christmas, thousands of worshippers dressed in Indian costume dance and sing in veneration of the brown Virgin who had appeared in the dress of an Indian princess at a place where water gushed out; it is now the most sacred shrine in Mexico, the Basilica of Guadalupe.

We ventured further afield via the magnificent bus system to Puebla, where the French were defeated in 1862. At Jalapa, I learned that red flags were not confined to communist parties, for the local peasants used them too, as did trade unionists on strike. At Guanajuato, the Spaniards who had worked the Indians to death in the silver mines had themselves become mummies in that dry climate. The mines had been Spain's strength and fatal weakness – once so abundant (now long exhausted) that the Empire thought it unnecessary to develop manufacturing industry at home. A single Spanish galleon captured by Drake (and another, centuries later, captured by Anson) had each financed the entire British state for a whole year, but were now exhausted. By far the most beautiful of the silver-mining towns were the pink buildings of Taxco.

The other major dimension of Spanish civilisation, Catholicism, was represented by the thousands of pilgrims at Chalma, about which Victor Turner had written a classic essay. Nearby were the remains of what had preceded it – Aztec shrines in caves, and on the mountaintop at Tepotzlán.

At Christmas time, we found that the chronology and liturgy of Christmas was not that of Europe, for the secular and the religious had become intertwined in colonial Spain in a distinctively different way from Christmas in Europe. After the Day of the Dead came the Noche Triste, which commemorated the night when the Spaniards had nearly been defeated at Tenochtitlán in 1520. The poinsettia was the symbolic plant at Christmas time, and the Festival of Los Reyes Magos, the Three Wise Men, at Epiphany, was given far more prominence.

Christmas gave us the opportunity to visit Yucatán, the heart of what had been the Mayan Empire, which had reached its height between 600 and 900 AD, and had not been finally broken by the Spaniards until 1697.

At Campeche, an inscription celebrating the repulse of an attack by Sir Francis Drake (who was buried at sea out in the Caribbean), described him not as a hero but as a 'pirate'. The name of Isla de Mujeres may reflect the myth current among the Spanish soldiers was that 'Amazon' women soldiers removed one breast to allow freer use of their bowstrings.) At Mérida, the capital of the state, the coat of arms depicted two Conquistadors resting their feet on the bowed head of an Indian. (In the palace Hernando Pizarro built in his hometown of Trujillo de Extremadura, in Spain, Atahualpa is surrounded by chained native chiefs.)

Back in Mexico, for the only time in our lives we lived in a luxurious American-style condominium apartment in Polanco, the equivalent of Mayfair. Even when our landlord had to return early from the US, after a bridging passage of hospitality from Larissa, we ended up in another marvellous house in Coyoacán, the colonial city where Cortés had lived.

Three centuries later, Diego Rivera and Frida Kahlo had also lived a few blocks away, and had given shelter to Trotsky next door. (She also gave him other kinds of comfort.) Paradoxically, she died in her steel corset gazing up at a painting of Stalin on the ceiling above her.

The machine gun bullet marks where the Stalinist muralist painter, Siqueiros, had brought a gang to try to murder Trotsky were still there. Stalin did succeed soon afterwards, when Trotsky's minder, a Communist named Mercader who had only been in the German Communist Party for a year or so, used an ice pick to smash his skull in. The books, in several European languages, which Trotsky was reading at the time are still on his desk.

A weekend at Lake Chapala, among the Indian fishing villages where D.H. Lawrence had written *The Plumed Serpent*, began to turn our minds to the giant country to the north. We took the overnight train to the border and passed through one the most disgusting cities in the world, Tijuana, where Americans go to use the casinos, to get laid, and to get their teeth fixed and buy medicines far more cheaply than in the US. At the border, we watched the very aggressive immigration officials rejecting people left and right with remarks like, 'You're an impostor!' When our turn came, it was, 'Welcome, Limey!'

The young hookers in the street outside our hotel in San Diego were pulled over by women police looking for needle marks on their arms. But the Zoo was magnificent. To us, LA was a smog-ridden city ruined by the automobile, where we stayed in a dismal hotel inhabited by senior citizens on Welfare waiting for death. But we made up for it in San Francisco, staying with friends in the North End, in a glorious haven of beauty and of culture: the Symphony Hall, Grant Avenue's Chinese restaurants, Merce Cunningham Dance at Berkeley, and Feydeau farce downtown. Returning across a desert full of decommissioned planes, we once more had nowhere at all to stay in Las Vegas. In a bus on the Strip, we were mentally prepared, at midnight, to go on two hundred miles to the next town, when a lady who originated from Blackpool offered us her spare king-sized bed in their hotel room (and free tickets for the floorshow). At the coffee shop next morning, the couple next to us had realised the American dream – they had won a million dollars the night before. (I won $25.) But next day the blue-rinse matrons were still, less ambitiously, 'working the slots', as they put it, at a quarter a time. I admired the dedication of the volunteers who staffed the museum dedicated to Liberace: his long trailing cloaks studded with hundreds of rhinestones, and the custom-built vehicle – a Cadillac front bolted onto a VW body – which he had used to come onto stage. Then came Death Valley, the Grand Canyon and the road to Santa Fe. There were more traces of Lawrence at Taos – Pueblo villages on the hills and more ancient abandoned Indian cliff dwellings and ball-courts – and abundant evidence that these Border states had once been part of the Spanish Empire. Not only did Santa Fe have the oldest Spanish church in the US, and boutiques in adobe buildings, but many of the whites outside Albuquerque and Santa Fe seemed to be bilingual. Then, past Los Alamos nuclear development base, it was with a sense of returning home to a less frenetic culture that we passed back into Mexico, even if it was to the horrid city of Ciudad Juárez where women were at great risk to their lives.

Brazil

Sheila went home; I went on to Brazil. I gave a lecture at San José in Costa Rica, then spent a ghastly night sharing a room with a Norwegian in the heat – even after midnight – of Panama City (Cristóbal Tuñon, my Panamanian postgrad at Manchester, told me that even they found the heat intolerable).

The bus ride into Rio was like a Formula One race, but worth every minute. To gaze up at the Sugarloaf from Flamengo in the velvet warmth was an enchantment. And breakfast next morning was bliss – *kaki* (persimmon) and Brazilian coffee distilled into a mere inch of fluid and sugar which set your heart racing furiously. I had to make my way to Belo Horizonte by bus immediately. I spent my days introducing myself to Brazilian anthropology by reading the very interesting work of my colleagues – one on the development theories of Fernando Henrique Cardoso, another on indigenous medicine, another on the Umbanda religion.

Umbanda was a mixture of two intellectual strands in Brazilian culture. One derived from Europe, particularly from France – regarded by nineteenth-century Brazilian intellectuals as the centre of world culture. Thus the inscription on the Brazilian national flag, 'Ordem e Progreso' (Order and Progress) is taken directly from the rationalistic Religion of Humanity invented by Auguste Comte, the founder of positivism (and sociology). But, Umbanda was a very different import a variant of European Spiritualism developed by a Frenchman, Allan Kardec. At the Père-Lachaise cemetery in Paris, later, I saw Brazilian visitors in ritual garb, with candles, still paying homage at his tomb.

The abolition of the slave trade in the British Empire did not lead to the abolition of slavery in the colonial plantations themselves, any more than in the southern states of the US. The trade simply expanded elsewhere, particularly in Cuba and Brazil – which explains why two revolutions occurred in Cuba within a century.

One cultural outcome in Brazil was the blending of Christian elements with religious ideas and practices which the slaves brought with them from Africa. Voodoo (Vodun), in Haiti, is the best-known such syncretic New World religion Europeans know about, but in Brazil the biggest religion that emerged was one unknown to people in Europe – Umbanda.

'South America' was now dissolving under my eyes. Firstly, we had lived among large populations of Indians in the Andes; then the mestizo-dominated culture of Mexico (albeit also with a sizeable Indian population dispersed over that huge country). Now we were in a country with a distinctive black heritage. All over the plantations, distinctions between blacks, mulattos and whites had been all-important. Though black and white were the basic categories of human existence, just *how* black you were mattered greatly too. In eighteenth-century Haiti, no less than 128 gradations of colour were recognised.

But by the twentieth century, blacks were only one in ten of the Brazilian population. Black girls in the fashionable parts of Rio wore gold neck-slave-rings as a fashion (and political) statement, for between 1960 and 1970 alone two million people a year had flooded into the country. By the 1970s, there were nearly one hundred million of them: people who had abandoned the poverty-stricken rural areas, especially in the arid north-east, but far more from abroad: a third from Italy; another third of people who had continued to come from Portugal; plus Spaniards, Germans and even Japanese in large numbers.

Brazil had been a strange political entity. Napoleon had forced the Portuguese Royal Family to move to Brazil in 1808. It was as if Queen Victoria had shipped out of London to be Empress of India in Delhi. But slavery had continued until 1888 – almost within living memory. The Republic was proclaimed the very next year.

In the evenings at Belo Horizonte, I even had the good fortune to watch a match between Cruzeiro and their deadly rivals from São Paulo. At the weekend, I could get to the old mining towns – Diamantina, Mariana and Sabará – which had given the state its name, Minas Gerais. The gigantic trucks full of ore which rumble to the coast are still the source of half Brazil's mineral wealth, but the older towns have now become beautiful tourist centres. In the square at Ouro Preto was a memorial to Tiradentes, the dentist hero of the abortive independence movement, inspired by the recent revolution in the US, to try and establish a republic and abolish slavery in Brazil. After being flogged at the pillory, Tiradentes' body was quartered and his head cut off and stuck on a pole; the pillory is now a monument. During Holy Week, the streets were magically transformed overnight with flower petals, and I joined the procession escorting Christ, to the accompaniment of the wailing music of the brass band, to His 'Crucifixion' outside the church, where He was suspended by the wrists and ankles.

In these old colonial towns, wonderful carvings in wood by Brazil's greatest sculptor, Aleijadinho, abounded. Born to a slave mother, he was so severely crippled that he had to have his chisels strapped to the stumps of his arms and only got about by shuffling on his knees. Yet he was able to carry out even such major works as the life-size statues in stone which dominate the front of the Bom Jesus church at Congonhas, now a UNESCO World Heritage Site.

The very first newspaper I had read in Brazil had contained a remarkable story about the African heritage. African slaves had run away from the plantations into the interior from the earliest colonial times and had formed *kilombos*, independent communities, often of considerable size. The most famous one was Palmares, a state which defended itself against regular Dutch and Portuguese campaigns to destroy it from the 1630s to 1694.

Researchers had now found a population of pure Bantu speakers, not in the remote north-east of the country but closer to its urban centres. My colleague Peter Fry, who had worked in Zimbabwe, had helped identify the language as pure Bantu, and from the few words cited in the paper, I too recognised such basic nouns as the words for 'man' and 'house'. The elder who was interviewed expressed his dismay; now that the whites had figured out their language, he said, the community would have to *cruzar as palabras*: mix their words up again!

I had my own language problem. The grammar of Portuguese made it look very similar to Spanish, which it is, structurally. But the pronunciation is something else. I listened to my colleagues with incomprehension. The commonest word seemed to be 'eh-wash'. This was in fact *eu acho* ('I think', or 'it seems to me'). In Spanish it would have been a nice clear *me parece*. The ending of words was worse – 'Ruth' became 'Rutee'. But I quickly retuned my ears because I had to teach a lot more at the University of Campinas, where I had excellent colleagues and postgraduate students, one or two of whom later came to Manchester to do their Ph.D.s.

Campinas was a lively city, with plenty of cultural facilities: Brazilian films; the splendid soprano sax of Paulo Moura; a performance of the *Misa Criolla* by the composer Ariel Ramirez, with orchestra and choir from Argentina, using Indian instruments, including my beloved tortoise-shell *charanga*.

At Aparecida, halfway to Rio, fishermen had hauled a statue of the Virgin out of a river in 1717; by 1930, Pope Pius XII had declared her to be the principal patroness of Brazil; now, thousands of pilgrims were still proclaiming 'Faith, Family and Country'.

By now, I had become quite an aficionado of bus stations. In Mexico, I had read the cheap *historieta* illustrated comics produced for my fellow travellers, which had no words, only drawings, because their 'readers' were illiterate. At the Rodoviario bus station at Campinas I bought the cheap *literatura de cordel* about which my colleague Antônio Augusto Arantes had written his Cambridge Ph.D. and which David Lehman, the authority on Latin America, has felicitously described as 'chap-books' – thoroughly Elizabethan tales written in rhyming couplets about heroes who rescued innocent damsels, especially bandit-heroes, notably Lampião, who were partly popular Robin Hoods struggling against social injustice, but who often ended up marrying the landlord's daughter.

I was tempted to visit Santos, São Paulo's port, because Pelé had played there for almost twenty years and had scored more than twelve hundred goals. I had seen Santos play wonderful football at Hong Kong after a monsoon that had covered the pitch with inches of water, but after the Pelé epoch the team went into sharp decline and didn't win the Brazilian Championship again for thirty years (in 2004).

So I opted instead to take the bus to the beautiful island of São Sebastião. Being a Brazilian bus, it left the road for the beach for fifteen glorious miles en route. At Ilhabela, painted in traditional Portuguese colours, rural idyll and industry went side by side. When I threw myself into the translucent sea, I was up to the calves in an oil spill. Nearby, at Angra dos Reis, Brazil was engaged in a race against the Argentine military dictatorship to develop not only nuclear power but also nuclear weapons (a race mercifully abandoned after both military governments fell).

I found a hotel which seemed odd – all the lights inside were red, and the room I was shown was already occupied by a woman. 'What kind of a place do you think you've come to?' asked mine host. I hadn't realised, so I found somewhere else.

I flew up to the annual conference of the Brazilian Anthropological Association at Recife in great pain, since swimming at São Sebastião had spread an agonising cold through my sinuses, intensified by the cabin-pressure of the plane. In a misguided fit of egalitarianism, I chose to spend the night in a nunnery in Olinda, the old capital, where the students were being lodged, a great mistake since they rolled in noisily drunk all night.

Several of us then went to a peace service at the church of Hélder Câmara, Bishop of Recife, where we held hands. At the conference itself, I heard the Grand Old Man of Brazilian anthropology, Gilberto Freyre, but got very bored at the business meeting, when names were called, one by one, to check membership; then whether they'd paid their subscriptions; all before an equally protracted vote was taken. It took hours. When I complained to my friends, they said, 'Peter, we don't have elections in this country. We're enjoying it!'

I saw nothing of the famous North-East, which was the first part of the country I had ever read about, when Guimarães, in the very first paragraph of her first essay for me at Manchester, had introduced me to the remarkable pioneer work *Os Sertões* (*Rebellion in the Backlands*) written in 1902 by the geographer and former army officer, Euclides da Cunha. It recounted the astounding history of the four expeditions sent by the Brazilian government into the arid *sertão* to wipe out the twenty thousand people of every kind of mixed descent who had taken refuge at Canudos in 1896 and armed themselves with machetes and other rural weapons with which they defeated successive expeditions sent to wipe them out with all the firepower of modern weapons. To me, it was especially interesting that the spiritual leader of the resistance had been a prophet, Antônio Conselheiro (the Counsellor). Then one of the greatest novelists of modern Latin America, Mario Vargas Llosa, though conservative in politics, had written another powerful and sympathetic version of Canudos in his 1981 novel *The War of the End of the World*.

On the seafront, I enjoyed being made the butt of the jokes of a *repentista* singer, who improvised witty verses, to the accompaniment of the *berimbau* one-string fiddle (of African provenance), about this funny foreigner. But I only saw the city. I was too ill to see more than the decaying Dutch churches of the Dutch (who had ruled there for thirty years), and the splendid old Santa Isabel theatre, so I took refuge on the sofa of an American woman participant in the conference, and lay the next morning recuperating under the trees on the beach, watching the fishermen balancing on their *jangada* balsa-log rafts. It was not raindrops but nuts which kept falling on my head, until I discovered that they weren't coming from the trees but from a prostitute who was trying to drum up trade. She had had lots of German and Scandinavian 'friends', she told me. I was too ill to take the moral high ground, nor was I honest enough to ask which of her swains had removed her top front row of teeth, so I just told her I was dying. 'Oh! You're one of those, are you?' she retorted – meaning racially prejudiced.

The doctor strictly forbade me from flying again, so I got the wonderful sleeper-buses, like first-class air, where you can recline/sleep and have meals too. At Bahia (Salvador) I stayed at the charmingly named Largo do Pelourinho (Whipping-post Square). But as soon as I got to São Paulo, I found an ENT specialist who, it turned out, had trained in the US. He whipped out a foot-long syringe with an equally long needle and said, to my alarm, that he was going to pierce my ear-drum to get the gunge out from behind the membrane, but assured me that the hole would heal over again (it did).

The last conference at Brasília showed me that the dictatorship was indeed winding down. True, the Rector (Vice-Chancellor) was an Admiral, but he held a meeting on campus, in the open air, where he fielded questions quite honestly from the students about their grievances. To run a state like Brazil, you cannot depend on even the most brutal use of force – torture. (The military dictatorship had given their thugs a very free rein.) There also has to be an efficient cadre of bureaucrats, trained (like the torturers) in the US, but in different institutions. People called them 'the Sorbonne'. This Rector was, apparently, a nuclear physicist (like Jimmy Carter, whom most people think of as a hick peanut farmer, but who was a graduate of the US Naval Academy at Annapolis, and who served for seven years in submarines, and specialised in nuclear reactors).

After months of this regimen, I was exhausted when I got to Rio, so I didn't want to do as much work as I had been doing. On the beach at Leblon, wearing nothing but minimalist Brazilian trunks, I was surprised to be approached by a young girl who wore even less – a few skimpy strands of string over her nether regions – but she was only interested in the only other item was wearing, my watch. 'Young man', she asked, 'Can you tell me the time?' I resumed reading the

Jornal do Brasil which announced on the front page that if you wanted to see the celebrated English historian, Prof. Eric Hobsbawm, you should go down to Leblon at eleven in the morning. I looked up, and there indeed was Eric (familiar with Brazil, he had his swimming trunks on already, underneath his street clothes). For Brazil is one of those cultures, like Paris or New York (but not the UK), which honours intellectuals. When world events break, novelists and philosophers, and not only politicians and journalists, will be asked to give their interpretations. One cannot imagine reading on the front page of the London *Times* that Susan Sontag was in town.

The Bay was spectacular, but such a large city has innumerable smaller attractions too: the tram up to Santa Teresa up to the small Chácara do Céu Museum of Impressionist paintings, though the museum devoted to Carmem Miranda ran at a close second. Although to Hollywood she came from some place vaguely labelled *Down Argentina Way*, she was in fact a Brazilian national cult figure. When she died, the queues at her state funeral went round several blocks for days. At the museum, I solved a mystery – the fruit on her head. She was so tiny that she had to be made to look taller by adding piles of fruit at one end, and standing her on enormous platform shoes at the other.

When I finally got to the Maracanã it was a great disappointment, for, though it could hold a spectacular two hundred thousand, hardly anyone was there. I had been part of the hysteria of the World Cup Final when people had rushed out into the streets after every goal, dancing the samba and firing off huge rockets from the rooftops. But Brazilian fans only turn out for big matches, and this was some minor team, so I was able to walk round the entire lower level, happy to get away from the din of the samba drums.

Now it was time to leave Brazil. The economy was rigidly controlled by the military government, and I was told that I couldn't take what money I'd earned out of the country. But the bank officials kindly directed me to the adjoining black market. My last brush with bureaucracy was at the airport. My luggage had already gone down to the plane when the immigration official told me I couldn't leave because my visa had expired, by one day, after some five months. I would have to get a *prorogacão*, an extension. My luggage was retrieved and I had to go back into the city. More legal paper forms to fill in; a fee; the hire of a typist; and, eventually, the *prorogacão*. But I enjoyed going across the lovely fifteen-mile bridge, as far as I could get on the Niterói side, to a quiet fishing village where I spent my last night.

CHAPTER 8

Globalisation

I returned to Manchester armed with the material I had collected on a whole continent new to me, Latin America, and immediately got down to work on thoroughly reworking my original book on the Third World.

When I first wrote about Afro-Asian societies, this was seen by many sociologists as merely a branch of the historiography of colonial society, not proper sociology. But Jamil Hilal, a Jordanian postgraduate who later worked for the Palestinian Liberation Organisation, soon showed me that the study of post-colonial societies was morphing into a new field of study called 'development studies' and, in particular, a new and important school of thought called world-system theory, formulated by André Gunder Frank and Immanuel Wallerstein.

It soon threw down a challenge both to orthodox sociology and historiography, rejecting not only the traditional and parochial focus of historians on internal history as explanations for the emergence of this or that nation state, but also challenging the treatment of everything else as something separate. In Britain, for instance, the growth of the greatest empire in world history had often been seen as if it was something 'external', distinctively different from the history of the UK, and usually labelled 'the expansion of the empire' – instead of recognising that this expansion had deeply shaped the way society had developed within the British Isles themselves.

The new world-system theorists, on the other hand, argued that the polity, whether British, French, Portuguese or Spanish, was not the relevant framework of analysis. Their model was basically one of political economy. It was the mode of production that explained modern society – and the new, emergent way of producing and selling goods was capitalism. And it was England and France, not Spain or Portugal, which had come out on top, because these countries used the profits from overseas trade to finance the modernisation of industry.

But the world-system model of the emergence of modern colonialism and imperialism simply as the activity of a handful of European states which had succeeded in parcelling out the entire globe between them left anthropologists and sociologists dissatisfied, since it had little place for the very different political systems and cultures not only of the colonized, but those of the metropolitan countries, especially as between Spain and Portugal, on the one hand, and England and Holland on the other, too.

Spanish colonialism, which I had only just become familiar with, seemed very different to me from the colonialism of Holland and England, and did not seem to fit a 'one-size-fits-all' world-system model. Protestant colonisers had been the purchasers of valued goods (spices, silks, etc.), but they had not necessarily grabbed the land itself (they usually weren't able to), nor did they directly organise production themselves. This they left to traditional local landowners and political classes whom they now dominated by force of conquest, but who still exploited traditional sources of labour, whether that of slaves, serfs or small peasants, to produce whatever the foreign companies now wanted. Entire countries were turned into coffee or spice plantations.

In Latin America, the Spanish state had controlled colonial expansion rigidly from the beginning, reaping gigantic profits which kept the European metropolis going for centuries. But Spain had failed to use the silver of the New World to establish industrial capitalism. Britain and France did, reorganising the entire state apparatus, the social system and the cultural order in the process, after revolutionary civil wars. British and Dutch expansion had been very different, not undertaken by the State, but via trading companies like the East India Company, which were not displaced until the nineteenth century when those countries finally established formal colonies which were then consolidated into new, rival empires.

World-system theory attracted more and more postgraduates. We invited Gunder to speak; he announced at dinner beforehand that he didn't want to speak at all – though he had already accepted and had arrived! I thought this bizarre, but assumed he wasn't serious. In front of a couple of hundred people, in an apparently catatonic stupor worthy of one of Oliver Sacks' patients, I had to try every trick in the diplomatic book to get him to speak. But he continued to sit there stolidly (why, I don't know), refusing to say a word. Eventually, though, he did crack.

I stuck my oar into the debate with a critique of Immanuel Wallerstein, the other major theorist of the world-system school,[78] arguing that the model of the single world-system established over the last three centuries was ahistoric in modern terms, since it ignored the coming into being of the communist world, and also the emergence of the Third World. I now have to acknowledge that though my argument was valid enough then, it is not today, when there is only one global economy, which even incorporates the state capitalism of China. The Third World, too, has collapsed as any kind of independent force. Yet the massive reactions in the Islamic world to US economic domination and invasions indicate that resistance to the sole remaining superpower has by no means eliminated cultural and political autonomy and resistance.

Ethnomethodology

Theorising about the world as a whole understandably did not interest those who were primarily concerned with lower levels of social organisation, down to the interpersonal. They therefore became increasingly attracted by a new kind of theory which emerged at about the same time – ethnomethodology.

The dominant modality of intellectual life in Britain which shaped early sociology was empiricism (that of France, on the other hand, theoretical). To the English, facts were what mattered, so doing science is still popularly thought of as a matter of collecting ever more facts by ever more complex technical methods; conversely, 'mere theory' is disparaged. The social sciences, which came into being very late, were modelled for decades on a fact-collecting model taken from the long-established natural sciences, which was thought to be the way those sciences worked, at least until Thomas Kuhn showed that the natural sciences also had their own 'dominant paradigms' – frameworks of thought (like the belief that the sun moves round the earth) which became so entrenched over millennia, and were so strongly backed by organised religion, that to challenge them involved not just a revolution in thinking but risked incurring the sanctions which society brings to bear upon deviants. At the dawn of modern science, the lives of people like Galileo could be under threat. Only centuries later could people like Darwin get away with unorthodox thinking because they followed a perfectly conventional style of life.

But facts always have to be analysed within some framework, so by the 1970s social scientists were searching for new paradigms. When I was trained, functionalism and Marxism were the main systems on offer. Today, to use a Monty Python phrase, they have both passed over to the other side; and newer theoretical schools have succeeded them. But none has lasted long, and the rate of turnover between one fashionable theory and the next has become ever shorter, and some have been transient fads only followed by small sects.

Symbolic interactionism was by far the most vigorous and productive school of thought in the 1970s. The next theoretical school of thought to emerge in the States, however, proved more divisive than influential. Ethnomethodology rejected the assumption that the kind of knowledge that sociologists look for is superior to mere 'common sense'. Scientists themselves, they say, use common sense thinking – not just when they are communicating with their friends, off-duty as it were. Along with the specialised methods the sciences have developed, they still make sense of the world in ways no different in kind from others insofar as this involves observing and understanding well-known clues that we normally simply take for granted. So the children of the household normally do not address their parents in the same way as non-members of the household: their mother is to them 'Mum', not 'Mrs Jones', nor do they need formally to ask their parents' permission to go to the lavatory. Those who do break these unwritten codes, which everyone understands and uses, may well be regarded and treated as 'nutters'.

One clue to understanding what people are thinking and doing is by studying how these different kinds of thinking inform what they are actually doing. So ethnomethodologists have looked at conversations, showing, in exquisite detail, that ordinary talk is a social interchange in which people follow rules, such as taking one's turn – you shouldn't, for example, all talk at once.

This was quite a novel, if scarcely exciting, insight, and can be extended to the analysis of any situation. The nanoscopic techniques developed by practitioners of 'conversational analysis', for instance, have been used interestingly to trace the conventions one can find in the speeches of Margaret Thatcher. But ethnomethodologists have rarely looked at such public figures. Most of their work has demonstrated how quite humble people follow such shared understandings in everyday situations. But showing that conventions, and manipulations of conventions, can be found anywhere in social life, and that even ordinary members of a society 'work' on that society in the niches they occupy – and that there isn't any fundamental difference in any of it – becomes rather monotonous after a while. Most sociologists want to go beyond routine interpersonal interactions to examine institutions and social structures of different kinds and at different levels – say, trade unions or community organisation.

Students, unfortunately, could get caught in the intellectual crossfire. One excellent Filipino postgraduate, who had come to Manchester to write up the mass of material he had collected on the dock workers of Manila, was told by his supervisor that he should have collected the dock workers' conversations.

I used my Presidential Address to the British Sociological Association in 1973[79] to tackle these growing theoretical differences, since I thought that even those sociologists reputed as theorists were carefully evading confronting them.

C. Wright Mills had distinguished between Grand Theory and what he called 'mindless empiricism'. Few sociologists were recognised as theorists. They dealt with substantive matters at a less general level: with particular kinds of kinship systems, say, or with absenteeism in different branches of industry.

But, I argued, this didn't mean that most researchers weren't just 'mindless empiricists'. They *were* concerned with theory, but didn't necessarily subscribe to any of the grand theories on offer as whole sets of ideas, but used bits and pieces taken from these wider theoretical systems which they found useful in order to illuminate the bit of reality they were looking at. (Like everyone else, they also used bits and pieces taken from ideologies current in the wider society, not just academic theorising.)

Their preoccupation, that is, was not with thinking in itself – and showing how these bits and pieces fitted together as part of a whole theory – but with thinking about something 'out there', beyond the study walls. They did not hesitate to use what Merton called theories of the middle range: general concepts like 'alienation' or 'status group', or what I called 'parameters' – found in some social situations, or in some societies or certain kinds of situation only, such as 'extended kinship networks' or Michels' conception of the 'iron law of oligarchy', which he thought characterised the way political parties worked.

They were least likely to be interested in the most general Grand Theory of all, the kind that didn't concern itself with any particular kind of society at all, or with the thorny problem of trying to classify societies into some sort of typology; even less with *process*, such as the problem of social evolution which had preoccupied the nineteenth century, or with modern problems of 'development'. In the extreme, for instance, the 'formal' sociology of Georg Simmel had been concerned with 'constants and universal properties, processes, dimensions, relations' – which he called 'forms'. These included subordination and superordination, the way size, number, or scale, for instance, affected social life in general, not simply in a particular society or kind of society, or even bit of society, at this or that period in time, though he didn't distinguish, say, ephemeral encounters from long-lasting forms of social organisation. (Simmel, though, did not deal exclusively in formal sociology for he complemented his formal sociology with no less than two other kinds of sociology: a 'general' one and a 'philosophical' sociology.)

Ethnomethodology certainly wasn't the study of abstracted 'forms', for it placed social actors at the heart of their sociology. They also studied whole situations: how people used bits and pieces from different sources, drawing on their life-experience and that of others around them, and on ideologies current in the wider society, to make sense of the world around them. Yet the ethnomethodological studies, it seemed to me, like those of the symbolic interactionists, dealt with a world in which there were only 'situations' and 'social actors', and stopped short of constructing any model of the social structures and institutions within which situations occurred and actors acted. Herbert Blumer, the great theoretician of symbolic interactionism (and I'm not being sarcastic) had put it classically long ago: Marx's classes, he wrote, were not real at all; they were merely intellectual abstractions or categories. It was people who acted: 'instead of reducing human society to social units that do not act – for example, social classes', he wrote, 'we should recognise that the individuals who compose human society ... do not act towards culture, social structure or the like; they act towards situations' – anticipating by decades Margaret Thatcher's famous claim that 'there is no such thing as society'.

This, I said, was a 'denuded' sociology. As well as denying any place to social structure and institutions, it did not examine how culture – which guided what social actors did within situations and structures – was produced in the first place, and how it was then communicated. Studies of how people managed the first five seconds of conversations, or the implicit rules they followed in exchanging 'Good Mornings' might show how people 'worked' those limited areas of social life, and thereby widen our understanding, but they didn't deepen it, because they didn't examine the pressures exercised by 'significant others' who controlled institutions to follow the rules *they* wanted followed – how they exercised *power* over other, less powerful social actors. They showed how people were stigmatised; less often how they were exploited.

This address was very warmly applauded. It also resulted in something I didn't want – re-election as President for another year.

The gulf between this kind of theorising and ethnomethodology meant that there wasn't much room for shared understandings. Many pioneer ethnos had come up through Trotskyite sects, where they had learned 'caucus' methods of organisation which they now applied to recruiting bright postgraduates. Though only a handful, they were singularly active proselytisers. The non-ethnos simply evaded any confrontation with this now highly organised sect.

The new vogue in Manchester even reached the Press, when the *Times Higher Educational Supplement* reported the new triumphalist programme of the ethnos. They wanted, they declared, 'to do for the social world what linguistic philosophy had done for language. They would, for instance, be more interested in studying the way people used the word class than in developing a concept of class as part of a theory'. Conversely, 'Left wing sociologists who got involved in practical work were just heading for nervous breakdowns'.[80] We still await the fulfilment of this programme today.

Teodor and I nevertheless tried to accommodate the new trend. When two highly qualified ethnomethodologists applied for, and were appointed to the next two available posts in the Department, though, this olive branch was only taken as an incentive to step up the campaign to spread the gospel.

Our next olive branch was to invite the very leader of the movement, Harold Garfinkel, to Manchester. I had arranged for him to use one of my lecture times for his opening talk, but I could scarcely get into the room myself because it had been invaded by people who were not even members of our university, for the news had been spread by the ethno staff even to undergraduates from as far away as Lancaster.

When a new Chair then became available, we tried to tackle the underlying source of staff hostility – the appointment of Teodor instead of the candidate unanimously backed by the staff. This person was a very good sociologist, but had published only one (excellent) paper, which seemed to the Appointing Committee to be not enough to justify appointing a man as a professor. Teodor and I now took the staff's enthusiastic support for him as a signal to try and appoint him again, this time with the support of the professors – at which the staff did a complete *volte face*. They didn't want their candidate any more. (I forget whom they did want.) There followed a bizarre sequence in which Teodor and I stood by 'their' candidate – who had now secured the approval of another Appointing Committee – despite their having now abandoned him. The Vice-Chancellor, though, wanted to avoid alienating the staff and to drop the candidate – at which Teodor and I said we would both quit the university. It was the candidate himself who resolved the situation by buckling under the strain and withdrawing from the fray.

There followed a divergence between Teodor and myself, which was, however, resolved. He was a very ambitious man, and fell under the influence of the Shah of Iran, who had introduced a form of land reform and now used his wife as the soft face of the regime to propose setting up an international Institute for peasant studies in Iran. Teodor was given money to finance an initial exploration by inviting a group of distinguished senior people who had specialised in peasant studies to Manchester, including Eric Wolf and Eric Hobsbawm. Only a few weeks before, students returning home from Leeds had been tortured by the SAVAK secret police, so I said I would make public my opposition to any academic collaboration with the project. The majority agreed with me, and Teodor was sensible enough to respect his comrades' views and dropped the project.

His international vision finally led him to a project much more worthy of his talents: the exchange of postgraduate students between the USSR and the UK. This began in Manchester and culminated, despite the inevitable serious difficulties at a time when the USSR was becoming Russia, in the establishment of three institutes financed by George Soros: one in Moscow headed by Teodor, one in Prague headed by Ernest Gellner, and one in Budapest. The Moscow institute proved so successful, despite the inevitable serious initial difficulties, that it soon had hundreds of students from many Eastern European countries, some of whom I later heard giving excellent papers at Kent. Teodor was given the recognition he deserved when the British government awarded him an OBE.

The student revolution had been bad enough, but this schism within the staff and the simmering discontent which ensued had destroyed what had been a harmonious department. So when an invitation came to go to New York for a couple of semesters, I was only too glad to take it up.

New York, New York!

After Latin America, I had been trying to grapple with developments in the Third World, but had had little time to do so. Now I could do so at CUNY (City University of New York) Graduate Center in New York, at what seemed to me the best address in the world – Fifth Avenue and 42nd Street – with the New York Public Library across the street.

I had far more time to write, as I only had to do the normal Visiting Professor's stint of two two-hour seminars per week. There was more to it than that, though. This was a capitalist market culture, unlike the state-sponsored grant system of the UK. Our students were excellent, but there was a special edge to these American postgrads – firstly, because the competition to get into such a prestigious university in New York City was immense; secondly, because the students had to pay huge tuition fees from their own resources, which meant that they were not only highly motivated but also more demanding than British students, since the relationship was much more that of a direct cash nexus. They also expected you to work hard, in the form of essays, made demands on your time, and so on. Thirdly, getting a Ph.D. took far longer than in the UK. One study I read, called, appropriately, *Of Time and the Doctorate*, not about Ivy League Universities but about very prestigious universities in the South, showed that the average interval of time between starting one's Ph.D. and finishing it was 10.4 years. First, one had to do coursework for two years and pass an exam; then formulate a dissertation project, which was very critically scrutinised by one's teachers; then do the fieldwork for the Ph.D. (which took several years); and then write it up; then have one's thesis accepted. American teachers were often openly contemptuous of our much shorter and more permissive programmes. Nor were postgrads under any illusions that this was a ticket to paradise, anyhow. 'When you finish', one of them cynically remarked, 'You can compete with a few hundred other people for a starting job in a community college in Oshkosh'.

Under Reagan, market competition linked to financial rewards increased. I was unhappy about having to take on a Research Assistant whom I did not need to do chores like look up material in the library for me, until it was explained to me that this would enable her to eat. She was outstandingly good and was ranked for two years in succession among the very top postgrads in the whole country. That wasn't good enough, however, so, unlike Sylvia Plath, she was eventually forced to retrace her steps back to the Midwest. Though food in Manhattan cost half what it did in England, accommodation was an expensive nightmare: it was not the fun and games of Monica and Chandler, Rachel, Joey, Phoebe and Ross. Some of my students were too embarrassed even to let me see inside their shared apartments.

The main centre for anthropology in New York had long been Columbia University, with a succession of luminaries like Alfred Kroeber, Ruth Benedict, Ralph Linton and Julian Steward. By the 1930s, Franz Boas was the major force. Though his own fieldwork never excited me (yards of texts in Kwakiutl), it nevertheless did play a big role in developing fieldwork as the major technique of research, and further developed the intellectual tools with which to understand society and racism.

Boas' anthropology, that of an immigrant who had fled Nazism, resonated with a wider public because he engaged himself in the fight against racism and anti-Semitism, not only by his public opposition to those doctrines, but by developing the intellectual tools with which to understand them, particularly the concept of culture.

After the Second World War, a new generation of veterans, with 'materialist predilections and ... interests in politics', in Sydel Silverman's words,[81] arrived at Columbia. Some of them then formed a 'Mundial Upheaval Society'(M.U.S.), which included future anthropologists such as Eric Wolf, Stanley Diamond, Marshall Sahlins, Sidney Mintz, Morton Fried and John Murra – who all became very distinguished.

For all their brilliance, their writings were too Marxist for orthodox journals like the *American Anthropologist*. But when Leslie White arrived for a short stay at Columbia, his interest in the theory of cultural evolution (though it differed considerably from the (then) hard-line materialist evolutionism of Sahlins) resonated with the Young Turks of the M.U.S. White then opened up the pages of the *Southwestern Journal of Anthropology*, which he edited, to people like Eric Wolf, who was able to publish his seminal articles on 'closed corporate communities' in Latin America and his erudite comparative study of *compadrazgo* (fictive or 'pseudo'-kinship, such as god-parenthood). White then took Sahlins, Elman Service and Wolf back with him to Michigan.

The M.U.S. surfaced again in the 1970s during the Vietnam War, when Eric, now Chairman of the Ethics Committee of the American Anthropological Association, blew the whistle on anthropologists who were collaborating with US military Intelligence in Thailand.[82] Marshall Sahlins invented and organised the first anti-war teach-ins at Michigan. And Stanley Diamond, who had done fieldwork in Nigeria, went with Conor Cruise O'Connor to Biafra and used the pages of the *New York Review of Books* to denounce the Nigerian government's brutal suppression of the struggle for the independence of Biafra between 1967 and 1970, which left two million civilians dead from starvation.[83]

By the 1990s, two dynamic anthropology departments had emerged in New York, both headed by 'graduates' of the M.U.S. – Eric Wolf at CUNY Graduate Center, and Stanley Diamond at the New School for Social Research.

Eric had been born in Austria. I first met him when we were attending a conference in that country and were taken on a coach trip to Vienna, where they specially opened up the Ethnographic Museum for us. On the way there, looking out of the window, I remarked to Eric how beautiful the park was. 'Yes', he replied, 'I remember it well because that's where I first saw a man being beaten to death.' He returned to Vienna in a tank.

At the museum, they asked what we would like to see. I was about to have a long-held wish fulfilled. I said I wanted to see the Moctezuma treasures sent to Charles V – which was granted. But Marshall Sahlins' request to see the famous collection of Captain Cook memorabilia from Hawaii brought a rueful response. 'Oh dear!' said our host, 'I'm afraid those things are away in Hawaii on loan. However', he brightened up, 'we do have a reciprocal exhibition they've lent us on "Waikiki Today"'. The look of disbelief and despair on Marshall Sahlins' face beggared description.

At CUNY, Eric ran a course on theory every week, and, as the leading US specialist on Latin America, another on that continent – which was right up my street.

Visitors from all over the world attended the very lively theory seminar, while his Latin American seminar attracted such distinguished anthropologists as Darcy Ribeiro. (In Rio, I had felt I was getting somewhere with my Portuguese when I could tell him jokes in that language.) Darcy was not only the outstanding authority on Amazonian Indians but a man of many other parts. His novel, *Maíra*, for example, which appeared while I was in Brazil, was a prophetic picture of something which was happening all over Latin America – the spread of well-endowed US high-tech fundamentalist Protestant evangelist sects which installed themselves among remote tribes; in Brazil's case, the Indians of the *selva*. Darcy was not a partisan of the new Labour Party headed by 'Lula' (who eventually became President). Rather, he was one of a long line of radical Populists that went back to Getúlio Vargas and, later, João Goulart, the President exiled to Uruguay when the military seized power in 1964 because of his support for Cuba. Darcy was the ally of a newer Populist, Leonel Brizola, who now became Governor of the state of Rio de Janeiro and appointed Darcy as his Vice-Governor, giving him the opportunity of democratising education by introducing free meals for poor schoolchildren (he also tried to lure me to Rio to help him in higher education). More contentious was his transformation in Brazil's foremost cultural institution, the annual Carnival competition between the schools of samba, which are organised like British football divisions, with annual promotions and demotions. It had always taken place in the streets but Darcy now showcased it in a newly constructed 'Sambadrome'.

In the US, which is a continent and not just a country, there are very large populations of almost every cultural group you can think of, from Chicanos in California to fundamentalists in the Bible Belt and gun-crazy Mid-westerners, through to New York, which houses a marvellous intellectual population. There, apart from my two universities, I found a third intellectual centre – not a university, but a high-quality Marxist journal, *Monthly Review*, run by two people who could have held down distinguished Chairs anywhere: Paul Sweezy and Harry Magdoff. On Roosevelt's desk at the Pearl Harbour crisis was a document from Paul on reorganising the US economy. He came from a wealthy banking family, which had enabled him and Leo Huberman to start the *Review* and keep it alive. Harry had been very successful on Wall Street, where he had also accumulated enough material, which he kept in steel filing cabinets, for half a dozen books on the workings of the Financial District and other economic subjects – until they were reduced to ashes in a fire. But both of them had dedicated themselves not to making money but to keeping left-wing ideas alive, and had supported Castro in Cuba, Allende in Chile, and Daniel Ortega's Sandinistas in Nicaragua. They were a singularly open-minded pair. Harry had now become interested in Liberation Theology, so you would find such interesting people as Cornel West at the *Review*'s Tuesday morning 'seminars' as well as Lefties from Europe and Latin America. It was, for me, paralleled socially by the flow of fascinating people through the *salon* at Harry's Upper West Side apartment – mostly academics, others politicos, like the mother of Harry's wife, Beadie, a founder member of the Bolshevik Party and a militant from the days of the famed International Ladies Garment Workers' Association. She still lived with them, and was quite open about her condescending attitude towards the younger people clustered around a mere journal.

We lived in Greenwich Village, though Sheila was once more disappointed that our apartment wasn't what she'd expected from the movies. In deep midwinter, street people had to sleep on the sidewalks by gratings where hot air came out, though when the streets really became ice-rinks, they were moved to the armories (the equivalent of Territorial Army halls). More fortunate were the intellectuals, which the Village was full of – the server at your table in the restaurant was likely to be a budding ballet dancer. We were privileged because we had a lavatory inside the apartment; the others had theirs in the hallway. We couldn't understand the notice in every apartment telling us that the Exterminator would call on the fifteenth day of every month. This didn't mean Schwarzenegger. It meant the sanitary official whose job it was to spray every room to keep down the cockroaches, though they weren't too successful, as the insects still came out every night. One night, sleeping on a mattress on the floor because of visitors, I felt a tickling on my forehead. It was a two-inch long cockroach.

But the location was superb. We were living in the 'last bastion' of the Village's 'Little Italy'. Through the window was Our Lady of Pompeii, the church of Mother Cabrini, who had been sent by Pope Leo XIII in 1889 to take care of immigrant girls. The first US citizen to be canonised, she became, appropriately, the patron saint of immigrants.

A somewhat different Italian institutional import was the Mafia, which, it was widely believed, we had to thank for the relative crimelessness of the streets. Some of the older residents in our apartment block were of Sicilian origin. John, in his eighties, was blind, and sat on a chair in the stairway so that he could chat to people as they passed by. I asked him one day about a double murder that had occurred in the 1930s which the local paper had just written about. 'I suppose, now', I said, 'that people know who did it?' No reply. I thought he hadn't heard me, so I repeated the question. No reply again. I was in the presence of *omertà*.

Warm cinnamon bagels for breakfast were available only two doors away; Zito's, where Frankie Sinatra had bought his bread, was just around the corner on Bleecker, as were wonderful Italian delicatessens where you could get *braciole*. Balducci's was very expensive; not so our coffee shop, the *Lucca*, just outside the door, and on my way to the marvellous New York University Library – the Bobst (Mr Bobst had made his money from ladies' foundation garments) – across Washington Square, I could pop in to the *Reggio* on MacDougal. Cheap and good restaurants – Vietnamese, New Orleans, Szechwanese and Thai – were all around. At the thrift store at St Luke's church; at neighbourhood concerts or using the Jefferson Market local library, we began to feel like proper residents of the Village.

When not teaching, I worked long and hard at my book. But we had time to make up for those years in the African bush and the Australian outback by watching fifty-seven movies in six months. New York might only have one world-class orchestra compared to

London's five, but it was a far better place for modern dance. And there were Zefirelli productions at the Met, while a mere block or two away I could stroll to the Village Gate or the Village Vanguard to hear people like Benny Carter or Kai Winding. When the South Street Seaport opened, a few older people jitterbugged nostalgically to Lionel Hampton and Nelson Riddle. There were street vendors selling books on the pavements and big chain bookstores where you could shop at 10.30 at night. The museums were wonderful, and if we missed Europe we could always go up to the Cloisters at the northern end of the island. My favourite place, where I always took visitors, was the World Trade Center. I even thought about studying it, though with two commodity exchanges and thousands of offices this was a crazy idea. But while other visitors to the lookout on the 107th Floor (all of four minutes to get there) looked out at the Financial District spread before them, I read, and had copied, the display on the inner wall, which told the history of the world according to Rockefeller – it was the history of trade.

A totally unexpected letter now arrived from Manchester University: all the senior staff were offered early retirement. Financially ignorant, I wrote to Phil Leeson, a Communist economist at the university whom everybody loved, asking his advice. He replied that it had taken him three minutes to make up his mind. If it was good enough for Phil, it was good enough for me, for after the student revolution and then the staff upheavals I had lost the enthusiasm I had felt as a new lecturer starting out in life.

First, I had shed my huge first-year lectures. Now, as had long been the case in the US, where students never saw the distinguished names on their staff lists, lectures were given by teaching staff, not necessarily by the professoriate, and were tutored by younger teachers. Then I dropped second-year teaching; then, though I still taught as many hours as ever, I retained only the third-year theory course and a postgraduate seminar, in which I could teach what I liked. What I now increasingly liked was comparing Western medical systems with non-Western ones. But the truth was that, this postgraduate teaching apart, as a city, Manchester no longer attracted me, apart from watching United.

We had been spoiled by New York. From Manhattan we had been able to take the train up the breathtaking Hudson Valley to Montreal and Toronto to give lectures, which were opportunities to see old friends again, and we ended with a Greyhound expedition to the South to as far as we could get, to Nashville, where we saw Elvis' gold Cadillac, the Grand Ole Opry, and the decayed gardens of the

Vanderbilt estate at Asheville where Chance, classically portrayed by Peter Sellers in *Being There*, had been in real-life charge of the garden.

So when I went back to Manchester, it was to retire from active service. New York had been such an exciting city that I said that if I could start my life over again, I would start it there. It had given us a taste for world-class cities, and as our daughters were now in London, we decided to move there. Then followed the grim business of buying and selling houses, and classifying and disposing of three thousand books to a Japanese university.

My last exit, though, was bizarre. André Singer, an Oxford-trained anthropologist who had done fieldwork in Central Asia and written an excellent book on the *Lords of the Khyber*, had then worked for Granada TV in Manchester for years producing an outstanding series of anthropological films collectively entitled *Disappearing World*. When Granada started to go through a period of financial constraint, they realised that they had only used four per cent of this anthropological footage stored in their library. So they came up with the bright idea of capitalising on some of the other ninety-six per cent by making films comparing the 'tribal' footage, which was superb, with new film, specially shot, on British society and culture.

It all went swimmingly. They tested me by making me explain to the cameraman what anthropology was all about, and the producer said that my interview was the best he had ever seen. Then, over two years, together with Peter Bicknell, another Oxford-trained anthropologist, experienced in working for TV, we wrote the scripts for half a dozen films, then shot them. They ranged from *rites de passage* ('Staying Alive' [differences in cultures], 'Throwing Your Money Away', 'Growing Up' [primary school playgrounds in Salford], 'Men and Women', 'Passing Through Life', 'Out of this World' [religions], 'Body and Soul' [illness and death], 'Making a Living') to how people used their leisure time (holiday-makers at Manchester Airport). We then tried the films out on different audiences, such as WEA classes and Manchester University evening classes, and they went down very well indeed. The production team at Granada was thoroughly happy too, so much so that we were told we would be given a very prestigious slot right next to *Coronation Street*. But I cannot now honestly remember the details about every film because it all went pear-shaped.

All that was left was to put the soundtrack onto the last film. I was actually standing in the empty house we were just leaving when the phone rang. I had already been struck by the, to me, extraordinarily hierarchical nature of TV in contrast to the way universities worked, which in comparison were models of democracy (especially after the student revolution) in that people expected, and were given, considerable latitude about what went into their lectures, and had the major say about the uses to which their teaching was put. But in the media world, it seemed, new decisions could be made and further approval had to be won at successively higher levels, even though an in-house team had been working consensually for years. From having been promised the prestigious time for our programmes, I was now suddenly asked to remake them in a more popular way ('magazine format'). I wasn't prepared to do this. The conversation ended with my slamming down the phone, declaring that I had better things to do with my time than being messed about for a medium which was ephemeral anyhow!

Granada then hired other people to remake the series, which received very negative reviews. When I was persuaded to protest at this treatment, I was told by a very senior Granada executive that this happened all the time in TV, and when I recounted the story to an audience of the Learned Societies in the Social Sciences, people asked why I had been surprised: surely I knew the history of how even such eminent figures as Scott Fitzgerald had had their scripts mangled in Hollywood, and where a work like Eisenstein's film *Que Viva México!* never even reached the screen. Today, I don't even have a single copy of any of the films we made.

CHAPTER 9

London Town

In Manchester, I had been constantly badgered on the phone by a Ghanaian, Kofi Buenor Hadjor, who was starting a new journal, the *Third World Book Review*, so I gave Sheila strict instructions that she was to divert him if he continued to ring me in London. I didn't allow for his elemental force, however, which was quite equal to that of Teodor. Before long, I was Chairman of the *Review*, though this only entailed as much time as I was prepared to give, and I lived near the fine office, anyhow. Kofi, in any case, ran things like a stereotypical African chief. The masthead of the journal listed just about everybody of repute on the Left in development studies, plus some real professional politicos, notably A.M. Babu, a firebrand from Zanzibar who had founded the Umma Party, been imprisoned by the British for two years before Independence in 1962, had then become a Cabinet Minister in Nyerere's Independence government for eight years, but was subsequently arrested in 1972 and imprisoned by Nyerere for six years. When he returned to Zanzibar in 1995, he was prevented from engaging in politics any more.

Despite the distinguished names on the masthead, the reality was that the Board never met, and Kofi bestowed and altered titles at will. I, allegedly 'Chairman', never saw any accounts at all. But Kofi had a good track record of commitment to progressive Third Worldism at a time when the wind of change had blown in Africa. He had been Press Secretary to Nkrumah, with whom he went into exile in Guinea when Nkrumah was overthrown by a coup whilst on a visit to China, and was present at Nkrumah's death. Then he went to head up a UNESCO-backed School of Journalism in Dar es Salaam, Tanzania. Now he had secured funding from 'neutralist' Scandinavian countries to launch the journal, which produced several excellent issues.

Then the journal started coming out behind time. As Chairman, I was constantly getting letters from aggrieved people who had lent him money or worked for him – even, when I was teaching in New York, one from Judith Hart, who had been Minister of Overseas Development. Eventually, one issue was so late that Kofi made up for the non-appearance of what should have been the next issue of the journal by giving our readers a collection of articles I had made on the proliferation of nuclear weapons in the Third World, *On The Brink*, as a book.[84]

The final Act was a mysterious petrol-bombing which destroyed the office, situated on the edge of Hoxton, which, when I was Chairman of the Board of Governors of a local school, was the poorest district in the poorest Borough in London. Now a trendy area, it had been a notorious Fascist stronghold in the Mosley era: my friend Andy Windross, Vicar of the adjoining church, told me that in the 1930s the Church of England incumbent at Hoxton had run up a British Union of Fascists flag over his church. Canvassing for the Labour Party forty years later, I was asked in two different shops whether I preferred to leave of my own free will or be thrown out. So when the mysterious fire broke out, I attributed it to racist right-wing extremists. Whoever did it, it was the end of the *Review*. Kofi ended up as Professor of Black Studies in California.

An equally alarming incident was purely domestic. Next door to us was one of the last proletarians in this now bourgeois area: a man who worked at Ford Dagenham as a nightwatchman, but who was otherwise a total recluse. No one ever saw him, and if you did run across him he avoided eye contact. One day we had a serious overflow which affected both our semi-detached houses, so I had to go and find him.

Nothing was locked in his house, so I went round the back, let myself in and found myself in a pure stage-set for Steptoe and Son: a vast assemblage of furniture, most of it decaying, piled from ceiling to floor. You could just squeeze through, watching out for the holes in the floors and the stair-treads.

Then I didn't see him for months, until one night there was screaming at midnight and the sound of blows and fighting. I saw him sitting on his front step with blood pouring down his head, and so called the police. Apparently he had been followed home from a drinking club and had been struck over the head to get his money.

That was nothing compared to my next encounter with him. Unusually, I was working at home because Sheila and I were going for a second honeymoon to Amsterdam next day and I had to read and finish quickly a book I had been able to borrow from Sweden.

It was about the death of Betty, the wife of a colleague, Cyril Belshaw, whom we had known in Canberra and with whom we had subsequently stayed in Vancouver.

On Cyril's sabbatical year they had rented a villa in Switzerland. According to his account, they had then travelled to Paris where he was attending a meeting of the world organisation of anthropology, of which he was President. He had then left her at the Métro, and she went off to do her own work at the Bibiliothèque Nationale.

He never saw her again. Weeks later, a body was found, not in Paris but down a ravine in Switzerland used for dumping rubbish, gnawed by wild animals. The Swiss police concluded that it was Betty's body.

The whole story, written up by Ellen Godfrey, a Canadian journalist who specialises in writing murder mysteries,[85] is far more intriguing than any of her fictional works. Belshaw was extradited to Switzerland, imprisoned there for 394 days, then put on trial for the murder of his wife. There were many unexplained mysteries: the absence of records of the journey from Switzerland to Paris; how the body could have got from Paris to Switzerland; Belshaw's frank admission that he had falsified his wife's dentition records which he had got for the police from Canada; the revelation that he had had an affair known to the Vancouver police and which was continued in the villa in Switzerland; and many other matters.

At the end of her meticulous account of the trial, Ellen Godfrey comes to no conclusion at all; Belshaw himself had no explanation whatsoever as to how his wife had disappeared or how her body came to be found not in Paris but in Switzerland. The Swiss court itself finally released him, 'by reason of doubt' – rather like the verdict of 'not proven' in Scotland.

This was not the only corpse I was to deal with that day. I had reached the climax of the book, recounting the trial, when there was a knock at the door. The young man standing there was practically incoherent, saying things like 'wicked' at regular intervals. I could also make out something about a dead body. It turned out he had been inside the house next door and had found the corpse of our neighbour, covered in maggots. When I rang the police, he walked out into the street and started to disappear altogether. 'But you're the principal witness', I said, 'and the police will want to talk to you. What's your name? Where do you live?' He waved his hand vaguely northwards and was disappearing when a police car came round the corner. 'Oh', said the policeman, instantly recognising him, 'It's you!' He was evidently a well-known burglar. But our neighbour had obviously just died, and the burglar obviously hadn't done it, so no one was subsequently charged.

* * * * *

Two other activities now supervened – the first, deriving from my long-standing interest in non-Western medical systems, which took me back to Mexico several times; the second, helping to get a

Commission on Peace Studies off the ground, sponsored by the world organisation of anthropology, the International Union of Anthropological and Ethnological Sciences.

After my stint at the Colegio, the great and very democratic Mexican anthropologist, Guillermo Bonfíl, who ran the postgraduate school in Tlalpan, in Mexico City, got me to spend a couple of months teaching, not well-heeled postgraduates in the city but highly intelligent teachers and health workers in the beautiful lakeside town of Pátzcuaro, out in Michoacán.

The reverberations of the 1910 Revolution had lasted right into the 1930s, not only in terms of economic and political repercussions such as the nationalisation of oil, but cultural ones too. Hostility between church and state was nothing new, but it had not been a simple story of liberals versus conservatives. As long ago as 1767, in the epoch of the Enlightenment, the Jesuits had been expelled from all Spanish territories, including the colonies, which so infuriated the quite provincial and conservative Mexican-born *criollos* that it helped set them on the path to independence. A century later, after the Revolution of 1910, fifty thousand conservative and devout peasants took up their machetes in the total war of the Cristeros against a revolutionary government, not because that government was redistributive but because it was anticlerical. Seminaries and churches providing for ten million of the faithful were closed down; people had to flee across the border to El Paso in Texas to seek refuge, to go to Mass or to get married. Many priests were slaughtered. In 1926, the church hierarchy took the astounding step of withdrawing the provision of the Mass and other sacraments and public religious services from the congregations. In the short run, the US Ambassador was instrumental in bringing about a reconciliation, but as late as the year 2000 the Vatican was still canonising twenty-five martyred priests.

During this epoch, the colonial church in the main square at Pátzcuaro had been converted into a public library. On the wall above the former altar, Juan O'Gorman, the revolutionary artist, had painted a dramatic mural, not, though, of the modern struggle over religion but of the Conquistador – described as a '*sádico vil*' – who had sacked Tzintzuntzan nearby and murdered its people.

Tzintzuntzan had been the capital of the Tarascan Empire, which had rivalled that of the Aztecs until the Spaniards conquered and destroyed both.

A visit to the ruins of the Tzintzuntzan pyramids had bizarre consequences. I asked the guide whether he knew of the book written by an American anthropologist, George Foster, about the town. Yes, he did. 'And was it a reliable account?' I asked. 'Yes, but ...' 'But what?' I asked.

Central to George's celebrated study was the concept of the 'limited good'. Tzuntzuntzeños had no expectations of a better life (on this earth at least). There was only a limited amount of anything in the world; nor was the future likely to promise much better. This gloomy world-view included a mistrust of outsiders, whatever the latter purported to offer. Foster recounts one anecdote about a party of townspeople who had visited Mexico City, where they had bought tortillas, in one of which the hand of a small child was found. This, the guide said, was a most unlikely story. 'They might have found a finger', he argued, 'or even two. But a whole little hand (*manito*), no way!!'

I thought it worthwhile sending a note to Foster at Berkeley, telling him about this rare judgement by a 'subject' of anthropological study about the accuracy of the fieldworker – which resulted in making a contact that was to prove important.

In the Plaza at Pátzcuaro, I was also struck by the stalls where innumerable cures were on sale for:

> ordinary coughs, asthmatic coughs, varicose veins, phlebitis, rheumatism, diarrhoea, skin complaints, gastric ulcers and gastritis, wind, vomiting, allergies, kidney and urinary complaints, high and low tension, and nervous attacks, illnesses defined in Western terms, but treated mainly via traditional remedies: herbs, seeds, leaves and roots, but also snakeskins, coloured fluids, rubbing ointments for both head and chest, 'witches' brew', and foetuses, as well as holy pictures. (*Knowledges*, pp. 217–18)

But they also offered medicines which would 'tie and nail down your lover', or ensure success in examinations – hardly the Western distinction we draw between physical illnesses and social problems.

This inspired me to start putting together material I had collected for ten years on the diagnoses and therapies used by non-Western doctors, which I had been giving in postgraduate seminars in medical sociology at Manchester. Now I wrote up and published this material.[86]

In Pátzcuaro, I was rung up by Stanley Diamond from New York (who, being an American, had grown up with a telephone line where his umbilical cord should have been) inviting me to stop at the New School for Social Research in New York on my way home. There, I gave my paper on non-Western medicine, the result being, a few years later, an invitation to come and teach for a semester at the New School.

In the meantime, I also received a very different invitation: to go back to Mexico to help design a research project in the field of traditional medicine.

Mexican Presidents, like US ones (e.g. Reagan and Nixon in California), use the gigantic collections of papers accumulated during their presidency and can call on global corporations (in Nixon's case, a Japanese bank) to found research libraries and institutes, or foundations when they retire – the purpose of these being to create a retrospective myth of themselves as statesmen and patrons of culture. Few of them had so much to hide as Luís Echeverria, who had been Minister of the Interior in 1968 when three hundred people, demonstrating for democratic reforms, had been killed in the notorious massacre in the Plaza of Tlatelolco in Mexico City, for which he was only indicted thirty years later. As I write, over forty years later, he has been charged with genocide. But in 1970 it hadn't stopped him becoming President; he then tried to develop an image of himself as a Third Worldist (and turned up at Kofi's office in London on this quest). He further set to work to clean up his image by founding a research centre across the road from his Palacio, spectacularly decorated with Indian masks.

The research project was never adopted, alas (whether for financial reasons or failure of nerve, I never found out), and was replaced by a routine bibliography on indigenous medicine.

Back in Europe, in my new London home, without the constraints of departmental administration or publishers' deadlines, I now began work on a book which was to take me four years, and which I ultimately entitled *Knowledges*. But I did have time to interrupt this work and do less protracted things along the way. One such thing was to tackle the application of the concept of culture to theories about development.[87] Another was a summary overview as the end-piece of a huge book of over a thousand pages, written by various authorities on every possible aspect of anthropology, which the editor described as 'absolutely terrific' and could not 'think of any possible improvements'![88] (Me too.)

Yet another was the production of a slim book on *Marx and Marxism* as the flagship volume of a series of slim volumes aimed at introducing beginner students to the theories of key sociologists.[89] Though a massive topic, it did not take me more than a few months because I had spent decades thinking about it. Discussing it in a limited space, though, was anything but easy, especially since it involved coming to terms with my own intellectual history both as an academic and a political animal. But I knew what I wanted to say and did it in a few months.

I traced the three strands that had gone into the intellectual and political formation of Marx and Engels – German philosophical idealism, French revolutionary social and socialist theory and British political economy – and the ways in which these sets of ideas had given rise to a variety of political movements, greatly shaped by the very different histories and cultures of the countries in which they took root. At first, many had been only very small sects, mainly of intellectuals; later, major Communist movements, notably the pre-1914, very parliamentary German Social Democratic Party, and, in Russia (an agrarian society with a repressive political culture) the very different revolutionary Russian Bolshevik Party.

And when communist ideas took root in underdeveloped countries, the stamp of national history and culture, in agrarian countries which had recently been colonised by European imperialist powers (some, indeed, still colonies) produced outcomes which differed from anything in Europe itself. Most notable of these was China, the biggest country on earth, whose version of communism had little in common with either the Eastern European version (mainly the outcome of Soviet domination) or the Western European version, notably in France and Italy, where large Communist Parties were nevertheless safely contained by parliamentarism and prosperity.

And in the rest of the developed world communism was largely a movement of radical ideas, not one which threatened to seize power. In intellectual milieux, this was fertile ground for the proliferation of fashions in Marxism. In the nineteenth century, the most prominent versions had been evolutionist Marxism, which saw development of human society as an inevitable process (even revolution could be premature); and reductionist or materialist Marxism, which stressed the economy (in particular the mode of production) as the overriding determinant. Hence class conflict was the motor of human development. Functionalist Marxism, conversely, emphasised that everything in society fitted together, even institutions like the family; dialectical Marxism saw contradictions as between different social institutions, including contradictions in thought. Historical Marxism, which recognised the importance of social and cultural institutions that persist over long periods of time, differed from those forms of Marxism which emphasise the revolutionary power of action to transform society, or which emphasise that the ideas of thinking, active subjects give them the power to interpret and thereby change the world – that they are not determined by the objective social structure in which the subject lives. More modern versions of Marxism indeed have argued that what the nineteenth century dismissed as mere 'superstructure' is therefore crucial, including political institutions or the cultural apparatuses which shape and manufacture consent (such as religion or control of the mass media).

All of these ideas can be traced back to the original corpus of ideas with which Marx and Engels started out. But they have been immensely elaborated by successive generations of Marxists, especially once Marxism became a subject of academic study and exegesis in the academy. So we have experienced a succession of fashions in Marxism, some of which have only lasted a short – and, it seems, ever-diminishing – time, and often written in language so arcane that virtually no one except French intellectuals can understand them (certainly not Chinese peasants).

This is not to say that Marxism can mean anything you like, for it embodies more than a set of propositions that made sense to intellectuals. It also articulates and expresses an awareness among both educated and uneducated people that the world is highly unequal and unjust, as well as a rejection of that doom on the part of the underprivileged, for more than a century; and it has fuelled movements as varied as the West European parliamentary Communist Parties to the Maoists.

I found writing these books a relief from having to rely on colleagues who had only too often let one down, and was relieved to go back to the traditional lone-wolf style of work that anthropologists were more used to: not, it is true, fieldwork, but years of hard labour during which I totally rewrote my earlier book on the Third World, called *The Three Worlds*,[90] incorporating all that I had been reading in the meantime, and in particular my experience of Latin America. It became an academic best-seller on the University of Chicago's list.

Peace and War

It was well received outside academia too, so much so that I was immediately invited to go to a conference in Penang, Malaysia, hosted by an indigenous organisation dedicated to development and peace and funded by a remarkable local millionaire, S.M. Idris. I had acted as External Examiner at two universities in Malaysia before; now I could make contact with peace activists in the Third World countries. A few years later I went to another such conference. There were extremely interesting people there, mainly from southern Asia, like the man from Kerala who declared himself amazed to find himself on a platform sandwiched between two white men. Every year, they organised marches of intellectuals (teachers, medicos, etc.) across the state, using traditional styles of dance and drama to take to the villages messages relating to peace issues, such as the Bomb. Someone was interested in peace in the Third World at last.

The conference did not restrict itself to economic and political matters. On the cultural side, Garry Whannel, whose father Paddy I had known when he worked at the National Film Theatre in London, had become a specialist in the study of sport, and subsequently wrote a witty piece recalling how he had been trudging through a northern city in the rain when he heard the voice of a John Motson football commentary coming through a window. The northern city in question, however, was in Malaysia, not the UK.

Only rarely did going to conferences, wedged into gaps between other commitments, leave any time for tourism. But Richard Gott and I were able to do a bit of semi-academic tourism by visiting Malacca, now only a small town on an unimpressive river, but which had once been a crucial entrepot in the early spread of global capitalism, not only as between Europe and Asia but, as the graves in the churchyard showed, had involved Europeans from the Cape in South Africa – not Englishmen, but Dutchmen. And Saint Francis, whose name had graced my Liverpool school, had been buried there before his body was taken to Goa in India.

But on a second visit to Penang I was able to do something that was pure tourism, by visiting Bali – quite the most beautiful place I have ever seen. If you steered clear of the thousands of Australians who came for the surfing, like Kuta (tragically the scene of the terrorist bombing some years later), everything in a delectable town like Ubud, from the houses to the rice-fields, was a joy to the eye; it looked like a piece of heaven. I lay on my bed admiring the perfection of the bamboo ceiling and the spectacular view of a volcano and a lake.

But when I talked to the guide who took me round the island about the events of 1965, when the Indonesian military had massacred several hundred thousand supporters of the Communist Party in Bali alone, and some millions in the country as a whole, Bali sounded more like a Dantesque vision of hell. The CIA itself – which should have known, because it had a big hand in the process – described it as 'one of the worst mass murders of the twentieth century'. But as in the Rwandan genocide or the massacres in Pinochet's Chile, the 'West' made no protest even though this one was on the doorstep of people like the Australian Prime Minister, Harold Holt. They were after all only Communists, and the place hadn't any strategic or economic importance.

Several hundred had been killed in my guide's small town of a couple of thousand. He still woke up at night thinking about it, he said. And General Suharto, who had done all this, was still in power.

I did not experience any of this during my thoroughly enjoyable foray into tourism. A (male) anthropologist's wife and children, on the other hand, often suffer more than he does. When I went again to Hong Kong as External Examiner in 1988, I could at last afford to take Sheila with me under conditions that should have been optimal. Alas, stopping off in Sri Lanka on the way back to the UK, she picked up a stomach infection that is still with her – and incurable – sixteen years later.

A quite different peace initiative now emerged on the other side of the world when I was contacted by Mary Foster, a linguist from the Berkeley Anthropology Department, the wife of the Tzintzutzan anthropologist to whom I had written earlier.

She and others were setting up a group to encourage anthropologists both to study and work for peace. At the Vancouver meeting of the world organisation of anthropologists – The International Union of Anthropological and Ethnological Sciences – we were accepted as a Commission of that organisation and held our first meeting at Harrison Hot Springs in British Columbia, with mainly Americans but also the participation of a Soviet anthropologist and Silviu Brucan, a career diplomat from Romania who had been Romania's representative on the Comintern, then abandoned his Stalinism and became an academic. (Later, he was to be one of the crucial group who took the decision to have the Ceausescus shot.)

The least open-minded was also a career diplomat: an American ex-Ambassador (they retain that title even when retired) who reacted in a very hostile way when I suggested that the new plan to build a natural-gas pipeline from the USSR to Western Europe would help make the two economies more interdependent.

Two books came out of these meetings,[91] but I was disappointed when a notice inserted in the IUAES journal telling my colleagues about the new Peace Commission resulted in precisely zero responses. But there were enough, like Paul Doughty, who persevered and produced a journal devoted to peace issues.

When the Fosters then came to stay with us in London, UNESCO rang asking us to send a representative to Paris next day, so I was drafted to attend. Then we were invited to Moscow by the Academy of Sciences, where anthropologists from the USSR and from Hungary and Czechoslovakia produced very good papers. The same could not be said of the statutory politico who was foisted onto their team at the Peace Institute, who had reached the lofty heights of the Ambassadorship to the People's Republic of Benin, in West Africa (which went through a brief pro-Soviet period). He accused me of pro-Americanism, at which I protested that I had spent some of the best years of my life picketing US airbases in Britain, even though we were only too aware that British air defences were designed to cope with the threat not of US missiles but of Soviet ones programmed to wipe out London and other cities. This despicable creature then declared that he didn't care about the destruction of London – at which I stormed out. There followed the usually 'hard man/soft man' routine when one of their anthropologists was sent out to mollify me.

The next initiative was an invitation to the Commission to go to Peru. I went via Rio, not New York. I had to go all the way to Brazil to find out that according to Alba Guimarães (now once more Zaluar), the finest novelist since Dostoevsky was an Albanian called Ismail Kadaré. I then read everything I could find by him. Today, as I write, he has been awarded the first Man Booker International Prize.

Getting to Lima involved a stop at Santa Cruz, the capital of the lowlands of Bolivia where Guevara had fought his last, tragic battle. Richard Gott had been teaching in Santiago, Chile, nearby, but since in the Allende period the University was constantly shut down by student strikes, he had had time to write a brilliant book on the 'Land without Evil' – Paraguay – a country virtually ignored today but which old maps show as once the largest country by far in South America. Ancient myths, from time to time, had led Indians to set out en masse for the far-distant coast in the east, where they believed liberators would arrive who would usher in an epoch when evil would be unknown. Conversely, the Spaniards and Portuguese had their own myths, a materialist one about the land of gold, the realm of El Dorado in the interior, which took them in the opposite direction. The Jesuits, as ever, pursued different, religious ends by creating communities under their rigorous control, called *reducciones*, which, as the film *The Mission* dramatically showed, were finally wiped out by slave-traders.

But Richard suddenly found himself catapulted into modern, not early colonial history, when he witnessed the bringing in of Guevara's body (duly attended by CIA personnel).

La Paz, Peru's capital, is the highest in the world. The moment I landed, my head started aching and I felt sick, but now I knew exactly what it was: the *soroche*, the mountain sickness. I also knew what to do about it, which was to go to sleep immediately for twenty-four hours. It worked.

I have already described, in *The Three Worlds* (p. xi), what happened next, which was so dramatic that I do not apologise for recounting it again:

> A peasant in a poncho stopped me in the street, begging for money. He didn't use words, because he couldn't. He simply pointed to his mouth, from which strangled sounds issued. The inside was filled with a swollen yellow thing. It was his tongue. In horror, I recoiled, shoving a note into his hand, and fled. Then I turned back, racked with guilt, and stuffed more money into his hand, for antibiotics, than he could have earned in a month.

It was little surprise that Peruvian anthropologists were concerned about peace, for guerrilla struggle was still going on. The 'Shining Path' Maoist guerrillas had been waging a bloody war in the mountains for years, their prime targets being officials such as judges and local government workers. (Information about these killings was generally tucked away on the back pages of the Lima newspapers, under 'Police News'.) This very violent civil war which, some say, brought two-thirds of the country under their control, went on for years until 'Chairman' Abigael Guzmán, the Maoist leader, was finally captured.

Peruvian politics, though, still continued on its ever dramatic, unpredictable way when Alberto Fujimori, born in Lima of Japanese parentage, beat the world-famous author Mario Vargas Llosa in the presidential elections, and remained President, legally and illegally, for over a decade. His first economic innovation was to privatise hundreds of state enterprises and give free rein to foreign-owned enterprises to take over mining industries, which made him popular with the US. After a noisy public divorce from his wife, whom he stripped of the title of 'First Lady', Congress turned against him, not because of this marital scandal but for his glaring corruption, at which point he staged an 'auto-coup', and dissolved his own Congress. But he remained popular with an electorate which had no time for the corrupt ruling families and their political parties which had always ruled Peru, and which made ordinary people's lives a misery and reduced the country's politics to chaos, so that he was able to win the Presidency once more by spectacularly defeating yet another Peruvian with a worldwide reputation: the ex-Secretary of the UN, Pérez de Cuéllar.

His victory over the Shining Path had not signified the end of social revolution, though, for in 1996 a second revolutionary movement, named after Túpac Amaru, the Inca who had led the revolt against the Spaniards, seized the residence of the Japanese Ambassador in Lima, taking four hundred diplomats, government officials and other dignitaries as hostages. After a four-month standoff, the residence was stormed, with Fujimori standing among the bodies of the dead insurgents with a gun in his hand.

In 2000, though, he was finally charged with appropriating two billion dollars, and fled the country to Japan. Three years later, at the behest of the Peruvian government, which had declared him 'morally unfit' to govern, Interpol issued an international arrest order against him on charges of murder, kidnapping and crimes against humanity. But as late as 2005 he still had supporters who announced that they were going to try to revive his political fortunes by marketing a new drink 'Fuji-Cola'; and in November of that year returned to South America, to Chile, from whence he announced his intention to return to Peru. He was then arrested and extradition to Peru applied for.

I had visited the fringes of the Amazon from Ecuador, but had never been able to see any of the major confluences of the river, so when the conference finished I asked Ernesto Yepes, a former Manchester postgraduate who had worked down there, what it was like. '*Es un encanto*' ('It's a dream'), he replied, at which I decided to go there immediately. But, he added, it would continue to be an *encanto* only for a week or two; then it would become really boring. I decided to see this contradiction for myself, so flew down to Iquitos, the capital of Peru's piece of Amazonia, which still had the beautiful wrought-ironwork house inhabited by the legendary Fitzgerald, about whom Werner Herzog had made the astounding film, *Fitzcarraldo* (as the locals pronounced 'Fitzgerald'). He had made a fortune ruthlessly forcing Indians to bring in wild rubber from the jungle, using some of the profits to build the Opera House at Manaos, to which he brought Caruso all the way from Europe for the opening performance.

Today, Iquitos contained the largest and sleaziest slum I had ever seen, so I immediately headed for what I had come for: a tourist camp in the jungle. It did, indeed, prove to be an *encanto*. An Indian guide showed me the medicinal uses of dozens of plants. You had to avoid the *beso del novio* ('lover's kiss'), though, because it produced what Oscar Wilde had described as 'bee-stung lips'. He also instructed me in how to use a blowpipe to fire the cotton-tipped darts which he sharpened on a *piranha* tooth which he wore round his neck. I did quite well at this.

Apart from the sound of dry leaves falling on the roofs, during the day there was total silence. Night-time was different. We headed up-river in a canoe, under an overhead magic carpet of stars, but when we switched off the outboard, the engine noise was replaced by the *concierto nocturno* of millions of insects and animals in the surrounding jungle.

* * * * *

I had done much of the work on *The Three Worlds* in New York, where Stanley Diamond had invited me to teach at the New School of Social Research, at a wonderful location on Fifth Avenue. The New School, which had grown out of a great tradition of providing evening education for the less privileged, had also sheltered eminent refugees like Horkheimer and Adorno from the Frankfurt School, and had been a fitting home, later, for Lévi-Strauss.

It was just the place for Stanley, who, like Eric Wolf, been a veteran of the Second World War and a founder member of the Mundial Upheaval Society at Columbia. He had been a veteran, though, not of the US Army but of the British Army, for he had been so keen to fight fascism that (America being neutral), he had volunteered to join the British West African colonial army, and from there served in North Africa, acquiring along the way a strong distaste for British imperialism, but also an experience and appreciation of British and European culture and institutions. At Columbia, he became research assistant to Leslie White.

Stanley's fieldwork, on the Jos Plateau in Nigeria, was not wonderful: significantly, one of his best articles was about the difficulties he had experienced in trying to penetrate that culture. Rather, he was a thinker, indeed a guru, and a poet as well as an anthropologist, who once cornered me at prestigious Bard College of up the Hudson, for a couple of hours while he read his latest, compelling verse. His last appointment at the New School was as Poet-in-Residence.

His sheer charisma, and his imaginative anthropology, though, attracted excellent students and won the department – which only had a small teaching faculty – the highest rating in the academic exercise which evaluated the standing of the dozens of departments in the Greater New York area (including Columbia and CUNY Graduate Center). It also enabled him to attract the support to run a journal of world-class standing, *Dialectical Anthropology*.

Living in Manhattan again, in Chelsea, we were close enough to our old stamping ground in the Village for me to be hailed from across the street by former students. We felt that we had come home.

This time, I ventured on something midway between fieldwork proper and library study, exploring such icons of US culture as the World Trade Center and the Brooklyn Bridge, and got special permission to visit the Statue of Liberty, which was being refurbished at the time. I also followed up an interest sparked off by a visit to the original Disneyland, at Anaheim in California, and collected as much material as I could in the New York Public Library on the rise of the Disney empire. When I got home, I incorporated this material and the material on the Statue in my next book, *Knowledges*.

During this time I met up once more with Archie Singham, a Tamil born in Burma, whom I had known when he was a senior political scientist researching at Manchester. Archie still did his university teaching, but also organised a network linking left-of-centre Third World groupings at the United Nations, such as the Cubans.

I vividly recalled, later, standing at Brooklyn Heights looking across at the World Trade Center, when in a prescient moment he suddenly asked, 'What are those buildings saying, Peter? Don't they mean "Two fingers to you, the rest of the world?"' – exactly the interpretation that led to the twin towers being singled out for destruction in the most ominous terrorist outrage since the assassination of Archduke Franz Ferdinand.

* * * * *

Back home, out of the blue, my work was interrupted when I was asked to a conference in Berlin, just at the time when the *perestroika* and *glasnost* introduced into the USSR by Gorbachev had sparked off not only the collapse of the USSR, but also of the entire Soviet bloc – most dramatically when massive street demonstrations broke out in the most rigidly Stalinist country of all, East Germany. This gave me the opportunity to cross the divided city to meet up, after so long, with Fred Rose, in exile from Australia but now a distinguished Professor of Anthropology at Humboldt University in East Berlin, where he published his classic study of Groote Eylandt kinship.

Something seemed awry in the Rose household. Indeed, I could hardly have arrived at a more disastrous moment, not because of the political crisis but because the Roses told me that their son, who had studied nuclear physics in Moscow, had just committed suicide – despite which they were eminently hospitable. Another exiled couple, Len and Mary-Lou Goldstein, American victims of McCarthy and equally strongly attached to the regime, then invited me to their home outside Berlin.

Len had fought at Iwo Jima, so was perfectly prepared to take on the East German bureaucracy. In those days, visitors had to notify the authorities that they had brought a certain amount of US dollars with them. The duration of your permitted stay was, as is normal, stamped in your passport, but so was a note of how many dollars you had brought. I had twice the necessary amount, but wanted to stay a bit longer, so Len and I went to the local police station to get my visa extended. We had not reckoned, however, with East German bureaucracy. I would have to go back to Friedrichstrasse station, where I had entered, and do it all over again. Len protested; the uniformed policewoman and he then got into an argument which culminated with Len shouting at her that he had been a member of the Communist Party when she was in diapers – at which she stood up, screamed '*Raus!*', and threw us out. Once we had conformed with the dollar protocol, however, and re-registered, bureaucracy was satisfied.

This enabled me to stay at the famous *Elephant* hotel at Weimar (whose guests had ranged from Mozart to Hitler), where I was utterly entranced with Goethe's Gartenhaus, which induced me to read his astounding novel, *Elective Affinities*. I also visited the extraordinary legacy of Frederick the Great at Potsdam and attended a performance of *Parsifal* at Dresden with an audience made up of comfortable apparatchiks who regaled themselves and what Alexander McCall Smith would have described as their 'traditionally built' wives with champagne in the interval, much in the style of the pre-War bourgeoisie.

I was determined, however, to see something infinitely less pleasant – the concentration camp at Buchenwald. It is only a bus ride away from Weimar, with highly visible huge marshalling yards for the trains which had once brought nearly a quarter of a million victims, of whom 43,000 were killed. (In 1945, people were asked to believe that no one in Weimar had been aware of this massive camp or what it had been used for.) The site, the size of several football pitches, had since been levelled, apart from the cells in which Ernst

Thaelmann, leader of the Communist Party when the Nazis had come to power, plus the Chairman of the Social Democrats in the Reichstag, and prominent churchmen, including Catholics, had been imprisoned. The only other buildings still standing were the 'laboratories' in which medical experiments had been performed on prisoners, the gas-chambers, and the ovens in which tens of thousands of corpses had been incinerated, supplied by corporations whose name-plates were still on the ovens.

*****

Over the next few years, I worked steadily at my book which was to eventuate in 1997 as *Knowledges*.[92] As I was doing it, I was swept up in the information revolution, so like everyone else had to master the art of word-processing, beginning with second-hand Apple Macs; then went on to Alan Sugar's little Amstrad; then graduated to a hard disc; and ended up with this nice laptop. But in those days, there was nobody to help you, if like me you weren't in a university any longer, and teaching oneself wasn't easy.

I had been used to publishing best-sellers, and fully expected that this book too would be a considerable success, because, in my view, it was the best thing I had done, ranging as it did from a comparison of Australian Aboriginal ways of classifying plants and animals as compared with Western biology; how the Polynesians had navigated the vast stretches of the Pacific; religion in Africa; the variety of ways humans had tried to understand and cope with sickness; and culminating with my Statue of Liberty and Disneyland material from an industrial, urban society – all within a theoretical framework of theoretical discussion of culture, counter-culture and sub-culture.

It did get a few favourable reviews, but at the end of the day fell into the category that Cedric Belfrage – more used to swimming against the tide because he had run the left-wing *Guardian* newspaper in New York in the 1930s – used to describe his own writings: that they had all been 'worst-sellers'.

New Life and the Third Age

We had virtually given up hope that we would ever have any grandchildren. But women these days are having babies later in life. Suddenly, within three years, we had three; now there were other things more important in life than books, academia and world development. Rex, the first child, was premature, so put us through agonies of worry which were soon resolved at the wonderful NHS hospital at Chelsea and Westminster. Within weeks, our neighbour was describing him as 'the beauteous Rex', and once he got going such was his lust for life that he slipped out of the front garden gates on his own, across the main road, en route to the swings in the park, trailing behind him not clouds of glory but a roll of lavatory paper, like the puppy in the Andrex ad. The woman who rescued him was upbraided by a passing motorist for being a careless mother.

The second grandchild, Holly, through a twist of fate, came to live with us for ten blissful months. Writing now had to be interspersed with playing 'Fish'. Holly would imperiously select one of my fingers, wrap her own little hand round it, and haul me off to the 'jun-gell' at the top of the garden. And she gave me a new vision of a child's hopefulness. When Princess Diana was killed, she assured me that it would be alright, Grandpa, because the Prince would come along and give her a magic kiss to make her better.

I worked from home now, but, without the demands of the academy, had more time to take up other opportunities. I had always refused any invitation to South Africa, but after Mandela was released I accepted an invitation to a small university, Rhodes, in Grahamstown in the Eastern Cape, where the distinguished anthropologists, Radcliffe-Brown and Monica Hunter, had pioneered anthropology in the 1930s.

Drake had described Cape Town as 'the fairest cape we saw in the whole circumference of the earth'. Nature was indeed a delight: this tiny strip of land supported 2,600 different kinds of flowering plants, more than the whole of the UK.

What man has created was more equivocal. Driving in from the airport, we were shocked at the miles of appalling shanty towns on all sides. White Cape Town, on the other hand, was different. The omnipresent black servants apart, what with the white café society we saw on the glorious beaches, the world-standard production of *Cabaret* we watched at the Nico Malan theatre and the IMAX show, we might well have been in California.

But the city is also a palimpsest of colonial and imperial history. To the Portuguese, in a hurry to get their hands on the spices of Asia, it was little more than a watering-stop, the turning point of Africa they had sought for so long. Their Dutch successors, though, came to stay. In the great castle they built some of the culture of the Dutch, was preserved including one of the most elegant pieces of furniture in the world – the dining-table of the officials of the Dutch East India Company, who organised the planting of a garden to grow vegetables needed for the long onwards voyage to Asia.

To supply the labour, the Dutch brought in slaves from Madagascar, India, Malaya, Ceylon and Indonesia, many of them Muslims, whose descendants in the Malay Quarter (Bo-Kaap) fiercely preserve their Islamic culture, including its distinctive, spicy cuisine. (Some claim that the seven *kramat* graves of Muslim holy men surrounding the city form a protective circle round it.) The graves which I had seen in Macassar, in Malaysia, were of Dutchmen who had come there from the Cape; here, there was still a place called by the same name, 'Macassar', only a few miles from the trendy restaurants of Sea Point.

Long eclipsed by the spectacular Kirstenbosch Gardens, the Company's Garden was a pleasant open-air café area where the young South African national football team were now able to stroll. Kirstenbosch itself still retained one ominous early feature of the Dutch settlement – the hedge planted to keep out the natives-while the museum still displayed African culture as a part of the country's natural fauna and flora. Pensioners living off British state pensions found the city a lovely place in which to spend their declining years; more affluent immigrants like Mark Thatcher lived in splendid gated mansions around Constantia from whence they could plot the overthrow of oil-rich African States, defended by armed patrols and fierce dogs. And only an hour away was the exquisite monument to a culture which had aimed at replacing African barbarism altogether – Stellenbosch, the centre of Afrikaner intellectual life.

But there were new currents now in a liberated South Africa. Harold Wolpe's dramatic escape from Johannesburg's Marshall Street jail had been vividly recorded by his wife, Anne-Marie. Harold had become well known to us in the UK because, like Ruth First, he had spent his exile teaching sociology there. Now, back in South Africa, he had been working for two years to transform the University of the Western Cape, which had been a second-class institution for blacks, into a major national university. When he died two years later, I was sure it was because of being over-worked. In the kaleidoscope of South African society, it was inevitable that he should run across the police colonel who had masterminded the manhunt for his arrest, now running an upmarket tourist cafe.

Grahamstown, where we were going, turned out to be a very different kind of town and academic institution. To us, socially, it was a time warp which took us back to Liverpool in the 1930s: the only department store still sent invoices and cash in containers which travelled in pneumatic tubes along wires and brought back the change. But Liverpool did not have a large black population like Grahamstown, where the Church of England Cathedral signified that the town had been founded as a pillar of white settlerdom, not of Boer frontiersmen but of stout British orthodoxy. Still divided in two across the middle of the town, it was overlooked by a memorial centre recording the town's history, that is, the history of white settlement.

The history of the large black population, though, went unrecognised, even the decades of successive Xhosa wars of resistance to the British, except for a memorial in the cathedral which described one of these wars as an act of 'treachery'. Even the war of 1819, when a Xhosa chief, Makana, very nearly took Grahamstown from the British. He then became one of the first political prisoners on Robben Island, where he died, in a line of honour that was to continue until Nelson Mandela. The hill overlooking the town, Makana's Kop, still bore his name. The students were still mainly whites, though times were changing: a few were from neighbouring African countries, and one of my postgraduates was the first black mayor.

When I had studied African history, long before I encountered the Cargo cults of Melanesia, I had read about the remarkable millenarian movement of 1856/7 when the Xhosa had killed off most of their cattle – the mainstay of their economy – as ancient beliefs about the return of the ancestors had become intermixed with newer Christian ideas about the Apocalypse. Inspired by a young girl, Nongqawuse, who prophesied that the ancestors would return very soon, the Xhosa, like the Melanesians, now ceased cultivating their gardens because the return of the ancestors would usher in a time of plenty for all. That time seemed to have come with the Crimean War. When the Xhosa heard that one of the British generals who had been victorious over them in Africa had died at the hands of the Russians, people flocked to the coastal hills, looking seawards for the arrival of the ancestors and their new brothers, the Russians. Tens of thousands starved to death.

I had hoped to meet J.B. Peires, a South African who taught at Grahamstown and had written a brilliant study of the cattle killing, and had even used the next words from the Biblical quotation which I had drawn upon as the title of my book, *The Trumpet Shall Sound*, which were: 'And the Dead will Arise', as the title of his own book.[93] But he was no longer in Grahamstown; he was now an ANC MP. It was disappointing not to meet him, but good to know that he was part of the new South Africa.

When I asked our uneducated African servant what she knew about Nongqawuse, she knew nothing, and when I showed her old photographs in Peires' book, she concluded that the people must be Zulu. When I discussed Africans outside South Africa with them, I found that they had no knowledge at all of Bantu other than themselves and the Zulu. And they were dreading the time when our hosts, the Dowses, would leave Grahamstown, and leave them to unemployment and dire poverty.

I had long realised why slave owners had fought so hard to keep what they had got when I had a superb dinner in the elegant classicism of the Faculty Club of the University of North Carolina at Chapel Hill, and, again, a wonderful lunch served by black women in eighteenth-century mobcaps on Robert E. Lee's plantation in Virginia. And at Monticello, Jefferson, an undoubted child of the Enlightenment had designed his own splendid clock at the front of the house. It faced inwards, however, because it was for the plantation-owner's use, not that of the slaves outside; they simply worked until told to stop.

At Graaf Reinet, in the Eastern Cape, we were comfortably housed in the former slave quarters of a Dutch administrative building, now transformed into an elegant hotel. The whole area was saturated with the history of the black-white encounter, and the legacy of English-Boer relations too. I had not been surprised when, at the top of Table Mountain, I met with a resounding silence when I pointed out Robben Island to other visitors. Nor did I ever find anyone who had voted for the Nationalists.

But Graaf Reinet had a much more unambiguously Afrikaner cultural legacy than Cape Town: in 1789, inspired by French revolutionary ideals of liberty, equality and fraternity, it declared itself independent, together with another small Afrikaner town, Swellendam. Liberty, equality and fraternity, however, were to be for whites only.

In Cradock, Olive Schreiner's town, we began to realise that we were encountering one trivial pinprick after another – would we please go back in the street and park our car nose-in to the kerb, not parallel (when there wasn't another car in sight); after waiting for an hour an a half for the table we'd booked at their request, it had been given to someone else, and so on. Eventually, the guide at the Graaf Reinet museum was honest enough to explain what underlay all this – when he found we came from England he wittily remarked that this was a 'good idea' (i.e. to leave that country).

Every little township had its story of violent clashes between the Xhosa and the whites. Down on the coast, at Boesmansriviermond, there had not been a live Bushman for very many generations. Instead, the English had created the little holiday resort of Port Alfred. Nearby was the site of a *padrão*, one of the stone pillars erected by Vasco da Gama to mark his landfalls on the epic voyage when the Portuguese finally rounded the Cape, and proceeded immediately to bring European civilisation to Asia, attacking the cities of Gujerat with 'more devastating destruction than had ever been done before, or ever dreamt of, destroying every place so that there was no memory left of them, and [butchering] everyone [they] captured'.[94]

Down in the black township at Grahamstown was other historical evidence, that of the final victory of the successors to both the Portuguese and the Dutch: the British. In a sordid graveyard covered with broken bottles were the graves of sons of Mzilikazi, the Matabele ruler who had fought the British Army. His sons had then been exiled to Grahamstown to prevent any moves to have them installed as potential successors.

Constitutionally, apartheid might have ended, but the town was still divided into two. During the township revolts sparked off by the uprising in Soweto, the main highway between Grahamstown and the next big towns still ran through the black township. But when white motorists had been attacked by stone-throwing Africans, a very expensive new road had been built to circumvent this inconvenience – at a cost which could have financed a lot of new housing. To visit the black township, so desperate was the unemployment, the poverty and the ravages of AIDS, that we had to be escorted by intermediaries.

The liberal ethos of the university, which had been pioneering and open-minded enough to welcome Radcliffe-Brown and Monica Hunter, was familiar. But there was a second school of anthropology in South Africa completely unknown to us in the UK – Afrikaner *volkekunde*.

Back in Australia, our department had been next door to the South African Press Office. When they heard we were anthropologists, they gave us their ethnological publications, which carefully documented every battle that had ever been fought in that part of the world, over centuries, not just between whites and blacks but between different groups of Nguni, Sotho, Bushmen, Hottentots, and so on, and the history of the migrations that had brought these peoples there and into one conflict after another. The conclusion drawn from all this was that it had been *nobody's* country for long. Successive incomers might have been dominant for a while, but ultimately one set of immigrants, of superior culture and social organisation – the whites – had come out on top.

Quite sophisticated theoretical concepts, going back as far as Fichte (through to Verwoerd!) were developed to explain it all: the primordial unit of society was a racial one, the *ethnos*, but the highest *ethnos* of all, 'divinely established', was that of the whites.[95]

During my time in Grahamstown *volkekunde* was still the leading school in Pretoria, under P.J. Coertze, who then handed on the torch to his son. It was also taught in other Afrikaner universities such as Potchefstroom and the Orange Free State universities. Today, mercifully, this school is fading fast.

Fort Hare, in the Ciskei, near us, originally established by missionaries in 1916, had been the only higher education institution in southern Africa which accepted Africans as students: Nelson Mandela, Robert Mugabe, Oliver Tambo, Kenneth Kaunda and many other future leaders of the liberation struggle had been lucky to win a place there, and were spared from exposure to this kind of racist ideology.

Now it was a university, and the mining association of the Rand had given it a splendid new art museum in compensation for the decades in which they had exploited the black miners. But in the café of the little capital town of Alice, we were the only people who ordered anything other than slices of bread, which was all that the African customers could afford, and outside the town was the grim sight of Keiskammahoek, where Monica Wilson had done a pioneer anthropological study of the hundreds of shanties on the parched open veldt where Africans had been forced to make their homes when their land had been seized by whites.

At Johannesburg, we stayed in the rich white suburbs of Sandton where our former neighbour from Hackney was having a luxurious new mansion built, complete with swimming pool. The restaurants and mansions were serviced by a labour force which had to travel twenty-five miles in to their work from the parallel city of Soweto, deliberately built well away from the white city: the houses formerly inhabited by Desmond Tutu and Nelson Mandela were eclipsed by the splendour of 'Winnie's Castle'. The Orlando football stadium had been the scene of a huge farewell for Joe Slovo when he was killed; his new wife's reminiscences included mentioning his liking for women and wearing red socks!

* * * * *

Back home, we were immediately plunged into a very different form of class struggle. I had spent my life fighting capitalism. Now I found that I should have been fighting feudalism, because my neighbour, a Tory MP who traced his ancestry back to the Conquest, owned the freehold of our house, and suddenly brought to an end fifteen happy years in our home. In Manchester, I had paid the freeholder, the Duke of Devonshire, £5 per annum, which he often didn't bother to collect. In Hackney, I was asked to pay seventy-three times as much.

Then, out of the blue, I received a letter saying that the ground rent would be increased, by our Tory MP neighbour, from £365 per annum to £6000 – which I obviously couldn't pay. We scarcely suffered the fate of the Irish peasants whose hovels were 'tumbled' about their ears during the Famine. Though there had been successive reforms of leasehold legislation, we fell into one of the very small remaining categories of leaseholder who had no protection whatsoever under the law. The obverse of the coin was that property values had rocketed under Thatcher, so we were lucky enough to make enough money out of the forced sale of our home to buy a flat very near to our daughters and grandchildren on the other side of London.

We had suddenly entered the Third Age when Sheila broke her femur during a routine visit to Saint Bartholomew's Hospital. Typically not wanting to bother the nurses, she got herself home in a taxi. I now had to take her meals up and down fifty-seven stairs.

When she recovered, an entirely unexpected visit to the US now came about from a visit to Brighton Pavilion. A 25-ton crane had crashed into our car a week or so earlier, and I was driving a new one. I parked outside the Pavilion and ruefully acknowledged to two people waiting for the building to open that I'd done better jobs of parking in my time, but wasn't used to this car. We got talking. They were Americans. Within a quarter of an hour, we had arranged to do a holiday exchange of apartments: theirs in Pentagon City, Washington, DC, ours in London. In the event, we ended up thirty miles away in suburban Virginia. Washington being the centre of Government, not an industrial city, we were not surprised to find that a lot of our new neighbours worked for various branches of Government, and were less than overjoyed to discover that these included the CIA and the plethora of military bases in Virginia (as everywhere else in the States). Indeed, our very hostess was married to a Colonel in the Rangers who had served three tours in Vietnam.

But this was America, and there are always progressive surprises. He had been all gung ho on his first tour, and had won two Purple Hearts. By the second, he was less convinced. By the third, he was against the war and his wife was actively campaigning in the Mobilisation movement against it.

Sheila was able, eventually, to undertake other long-haul journeys again: the first direct tourist flight from London to Samarkand in Uzbekistan, and filling in the blanks on our map of the US with a trip down the Rockies, even an adventure into the Southern States to Savannah and Charleston. We had seen Harper's Ferry, where the Civil War had started; now we saw Fort Sumter, the flash point for the Civil War in the South, and also found Catfish Row, where Porgy and Bess had lived. And in Florida, we watched the space shuttle take off at Cape Kennedy. It seemed to have finished as the rocket, six miles away, disappeared into the skies, until, four minutes later, the ground shook as the shock waves from the blast-off reached us. To the American spectators, it was all entertainment and achievement; to us, an ominous glimpse of the future.

In our very last hour, Sheila started vomiting. I was just able to get her back to the safe hands of the NHS for a gall-bladder operation. Then, in addition, her eyesight began to disappear first in one eye, then – which only happens to two per cent of the population – she lost most of her sight in the other.

So now, in our late seventies, it seemed high time to visit the friends in Australia Sheila hadn't seen for forty-five years – though, regretfully, we didn't get to see the Aborigines on Groote Eylandt, where the spirit which became our daughter, Deborah, had entered Sheila's womb.

We did an epic journey, of seventeen flights, to Disneyland and the Getty Museum in LA; to Pearl Harbor, where I stood on the deck of the USS *Missouri* where the Japanese surrender had taken place (and was taken out of mothballs to launch missiles in the Gulf during the Kuwait War); to Fiji; and then the incredible beauty of New Zealand; before seeing our friends and relatives in Sydney, in Canberra, Melbourne and Tasmania.

One of my great intellectual heroes is Robert Hughes, art critic for *Time* magazine for decades, and author of *The Shock of the New*, who has been described as 'possibly the best art critic writing today'. He is also the author of a superb social history of Barcelona, and a book of witty reflections on fishing, *A Jerk on the End of a Line* – written, he says, by a 'mediocre fisherman' who is just another 'jerk on the end of a line'.

Tasmania seemed to us an underpopulated oasis of peace. But Hughes' definitive history of Britain's penal colonies in Australia, *The Fatal Shore*,[96] shows that Tasmania had entered modern history as anything but. In the nineteenth century, it had been the scene of the appalling attempt to exterminate the Tasmanian Aborigines, when a 'Black Line' of troops had swept the island in what Hughes describes as 'an immense pheasant drive', to wipe out every Aborigine they met. They were singularly ineffective, though, because they only captured one man and a boy. But, as everybody knows, the Tasmanian Aborigines were finally exterminated when the last full-blood, a woman called Trucanini, died. Terrified of an indigenous evil spirit, Rowra, her nominal Christianity and her Christian burial did not prevent her body from falling into the hands of the white scientific surgeons – she was still dug up. But what everybody knows is not always correct, for the number of Tasmanians who identified themselves in the census as 'Aborigines' grew from 2,700 in 1981 to 16,000 in 2001, and some have even made successful claims for the restitution of their ancestral sacred burial sites.

Hughes' book took us to Port Arthur, the grim site of the brutalities inflicted not on Aborigines but upon the nearly thirteen thousand white convicts, the boys at Point Puer as well as the grown men – who were constantly subjected to sometimes hundreds of lashes from the cat o' nine tails, which reduced a man's back to the condition of 'Bullock's Liver'. The entrance we passed to get into this hellhole was Eaglehawk Neck, only one hundred yards wide, had once been guarded by a row of tethered dogs and a line of oil lamps, plus a chain of elaborate semaphore signals which could flash a warning of any escape from Port Arthur to Eaglehawk Neck in one minute flat.

After returning from this odyssey, and having spent so many years in the Third World, I began to think of putting into practice what I had always thought of doing – spending our old age less strenuously, visiting countries nearby like France, Italy and Spain, with occasional forays further afield to examine or lecture in Scandinavia. Helsinki proved to have a city-centre so quintessentially Russian, with all the apparatus of a repressive autocracy (the cathedral, the University, the police headquarters and the Army headquarters) all round the main square, that it was appropriately used in Warren Beatty's film, *Reds*, as St Petersburg. I paid homage to Sibelius' grave in the National Cemetery, and found that that what we had called the Russo-Finnish War, followed by the Second World War, were, in

Finland, simply the First and Second Russian Wars (the latter on the Nazi side).

And we got to know our own country very well from travelling all over it at four miles an hour in our ancient narrow boat. After twenty-seven years I was finding the maintenance work too arduous. But we continued to see a lot more of the changing cities, and the country too, not just its ancient villages but such wonderful modern innovations as Tim Smit's Eden Project – a demonstration that with more than a little genius it is still possible to drive through an enterprise which attracts like-minded creative spirits to convert a disused china-clay pit full of water into a place of wonder; and, organisationally, to persuade planners and bankers, from the local level to Europe, to back such a project.[97]

The Millennium Revisited

Since first publishing my book on Cargo cults in 1957, I had had nothing to do with New Guinea except to protest publicly when I found that this new country was still excluding anthropologists they regarded as Reds – in this case not me, but Daniel Tumarkin, the leading Soviet authority on Mikloukho-Maclay. (Finally, in the 1970s, he was given a week, on two occasions.[98])

I myself was in the ironic position of being seen as an 'authority' on Cargo cults, despite never having been to Melanesia and unable even to cope with the flood of publications on the cults published in the forty years since I had written my *Trumpet* book. Then Christin Kocher Schmid, a Swiss anthropologist with fifteen years' experience in the field, gave me the opportunity to catch up by asking me to write an introduction to a collection of nine short essays by different writers on New Guinea Cargo cults. I was particularly delighted that this collection was published in New Guinea.[99] I was then asked to tackle something much wider, for an international conference[100] – to appraise the much larger literature on Cargo cults which had appeared in the half-century since my original study had appeared.

The anthropology I had been taught had been a functionalist anthropology, which treated the peoples of Melanesia as 'structures', entities separated from each other by enormous mountains and swamps, and by the ocean, which had given rise not just to hundreds of different languages but to a large number of whole language-families.

Relations with neighbours were largely those of warfare (which stopped after a few casualties) and trade – not just utilitarian trade but also the exchange of objects of ritual value: ceremonial stone-axes traded for hundreds of miles from the Highlands, or the shell necklaces and armbands which the Trobriand Islanders exchanged on their famous Kula voyages.

The kind of anthropology which had been developed in the US, on the other hand, focussed on culture as the central binding force of society. Robert Redfield then made a further distinction between the Great cultural traditions – Hinduism, Christianity, Islam, Buddhism – and the Little traditions. British anthropology seemed to be concerned with neither, but with 'Tiny' traditions – discrete entities, 'tribes', the smaller being 'stateless' societies (island societies seemed to be the ideal type); the larger, state societies. There was no mention of modern imperialism, or of the rivalry between different colonialisms which had swallowed up not only the tribes but even sizeable states.

There were, in fact, common cultural sharings not just across New Guinea but across the entirety of Melanesia – primordial myths of origin, myths which explained why the world is as it is, and myths which foretold how the world would develop in the future – notably that not only would the world come to an end but that this could happen in the near future; a belief we label 'millenarism', though in Melanesian thought the 'millennium' was not, of course, one thousand years.

Traditional thinking, the anthropologist Ton Otto has argued, placed a higher value on knowledge, not – as Western economics has emphasised – on productive labour as the source of value,[101] while the purpose of producing wealth was to convert it into social status by distributing it to others. Yet in modern times, blacks did all the work, while white men, who did none, were still somehow able to collect goods from ships and planes because they had special pieces of paper – invoices, receipts, bills of lading – inscribed with mysterious symbols, which were part of the knowledge contained in the white man's most important book, the Bible. The most secret part of the Bible, however, was not available to blacks because it had never been translated into indigenous languages (most of the Bible has still not been.)

At the time when I first wrote about Cargo cults I had had to rely on scraps of information, mainly written by people hostile to the cult movements: missionaries, colonial administrators, even white settlers. Now I could draw on half a dozen studies by professional anthropologists, some of whom, like Andrew Lattas, had worked for a decade in the field, on and off.[102]

In the 1950s, there had been three different kinds of religion: traditional belief-systems; Christian teachings (of different kinds) in foreign, white-run missions and the Cargo cults.

But, following independence, newer kinds of cult had emerged which borrowed freely from all of these, resulting in a syncretic mix of doctrines which differed from village to village, and in differing modes of organisation too.

In the established foreign missions (mainly Catholic, Lutheran and low-church Protestant), leadership still came mostly from Europeans. But in newer cult movements and sects, missionaries now came from a variety of other foreign countries, including Pacific islands such as Fiji or Samoa. Some of the missionaries from the US were also black, and many were fundamentalist.

The world outside, by now, knew about the existence of Cargo cults, partly from my book, and from the play by David Lan – a good anthropologist (and now Director of the Young Vic theatre) – *Sergeant Ola and his Followers*. The highly educated audience at London's Royal Court Theatre, however, found the sight of people trying to get through to the ancestors on radio sets made of lianas to ask when the world would come to an end just too hilarious. Another Cargo play, *Jamais Vu*, about the 'Duke of Edinburgh' cult on Tanna (New Hebrides), was given the 'Best Comedy of the Year' award by the *Evening Standard*.

Members of these cults did not find them so funny – or all that different in kind from Christian notions. As early as 1960, Cargo cultists had become sensitive to foreigners who saw their beliefs as just so much 'superstition', and had worked out sophisticated ways of dealing with whites whom they suspected of disrespect for Cargo ideas. When a young David Attenborough asked followers of the John Frum cult on Tanna why they went on believing that their Messiah, John Frum, would return – even though he had been dead for twenty years – these illiterate villagers came out with a logical and theological response which was to become standard: 'Sam looked at me for several seconds before replying. "If you can wait for two thousand years for Jesus Christ to come", he said, "I can wait more than nineteen years for John Frum"'.

Paul Gauguin, a famous visitor to the South Pacific, on one of his canvases, asked three questions which not only underlie anthropology but are the key questions of human life too: '*Qui sommes-nous?*', '*D'où venons-nous?*', '*Où allons-nous?*'. ('Who are we?', 'Where have we come from?' and 'Where are we heading to?'). Across Melanesia, people are still looking for answers to those questions. Some of them cling to or revive traditional ideas. Others have long ago committed themselves to Christian teachings. But none of these ways of explaining what was happening to the world changed the way that world actually was, so those who were still dissatisfied with that world developed innovatory systems of ideas – the Cargo cults. They were singularly powerful because they drew upon not one but two kinds of millenarian belief – traditional ideas about the end of the world, when not only would cosmic changes take place (mountains would become valleys), but fundamental social change too – it would no longer be necessary to work, and the goods of the white men would become available to blacks. Such ideas seemed to be confirmed by newer Christian ideas about the Apocalypse and the return of the Messiah, ideas backed by all the authority and prestige of the white man.

So millenarism, Kocher Schmid found in her surveys, is still widespread and probably underestimated. Only five villages 'had no special expectations for the Millennium'. The cults are fuelled by 'feelings of dissatisfaction and disillusion with the modern state [which] are running high. … People do not feel that they are in control of their lives and their future … 84 % thought that the world too uncertain to allow planning ahead; 67 % thought that what happens in life is a matter of chance', and so on.

These are diffuse ideas, so diffuse indeed that respondents in London might come up with similar responses. But in New Guinea they were not simply loosely-shared ideas, but were the basis of actual organised movements. In areas where millennial ideas were strongest – where everybody was said to share a common belief in the imminent end of the world, Kocher Schmid recorded no less than twenty-eight widely varying denominations –in some villages up to ten cults, with an average of three per village. Many of those which had been introduced by 'parent' foreign missionaries developed new, deviant forms and doctrines once they became implanted in New Guinea.

In Kompiam, for instance, where the Baptist church had been dominant, people were now exposed to a whole battery of competing fundamentalist sects: a group which broke away from the Baptists abandoned traditional settlement sites and gardens, and began attending large rallies in remote places. There was also the PNG Bible church, which emphasised belief in 'rapture' (like ex-President Reagan); the Four Square Gospel Church, which stressed the Holy Spirit; and the Seventh Day Adventists, who practised camping out and eating bush foods in preparation for the Day; plus the even newer New Apostolic, United Pentecostalists and Revivalists.

Both the older missions and their enemies, the cults, have experienced marked rises and falls in membership. Cult members, now aware that in the outside world (e.g. Royal Court audiences) their belief in the coming of the Cargo by supernatural means is regarded as ridiculous primitive superstition, have now become ashamed of being labelled Cargo cultists and hide their beliefs.

Bastions of both mission and cultist orthodoxy still exist. But increasingly the village is no longer necessarily under the control of a single mission or even a single cult. Often, rather, what Peter Berger has called a 'market-place' of competing religious organisations has come into existence, giving rise to a virtual palimpsest of ideas, a gamut of concepts which even infects established missionary congregations. The usual distinction between 'radical' and orthodox denominations, Kocher Schmid observes, 'does not seem to apply', for Catholic, Lutheran and United churches 'appear to have equal levels of involvement in the millennial discourse'.

Within the cult spectrum, some are communitarian; others I have labelled 'totalitarian' because the cult leaders seek to control much more than orthodoxy of belief and conformity to ritual practice. In these petty despotisms, even the most detailed behaviours of everyday life are monitored: in one cult, in New Britain, smoking tobacco was forbidden, or the wearing of new shoes or socks. Fines for breaches of the new laws were kept in special bottles, which were regularly and rigorously inspected.

The collective life of the villagers was also radically reorganised. Under the influence of the Summer Institute of Linguistics (a fundamentalist organisation dedicated to the conversion of tribal peoples) the semi-nomadic Kasua physically moved the populations of their villages – previously islands in 'a sea of vegetation' – to new, equally-aligned gardens outside the forest altogether. And whereas in Western societies, death is kept out of sight in hospital morgues and cemeteries, in Melanesia, dead relatives live in the same villages as the living, and are far too important to be airbrushed out of history. Under the new cult, they were now moved to new cemeteries outside the village. Adherents of other creeds were fiercely rejected, one Italian anthropologist being suspected of being a Papal spy. Radical new codes replaced traditional relations between the sexes, as 'supereroticised' women became the medium for communicating with the dead, for whom the villagers also worked specially dedicated gardens.

We now have some evidence of the rise and fall of membership of cults and of mission congregations for some areas. New Britain alone has experienced 117 such movements since 1877.

In the outside world, many people have become aware of the existence of Cargo cults, but not about these newer kinds of religious innovation and pluralisation. To them, Melanesians are people who, for some inexplicable reason, cleave to millenarian ideas.

But where people do cling to these ideas, it is not because they are uncritical or singularly susceptible to the power of myth. Rather, colossal change – one might say, cosmic change – has been part of their real-life experience.

Firstly, various kinds of white man – Germans, Dutch, English and Australians – arrived and established their rival colonies. In the Second World War, these all-powerful colonial regimes and their plantocracies were defeated by a previously unknown people, the Japanese, who threw the masters into jail, and lost a quarter of a million men in the process. In turn, they were fought to a standstill by the arrival of vast numbers of a new kind of egalitarian Australians, who even gave natives guns to fight the Japanese. Manus, in the Admiralty Islands, then experienced the even larger and more traumatic arrival of another previously unknown kind of egalitarian white man, the Americans, one million of whom, including many blacks, arrived one day on 850 ships – on islands with a population of only thirteen thousand.

After the War, with independence came political transformation. Major leaders of cult movements now moved centre-stage as national figures – like Paliau Moloat on Manus, who had been imprisoned during the colonial period, then involved with the Japanese administration, and then had master-minded his own cult movement.

Some theorists have seen cult leadership as simply a modern manifestation of the traditional New Guinea 'big man'. But Paliau thought that tradition was precisely the problem – people needed to adopt modern ways. A magnetic speaker, given to marathon five-hour sermons (like Fidel Castro), he used them to ram home ideas similar to those of other such cults, but would at times suddenly introduce quite radical new ones, as when he renamed the movement Makasol, and gave it a new ideology ('Wind Nation'), with a panoply of new deities.

Neither traditional ideas nor Cargo beliefs, however, were any impediment to involvement in modern state politics. By 1964, Paliau had become an MP; in 1970 was awarded the Order of the British Empire; and when he died, he was given a state funeral.

Other cult leaders such as Golpak, in the part of New Britain studied by Helen Aquart, was similarly awarded the MBE and sent to Cairns to meet Queen Elizabeth.

On the national level, the persistence of old-style cultism, however, now seen as shameful and a sign of backwardness, was usually kept out of sight. But below the surface, out of view, it persisted. In the villages, particularly, new cults could emerge at any time.

These movements, then, do not exist frozen in time in some kind of timeless, functionalist 'ethnographic present', victims of some pre-modern, archaic cultural legacy. Rather, they have a history, and it is one which people think about critically. And constantly search for better ideas. When Christin Kocher Schmid received some new audio tapes, of Beethoven and Mozart, she found that the entire village had silently made its way to her house to listen too: 'What kind of music is this? We have never heard something like it! It is beautiful. It is certainly not 'white' music. It is not church music. It is not radio music. What is it?'

* * * * *

Because Cargo cultism has focussed on acquiring the white man's worldly goods (Cargo), some theorists have labelled them 'materialistic'. But the way this was to come about was anything but materialistic, for what was needed, rather, was a mystical, other-worldly one: access to the white man's *secret* knowledge.

Millenarian ideas persist because they are relevant to new problems. Economists show that the modern state of Papua New Guinea depends for its economic survival on three gigantic mines: the Panguna copper mine on Bougainville, which resulted in a breakaway armed resistance so strong that the mine had to be closed; on the main island, the copper, gold and silver mine at Ok Tedi in the western mountains; and the fifty-nine million tons of gold in the mine at Porgera further east (about which I had written as long ago as 1956[103]). All these mines have been described as 'ecological disasters': potassium cyanide goes into the Fly River from Ok Tedi; mercury into the Sepik from Porgera; and Panguna has been labelled a 'formidable toxic desert'. Since Australian corporations own the mines, this gives Australia political leverage over the state. Papua New Guinea may be constitutionally independent, but is de facto controlled by Australia. Australian direct grants constitute two-thirds of the national budget and subsidise sixty per cent of the defence expenditure.

Three-quarters of the national budget goes to the salaries of massive numbers of politicians and bureaucrats in central and regional government, a new political class – many of whom, like Paliau himself, are illiterate – which the anthropologist Alexander Wanek has termed the 'super-tribe'. The town of Lorengau thus has five hundred public servants out of a population of two thousand. Not surprisingly, the state is widely seen as corrupt. On the island of Manus, Paliau's movement dubs it 'Lucifer', just as Rastafarians label the secular world 'Babylon'.

But to millenarists, the mines represents something more – a new, cosmic, rape of the earth, the source of all wealth and the place where the ancestors live and are accessible at places which lead underground, such as waterfalls, volcanoes, caves or holes. In addition to the poisoning of the land and the rivers, other outsiders, notably Asian logging corporations, are destroying the forests. In a sacred land, nothing is sacred any more.

People know about these things from daily experience. But they can combine secular knowledge with quite mystical belief. Newton did. He spent most of his time not studying gravity or optics but alchemy, and examining the Bible, church history, theology, the chronology of ancient kingdoms and the prognostications of ancient prophets, searching for hidden clues, especially in numerical form, such as apocalyptic numbers like 666 (now fashionable among the young), which might be decoded by the exercise of the God-given faculty of reason. (He also urged researchers into these kinds of knowledge to keep their findings secret, while his Cambridge College further conspired to keep the documentary evidence of his preoccupation with such things out of the public domain for over two centuries more.)

In contemporary New Guinea, the provision of scientific information about the world outside is virtually non-existent. Knowledge is filtered through a religious screen. Such is the confidence (and arrogance) of the West that mystical beliefs like those which inform the Cargo cults must, it is assumed, be attributable to an indigenous primitive heritage. But state education, particularly in the villages where most people live, is very limited indeed. It is still the Christian missions which provide what schooling there is (often little more than catechism). Publishers only market textbooks and Bibles.

I have been taken to task for having argued in the 1950s that Cargo cults would gradually be displaced by secular knowledge. Millenarism is indeed weakest in areas with a longer colonial history and longest exposed to foreign ideas – especially the towns, where people are cut off from their roots in close-knit communities which number only a few hundred. But they are not necessarily replaced by secularism, and persist underground, covert, disguised, hidden, unpredictable and confused, and can jell into organised form when some new external stimulus – not only major disasters like tsunamis (quite common) but frenetically trying to make sense of any scrap of information about life abroad, especially what the white man is up to now. So world events can spark off ideological panics in remote villages: in the past, news about 'Masta Hitler', or Lyndon Johnson; in more recent times, a visit from the Duke of Edinburgh, or Pope John Paul (regarded by many non-Catholics as the Beast of Revelation), who spoke to them in Tok Pisin, the lingua franca. Garbled, partial accounts of new happenings filter through: rumours of flying saucers morph into stories that the whites have started to quit the earth in an exodus to the moon, leaving the blacks behind. Other signs of coming cataclysm have been reports about new political transformations – the reunification of Germany, the collapse of Communism in Eastern Europe, wars in Israel or the Gulf, or global warming. Technological innovations such as 'smart' ('savvy') social security and credit cards, which have long, new numbers on them which identify the individual, plus hitherto unknown symbols such as bar codes, are seen as having new significant but mysterious meanings.

Not all people who go away from the village become sophisticated urbanites, however. Far more people who leave the village still go to work on plantations – ninety per cent of men aged fifty to seventy in one part of New Britain. In the towns, too, they are more likely to develop a disgust for, and fear of, the *raskols*, the violent lumpenproletarians who make life in Port Moresby and Rabaul so dangerous for everybody.

When they come back home, the outside world intrudes more and more into daily life – Government, of course, but the familiar day-to-day presence of mission evangelists who dedicate themselves to indoctrinating and controlling their flocks and proselytising in order to recruit new members. The newer fundamentalist sects which focus on first and last things – the coming Apocalypse – grip the imagination of many. These new sects are often very well heeled indeed, backed by dollars and equipped with modern technologies of communication, initially with radio and aeroplanes, now with computers. I have participated in academic seminars in Fiji conducted by satellite with students in other islands, hundreds of miles distant. But regular flights also take not only missionaries, teachers and linguists, but even members of their congregations out of their mountain fastnesses to towns where they are exposed to high-tech religious evangelism in an exciting, 'happy-clappy' milieu in the company of hundreds of people from places they have never even heard of.

Not surprisingly, there has been, according to Ton Otto, a shift of emphasis in many cults: the arrival of the millennium is now seen not so much as a matter of acquiring the material Cargo but as the coming about of changes in the quality of life – the coming about of a dream of 'freedom' – the absence of ageing, the absence of illness, the absence of death and the absence of work. Such cults, that is, are still millenarian, but no longer Cargo cults.

And some cults once resistant to colonial government's efforts to foster cooperatives and cash crops have now become modernisers, adopting development strategies and dedicating themselves to *hatwok* (hard work), enthusiastically saving to accumulate capital which they invest in education, agriculture or business. In such areas, it seems, the Protestant Ethic has finally arrived. Some modernising cults have even gone on to internalise First World notions of aid, using their accumulated capital altruistically to help their poorer neighbours via regional, not village-based strategies. There are still cults which expect the end of the world and which therefore resist planting not only cash crops but even trees which provide staple foods such as nuts and oil. But tradition and modernity are no longer – as posited in most development theory – polar opposites.

Anthropology itself has contributed at times to negative stereotypes about Cargo cults. Early reports of them as 'madness' were predictable responses when they came from planters and missionaries. But it was an anthropologist who worked for the government, F.E. Williams, in his pioneer study of the movement he called the 'Vailala Madness', who gave authority to the notion that they were a form of collective hysteria.

The wider theoretical notion that anthropologists studied peoples who lived in some timeless 'ethnographic present' scarcely made sense of movements which suddenly erupted on a mass scale. Nor did more modern theories borrowed from Foucault's studies of the hospital, the prison and the asylum in nineteenth-century Europe, for those were closed systems different in kind from volatile sects. Some anthropologists seemed to throw up their theoretical hands in despair. Martha Kaplan, for instance, has written that studying them is akin to a world of 'chaotics' seen through a fog of 'systemic murk'.

I have objected in the past to the use of Weber's concept of charisma as misleading, at worst a mere trendy buzzword or fashion because it treats the cults primarily as responses to the personal dynamism of individuals, latter-day versions of the 'big men' who are so important in New Guinea cultures, but now writ large. Thus, Chief Tuk, who led the bizarre cult focussed on the Duke of Edinburgh on Tanna, in the then New Hebrides, might well have been the 'consummate fabulist' Nigel Evans described him as in the *Independent* (2 February 1994), but this is a judgement which diverts attention from the cults as *movements* – collective responses to social pressures of far more significance than any mere reaction to even the most spell-binding of individuals. It also undervalues the critical input of people who are constantly experimenting with new ways of thinking and acting in order to answer Gauguin's questions about the meaning of life.

Yet, however much the rise to leadership is a function not of the medium but of the message of hope they bring, remarkable spell-binding individuals do exist, and today we are literally able to see for ourselves something of the personal magnetism of older prophets like Yali, Mambu or Paliau, for Strathern has given us not only a biography,[104] but film footage of a more recent cult leader in action – Ongka – who in mobilising his audience blinds the viewer with science and talks a blue streak. For me he really does have charisma.

The Fourth Age

My colleague, Margot Jefferys, who specialised in geriatric medicine, always insisted that the majority of people who retired in their sixties were perfectly capable of carrying on managing their lives and doing valuable work or taking up things they had always wanted to do.

Academics are often particularly fortunate in this respect, because they have often accumulated mounds of data which they now have time to work through, or alternatively, can now sit and think through theoretical issues they never had time to confront properly. The sociologist Pierre Bourdieu has described this as the accumulation of 'cultural capital'.

But there comes a time when one has used up the empirical data in one's notebooks; a time, too, when one has nothing new that one desperately wants to say in theoretical terms.

The classic observation about growing old is that it is 'a series of relinquishments' – by which people usually mean relinquishing sex. But one has to relinquish, successively, all sorts of things. People think that playing the piano is one long romantic sequence of beautiful legato broken chords and arpeggios. I had enjoyed playing for more than seventy years until I found out that if you have arthritis the piano is also a highly painful, percussive instrument. Some people can be lucky – I heard Artur Rubinstein play two Liszt concerti in one night at the Liverpool Phil when he was over eighty, whereas Nathan Milstein, one of the greatest violinists in the world, had to give up playing because he was unable even to hold his instrument.

In the Fourth Age, the body more and more determines what can and cannot be done: in my case, making mobility problematic – even reaching libraries only seven miles away (and my medical problems are very minor compared with those of many people).

Some new technologies can even help with physical illness, for there is a whole repertoire of modern drugs one can resort to. But at the end of the day, as a Canadian friend of mine remarked, 'growing old is not for wimps'.

There are also social aids, notably the tender loving care of relatives, friends and professionals. A different kind of social aid is technical rather than human, the one in front of me: the word processor, on which I can not only do academic work, but also keep in touch with friends, and even reduce domestic labours by doing e-banking and by having groceries delivered to the house. The word processor is, indeed, probably the best thing since sex.

But technology doesn't solve everything, and the likelihood of ending one's days in suffering is still high. That is why I had to admire an old friend who once walked into a room and remarked to her companion that she'd slept with every man in it. She then exhibited the same boldness in managing her own death rather than endure further agonies from rheumatoid arthritis – not perfectly, because, sedated as she was, the black bin-liner over her head didn't do the job properly the first time. So she did it again – and succeeded.

Not all of us are as resolute as she was, and control of one's circumstances at the end may prove beyond our reach. Even then, medico-social intervention at the hands of others is still possible, like the hospice movement pioneered by another of my heroines,

Dame Cicely Saunders, near us in Hackney, which makes it possible even for the terminally ill to carry on 'living before dying'.

The End of the World?

Death, though, in the nuclear age, is a collective, not an individual prospect. Atomic weapons have a particular significance for people who live in or study the Pacific, because they were tested in remote islands in Micronesia and used in Japan.

I had been alarmed to find that an archaeologist on Groote Eylandt – about as remote a place as you can think of – had been using radiation fall-out from the first British atomic tests in the 1950s, hundreds of miles away on the Monte Bello Islands of Western Australia, to date objects she was finding on Groote more than a decade later.

By the 1980s, it was no longer only the major powers which had nuclear weapons, so in a book I edited about nuclear proliferation in the Third World, entitled *On The Brink*, I tried to alert people to this new proliferation of nuclear weapons – with very little effect.

The spectacle of entire populations who were expecting the end of the world had been ludicrous to a sophisticated Royal Court audience, for in England millenarian prophecy died out hundreds of years ago. Occasionally, Jehovah's Witnesses might knock on my front door, but the only regular encounter I had with millenarism was the man in a black bowler hat, a figure of fun at Old Trafford football matches, whose banner urged us to forget about Matt Busby and join the Lord's team.

Even if you were to grant that Melanesians did try to think rationally about the world, they lacked the empirical knowledge with which to do so.

Millenarism isn't entirely nonsense, though. We all know that the end of the world will come about, for it includes asteroids, tsunamis, hurricanes, volcanic eruptions, pandemics and epidemics like AIDS. We recognise that these are real prospects, but we do not spend much time worrying about them, for there is nothing much we can do.

I hold no brief for superstition or for anti-scientific irrationalism such as the trendy romanticisation of exotic Eastern religions that has been widespread in the West. All religions (and non-religious ideologies too) are complex products of intense human ingenuity, scholarship and thought, of ideals and self-interest, which produce amazingly complex belief-systems which can be interpreted many ways. People in Europe now realise that a religion like Islam, which preaches peace and community, is no more immune to visiting butchery on people of other cultural persuasions than that other religion of peace and love, Christianity. From Sri Lanka, I have learned that Hinduism is not only the saintly pacifism of a Gandhi, and that Buddhists who strive to renounce the world are equally capable of slaughtering the Hindus they live amongst.

Such complex bodies of belief and exegesis give rise to multiple, often conflicting interpretations. Theologians spend their lives examining the sacred texts, interpreting the Truth in many ways, affirming some interpretations and dismissing others as heresy. Islam includes suicide bombers, but far more millions are resigned to the will of Allah. But these complexities of belief can be easily reduced to simple oppositions, even by scholars whose criticality stops short of examining their own beliefs. It is the non-believer who is usually identified as the other – the enemy. To Al Qaeda, that enemy is not even those who live next door, but the historic Crusader who first invaded their lands centuries ago. But even those who claim to believe in the same religion, and therefore to belong to the same *umma*, are not immune to condemnation, whether by learned fatwa or the popular belief and prejudice which flourishes in the streets. Nor is the condemnation just intellectual, for it involves condemnation to death too. Sunni religious dogmatists condemn Shia belief; Catholics kill Protestant fellow Christians; Serbian Orthodox Christians murder Catholics and Muslims alike.

Melanesians have long recognised that the most real and immediate threats to human existence come not from Nature, but from the white man, and in particular his science and technology. These have given him so much power that he is rightly proud of his achievement. But they have also produced so many horrors, material and otherwise, as well as wonders, which confirm what traditional ideology had foretold all along: that the world would be turned upside down and, sooner than we think, may well come to an end altogether.

The Enlightenment created such confidence in science as a means of understanding Nature that it thought much less about understanding human society, especially the people who do the work of science. For scientists are induced to work in their laboratories and engineering plants not solely because they are interested in the pursuit of pure knowledge but because they are well rewarded or forced to do so. Their professional expertise apart, their motivations do not differ from those of the tens of thousands of ordinary workers who work in the huge UK armaments industry, because scientists too have lives and identities other than those they operate with in their work, and conform to national, ideological even religious – in a word, non-scientific – beliefs and identities. They have no monopoly of wisdom.

To the Enlightenment, the steady extension of rational thought and of natural science would be the means of eroding away superstition. Rationalists believed that all you had to do was to demonstrate that people cannot walk on water or that the world is much older than a few thousand years.

To the nineteenth century, industry was to be the agency which would put this new knowledge to use and liberate humankind from drudgery. Auguste Comte then advocated using the methods of science that had proved so powerful in studying Nature to society to formulate laws which would enable us to bring about a rational social order.

All cultures recognise the importance of finding out about the facts of life. They also have beliefs which prevent them applying the same attitudes to society. So diviners who specialise in the analysis of witchcraft do recognise that the oracles often produce forecasts which turn out to be erroneous. But they still believe in the general theory which underlies the specific predictions, and have alternative theories to explain away these theoretical malfunctions. Where statisticians see theories of chance or probability, they see accident, or the operation of extra-human forces.

However great the information we have, facts have still to be interpreted, and the meanings people look for are not just self-evident, empirical matters of fact. They are social facts, susceptible to different interpretations. 'Why me?' is the common response to sudden illness, especially when innocent children die while evil people flourish.

To latter-day humanists, science contains no moral imperatives about how society should be run, for science can be used for different, including disastrous, ends. Hence the greatest scientists have diverged over the ultimate uses to which science should be put. In 1939, Einstein wrote to Roosevelt urging the necessity of producing atomic weapons to prevent a Nazi victory. At the end of that war, he tried to stop the further production and use of the Bomb, but failed. 'I do not know how the Third World War will be fought', he later remarked, 'but World War IV will be fought with sticks and stones'. Instead, it was Robert Oppenheimer who won the day. These were not just differences of theory. After witnessing the explosion of the first atomic bomb, Oppenheimer knew exactly what that would lead to, quoting the Bhagavad Gita – 'I am become Death, the destroyer of worlds' – and went on to become the 'father of the atomic bomb'. Einstein who tried, too late, to stop the use of the atomic bombs in Japan, remarked that, had he known where his life-work would lead, he would have become a locksmith.

But the responsibility for bringing about our ability to destroy the world does not fall to scientists alone, or even politicians, though these people do have special power which enables them to hide what they are doing from ordinary people, or to force them to do what they want. But we are all still responsible for letting them get away with this.

At the end of the Second World War, peace had been imposed on the defeated Axis by the victors. But Cold War between the two superpowers had already started, and the American monopoly of nuclear weapons only kept the USSR under restraint for the four years it took for the Soviets to explode their first nuclear bomb. Then Europe was fractured along the fault-line of Germany. And in 1951 came the first US hydrogen bomb, followed two years later by the first Soviet hydrogen bomb.

It had proved impossible for the Big Five to continue to dominate the world through the Security Council. Now it proved impossible for the superpowers to maintain their nuclear monopoly. Britain exploded its first atomic bomb in 1952, and France joined the 'club' in 1960. Israel's nuclear capacity by now was an open secret, and she consolidated her newfound nuclear regional strength when she destroyed Iraq's only nuclear reactor (albeit by non-nuclear bombing). North Korea, too, continued its nuclear development.

But the historic breakthrough came when, in 1964, China, with the largest population on earth, became the first country outside the highly industrialised West to explode a nuclear bomb. The spread of the Bomb beyond the big powers was now unambiguous. By the time of the Cuban missile crisis, the already intercontinental threat reached its apogee: the US itself had to risk world nuclear war in order to make the Soviets withdraw missiles only eighty miles off the coast of Florida.

People have drawn comfort from the fact that though poison gas had been widely used in the First World War, it had not been used again. Winston Churchill, when Colonial Secretary, had been 'unable to understand' the 'squeamishness' of people who opposed its use against 'uncivilised tribes' in Mesopotamia, and was 'strongly in favour' of doing so, but was over-ruled. Instead, young RAF officers like Trenchard and Bomber Harris (a.k.a. 'Butcher' Harris), who thought that 'the only thing the Arab understands is a heavy hand', were allowed to learn their trade by bombing civilians. The use of gas was left to Saddam Hussein, in an independent Iraq, against the Kurds.

Nor have nuclear weapons been used again in war since Hiroshima and Nagasaki, an experience after which Japan renounced any attempt to build nuclear weapons. Other states which had actually embarked on the path to nuclear weapons – Argentina, Brazil and South Africa – abandoned those projects once democracy was restored in their countries, and, under Western pressure, Libya terminated its programme. Former Soviet satellites have also terminated theirs. Encouraged by such self-restraint, some people have concluded that the world will preserve itself from destruction.

Yet, as I write, North Korea has carried out its first underground nuclear test, bringing the number of nuclear powers to nine.

Most of these newcomers are not yet able to launch missiles from one continent to another, but they can launch them against their neighbours, with inevitable further consequences for whole regions – as the two oil wars in Iraq have subsequently demonstrated. Now Japan and South Korea are contemplating rearmament with weapons that would destabilise the whole of East Asia too.

The Indian sub-continent is already much further advanced along this path. Westerners still have a totally outmoded image of India as Gandhi's pacific India. But Gandhi was assassinated very soon after Independence, and as early as 1974 India went on to develop nuclear weapons. When she conducted further tests in May 1988, the immediate consequence was that Pakistan exploded her first nuclear bombs, opening up new vistas, not of the inter-continental exchange of nuclear missiles but of nuclear confrontation across what had hitherto been a mere line drawn on the map, within a gigantic sub-continent inhabited by tens of millions which has been the theatre of one war after another, over Kashmir, since Partition.

India is in fact one of the biggest Muslim countries in the world, and inter-communal war is not the norm for the millions of Muslims who live in India. Progress towards disarmament was made following the collapse of the USSR: sizeable cuts were made in nuclear arsenals when Presidents George W. Bush and Putin signed a treaty reducing nuclear arsenals to ten thousand warheads for the

US and sixteen thousand for Russia. Since each of these warheads is as powerful as the bombs which destroyed Hiroshima and Nagasaki, these are still enormous arsenals, together quite capable of wiping out human life across most of the globe. The US alone has eight thousand, two thousand of them on hair-trigger alert, launchable in fifteen minutes.

Contributions to destabilisation now come from many directions. The father of the Pakistani Bomb, Abdel Qader Khan, having equipped his own state with atomic weapons, finally ended up under arrest for supplying technological know-how to Iran, Libya and Iran. Apart from the eight countries which now actually possess the Bomb, at least twenty states have the technological capacity to develop nuclear weapons. So while President Bush limits his concerns to two 'rogue' states – North Korea and Iran – every existing nuclear power, and every would-be nuclear state, has its own list of potential enemies (principally their neighbours), quite distinct from George Bush's list. The double standard which justifies the pioneer great powers possessing Bombs – but not newcomers – does not persuade them. They look at Britain, the main partner of the US, which, having duped its people into participating in the Iraq War, has now decided to retain 'its' missile, though, '[for] half a century, it is the US [which] has sent Britain radioactive detonators, fuses, and blueprints for supposedly British bombs ... All the computer software, guidance, and missile technology is imported'.

Though the bombs are made at Aldermaston, their design is lease-purchased from the US and the means of delivering them – Trident – also comes from the US. A recent study of the future of Britain's Weapons of Mass Destruction concludes that 'the UK does not and never has had a fully independent nuclear capability – it is and always has been dependent' on US technology and supplies'.[105] Who these weapons might be used on is not made clear. After the collapse of the USSR, 'rogue' states are often given as the greatest, and unpredictable threat. The red enemy though is still Russia, which has thousands of nuclear weapons. So Britain refuses to reduce its nuclear capability or even to abjure a policy of 'no first use'.

After 9/11 and 7/7 people are only too aware that Muslim fundamentalism stretches beyond state boundaries. Less well known and less widespread ideologies, such as *Hindutva* in India – only one of several virulent spin-offs from Hinduism, well-documented by Praful Bidwai and Achin Vanaik[106] – do not attract any such attention, though the millennial cultural-religious divisions which underlie modern Indian nationalism have been strong enough for a party dedicated to Hindu dominance, the Bharatiya Janata Party, only founded in 1980, to become the Government of India from 1998 to 2004. Though the Muslim population had been reduced to one in ten of the population after the massacres which followed Partition, Hindu organisations pressed for India to develop its own nuclear arsenal to defend the country against Islamic Pakistan, and this came about in 1998. Even some Marxists argued that their country, and other Third World countries, needed atomic weapons – it was while combating these people that Edward Thompson, on a visit to India, exacerbated an illness which helped bring about his early death.

Religious fundamentalism is not confined to Muslims and Hindus. A virulent fundamentalism flourishes in an Israel which was once seen, even on the Left, as a new kind of society based on progressive secularism. The born-again Christianity of millions exercises similar strong pressures on the government of the world's greatest nuclear power, the US, which having tried to bomb Afghanistan and Iraq into submission, has now threatened to bomb Pakistan back into the Stone Age.

Western nuclearism, however, overall, has not been based on religious-cultural doctrines: the main kinds of racism and nationalism in the Western world, just as poisonous as religious fundamentalism, have been in primarily secular political cultures such as that of the UK.

Intentional use of nuclear weapons first brought death on a massive scale not to armies but to civilian populations. Since Hiroshima and Nagasaki, however, nuclear disasters have been unintentional and non-military: Windscale (1957), Three Mile Island (1979), Chernobyl (1986) (and very many less well known ones), though there have been military disasters, too, such as the crash, in 1968 at Thule, Greenland, of a US plane designed to ensure that that country would be able to deliver a nuclear strike in any eventuality, but where the crew had to bale out only seven miles from the airbase. Though the 225,000 tons of jet fuel on board, and the conventional explosive in the device exploded, spreading radio-active material over a wide area, fortunately none of the nuclear weapons detonated.

There are, of course, other weapons of mass destruction than nuclear ones. Nor are states, any longer, the only entities which contemplate acquiring and using weapons of mass destruction. One non-state terrorist organisation has already used a biological weapon, sarin, in the Tokyo subway, while non-nuclear terrorism has devastated New York, Madrid and London. Nuclear know-how can also be transferred from 'peaceful' nuclear reactors and used to manufacture bombs. There have been numerous cases not only of the transfer of nuclear know-how from one government to another but of the theft, smuggling and illegal sale of nuclear materials. In the case of plutonium oxide, eight small packets – the size of a cigarette packet – would contain enough to build an atomic bomb.

That Japan has renounced nuclear weapons is comforting, but that country derives half its electricity from nuclear sources; in Europe, France has long been heavily dependent upon nuclear power; while Taiwan derives more than half its electricity from nuclear reactors.

Some countries – Sweden and Germany – are phasing out nuclear power plants. But of those nuclear plants that have actually been decommissioned (such as Dounreay), none has yet been able to solve the problem of how to dispose of the radioactive waste. That is simply left to future generations, and it has been the cost of decommissioning that has deterred even the largest energy corporations from embarking on the construction of new nuclear plants – so far. Yet, paradoxically, responses to global warming, the destruction of the world's rainforests, and the search for an alternative to oil with minimal CO_2 emissions, have led to campaigns to turn to nuclear energy.

High-tech weaponry is not necessarily called for in genocide – in Rwanda, out of a population of only 8.5 million, hundreds of thousands were killed just with machetes. I do not subscribe to that kind of lazy geriatric pessimism that sees the past only as the story of mountains of human skulls, but a future of nuclear extinction for much larger populations is becoming more and more likely.

Like tens of thousands of others in Britain, I try to do what very little I still can do to hold back this drift, though I no longer belong to a Party which has replaced traditional, if inadequate, democratic socialism with focus groups, sleaze and cronyism. Like people of my age, I find the greatest of pleasure in watching my grandchildren grow up, and trying to help them mature and have fun. And whereas Voltaire saw cultivating one's garden as a kind of opting out, a privatisation of one's world, since that world seems hell-bent on destroying itself, I have enjoyed founding a local garden society and make no apology for seeing that too as a form of nurture. I also enjoy weekly conviviality in a West End pub, which would be too expensive for the one in five people over fifty who live below the poverty line or the seven million who may have bus-passes but have no access to public transport.[107]

So it is not just that I have grown old and lost the optimism of youth, but due to the sheer logical probability that one of the nightmare scenarios I've discussed will actually come to pass in a world so racked by divisions of inequality and culture that people regress to the fundamentalisms they read into sacred books.

Despite the still superior destructive power of the West, and its capacity to deliver its nuclear weapons anywhere, by land-based missiles or from submarines, it can no longer ensure even its own defence, let alone its ability to keep global proliferation under control. The source of this international instability is only in part cultural-ideological. It is built into the framework, of a global society founded on the market, and, within that framework into the social structure both of poor societies in the Third World (mis-named 'developing', though very many are not), and into the structure of equally mis-named 'developed' societies – where a microscopic handful are obscenely rich and monopolise political power; a third are comfortably off; another third lead a tolerable existence; but the last third are poor, sometimes desperately so. It is a sad conclusion to reach, but it may mean that to have spent my life trying to make the world a more rational place could prove to have been a delusion.

In an epoch of global warming, we are very conscious today of disasters which overtook the natural world, notably the extinction of the dinosaurs, though we are less aware of the numerous human cultures, from Easter Island to the great civilisation of the Maya (who were capable of developing their own written script and developed the mathematical discovery of zero as early as 36 BC), which have destroyed themselves in the past.[108] Today, it is not just a particular culture that may disappear, but human civilisation as a whole.

Notes and References

I have only referred to works that may not be so well known, and substantiated facts that others might challenge, and have omitted small pieces of my own later which were incorporated into more substantial articles. I have also watched out for what my friend, Bob Gollan, the Australian historian, has called the 'Dili factor', when he warned his colleagues not to rely on their memories but to check their sources, since he had once described how he had flown on a bomber sortie against Dili, on the Japanese-held island of Timor – or so he thought, until, on consulting his diary, found he had never bombed Dili at all. Conversely, I have been surprised how I have succeeded in remembering an awful lot once prompted by some detail, even if at the cost of lost hours of sleep.

Checking even the tiniest of tiny facts, or fuzzily recollected ones, can take ages; for one page here I had to read a whole Ph.D. thesis. A major asset has been my wife's prodigious memory for names, dates, places and birthdays. But much would have been unrescuable had it not been for the wonderful innovation of the search-engine, which allows me to call up factual information without even leaving my flat. Even when I was a Professor at Manchester University I was (only once) refused the use of the Inter-university Loan Service because it would have cost too much. Today, though I live only seven miles from the biggest specialist libraries in Britain, getting there is problematic for one who is losing easy mobility. But now I can go to my little local library at West Ealing, and be provided by the Inter-library Loan Service with books from the British Library's holdings at Boston Spa (including one published only in Australia, and another published in Portuguese in Brazil which even Cambridge University Library did not hold). None of this, though, is a substitute for being able to leaf through dozens of books and articles at leisure.

Chapter 1

1. Alan and Iris Macfarlane, *Green Gold: The Empire of Tea*, Ebury Press, 2003.
2. Jean McInnis, *Birkenhead Park*, Countyvise, 1984. See also Kate Colquhoun's *A Thing in Disguise: The Visionary Life of Joseph Paxton*, Fourth Estate, 2003, pp. 119–21, 134–36.
3. *Della Robbia Pottery Birkenhead 1894–1906*, Williamson Art Gallery, 1984.
4. 'Liverpool and the Atlantic Slave Trade', Information Sheet 3, Maritime Archives and Library, 2005. The first slave ship sailed from Liverpool in 1699. By 1750 Liverpool had overtaken Bristol, and by the 1790s controlled eighty per cent of Britain's slave trade and over forty per cent of the European slave trade. These facts were completely unknown to

me – or most people – in the l930s. The trade in slaves within the British Empire had been abolished in 1807 – a century and a quarter ago.

5. Quoted in Basil Davidson, *Black Mother*, Gollancz, 1961, p. 73.
6. Marika Sherwood, *Pastor Daniels Ekarté and the African Churches Mission Liverpool 1931–1964*, Savannah Press, 1994.

Chapter 2

7. 'Interesting Times?', *Socialist History 24*, Rivers Oram, 2003, with articles by Eric Hobsbawm, Roger Simon, George Bernard, Ralph Russell, John Maynard Smith, Cyril Claydon, Norman Lindop, Dorothy Wedderburn, myself, Dorothy Thompson and June Bean. Many who might have contributed, such as Martin Eve and Edward Thompson, are now dead.
8. F.H. Le Breton, *Up-Country Swahili Exercises*, R.W. Simpson, Sheen, 1946.
9. For another serviceman's account of these chaotic times, see John Saville, *Memoirs from the Left*, Merlin, 2003. Saville was given local leave by the Army in 1945/6, which he spent working for the Indian Communist Party, and writing pamphlets for the CP under a pseudonym. Mervyn Jones witnessed the machine-gunning by the British troops of people in Bombay during the 1946 RIN Mutiny. When he reported this to the Forces Parliament, the Parliament was closed down (pp. 68–72).
10. Thomas Spear, 'Being "Maasai", but not "People of Cattle": Arusha Agricultural Maasai in the Nineteenth Century', *Ethnicity and Identity in East Africa*, eds Thomas Spear and Richard Waller, James Currey, 1993, pp. 120–33. These differences in culture and economy have a lot to do with the distribution of water resources. The arid plains were only suitable for cattle nomadism; the higher slopes of Mounts Meru and Kilimanjaro, rich in volcanic soil and well watered, supported permanent agriculture; the in-between areas, shifting cultivation; and there were 'oases' like Taveta and Ngong in the middle of the arid zones. There were also market centres where pastoral and agricultural zones adjoined each other.

Chapter 3

11. P.M. Worsley and J.P. Rumberger, 'Remains of an Earlier People in Uhehe', *Tanganyika Notes and Records*, Vol. 27, June 1949, pp. 42–46.
12. Alison Redmayne, 'Mkwawa and the Hehe Wars', *Journal of African History*, Vol. 9, No. 3, 1968, p. 419.
13. Greg Blake, *Military History Magazine*, Primedia, 1977.
14. *The Wahehe People of Tanganyika*, unpublished D.Phil. thesis, University of Oxford, 1964, p. 245.
15. Richard Brown, 'Passages in the Life of a White Anthropologist: Max Gluckman in Northern Rhodesia', *Journal of African History*, Vol. 20, 1979, pp. 525–41; see also his 'Anthropology and Colonial Rule: Godfrey Wilson and the Rhodes-Livingstone Institute, Northern Rhodesia', in Talal Asad (ed.), *Anthropology and the Colonial Encounter*, Ithaca Press, 1975, pp. 173–97.
16. Max Gluckman, *Custom and Conflict in Africa*, Blackwell, Oxford, 1956.
17. Raymond Firth, 'Max Gluckman', *Proceedings of the British Academy*, Vol. 62, 1975, p. 493. I developed a parallel critique in my analysis of Max's handling of rebellions and revolutions in a paper originally given at the 30th World Congress of Sociology at Stresa, Italy, in 1959.

Chapter 4

18. See James Faris, 'Pax Britannica and the Sudan: S.F. Nadel', in T. Asad (ed.), *Anthropology and the Colonial Encounter*, Ithaca Press, 1973, pp. 156–62.

19. F.G.G. Rose, *Classification of Kin, Age Structure and Marriage among the Groote Eylandt Aborigines: A Study in Method and a Theory of Australian Kinship*, Akademie-Verlag, Berlin, 1960.

20. P.E. Josselin de Jong, 'A New Approach to Kinship Studies', *Bijdragen tot de Taal-, Land-, en Volkenkunde*, Vol. 118, No. 1, 1962, p. 66.

21. 'The Utilization of Food Resources by an Australian Aboriginal Tribe', *Acta Etnographica*, Vol. 10, Nos 1–2, pp. 153–90, Hungarian Academy of Sciences, Budapest, 1961.

22. J.A. Waddy, *Classification of Plants and Animals from a Groote Eylandt Aboriginal Point of View*, Australian National University North Australia Research Unit Monograph (2 vols.), Darwin, 1988. In writing my much later book, *Knowledges*, I was therefore gratified when this expert, who had spent fifteen years studying Groote Eylandt biology, linguistics and ethnology, found my original article worthy of praise (see *Knowledges*, p. 4).

23. 'A New Stage in the Development of the Aboriginal People', *Communist Review*, No. 153, September 1954, pp. 282–85.

24. Richard D. Chenhall, *Benelong's Haven*, unpublished Ph.D. thesis, London School of Economics, 2002.

25. 'Noun-classification in Australian and Bantu: Formal or Semantic?', *Oceania*, Vol. 24, No. 24, 1954, pp. 275–88. I was gratified to be told only recently that this paper is appreciated by Bantu specialists.

26. Review of Charles P. Mountford's *Records of the American-Australian Expedition to Arnhem Land*, Vol. 1, Art, Myth and Symbolism, *Man*, No. 241, December 1957; Mountford's reply (*Man*, No. 5, 1958); and my retort (No. 93, 1958).

27. 'The Measurement of Cross-cultural Differences in Intelligence: An Australian Experiment in the Construction of "Culture-bound" Tests' (unpublished).

28. David H. Turner, 'Tradition and Transformation: A Study of Aborigines in the Groote Eylandt Area, Northern Australia', *Australian Institute of Aboriginal Studies*, No. 153, Canberra, 1974.

29. 'Early Asian Contacts with Australia', *Past and Present*, No. 7, 1955, pp. 1–11.

30. Gavin Menzies, *1481: The Year China Discovered the World*, Bantam, 2002.

31. 'N.N. Mikloukho-Maclay, Pioneer of Pacific Anthropology', *Oceania*, Vol. 22, No. 4, June 1952, pp. 307–14. The definitive biography, published in 1984, is E.M. Webster's *The Moon Man: A Biography of Nikolai Mikloukho-Maclay*, University of California Press. (The title refers to scientific tricks Maclay used to impress the natives.)

32. 'Totemism in a Changing Society', *American Anthropologist*, Vol. 57, No. 4, August 1955, pp. 851–61.

Chapter 5

33. 'The Kinship System of the Tallensi', Curl Bequest Prize Essay 1955, *Journal of the Royal Anthropological Institute*, Vol. 56, Part 1, pp. 37–75.

34. Caroline Elkins, *Britain's Gulag: The Brutal End of Empire in Kenya*, Cape, 2005; David Anderson, *Histories of the Hanged: Testimony from the Mau Mau Rebellion in Kenya*, Orion, 2005.

35. Eileen Fletcher, *Peace News Supplement*, 11 January 1957, which begins with an article of mine, 'Kenya Faces the Future' (pp. 1 and 6), and has a contribution by Fenner Brockway, MP.

36. 'The Anatomy of Mau Mau', *New Reasoner*, Vol. 1, No. 1, pp. 13–25.

37. 'The Mau Mau Rituals: Tribal Religion and Witchcraft', *Manchester Guardian*, 19 March 1954, and 'The Magic of Despair', reprinted from *The Listener*, 29 April 1954, in *Order*

and Rebellion in Tribal Africa, Cohen and West, 1963, pp. 137–45, which also contains Max's celebrated wider theoretical discussion of 'Rituals of Rebellion in South-east Africa' (pp. 110–36).

38. Peter Lawrence, *Road Belong Cargo: A Study of the Cargo Movement in the Southern Madang District, New Guinea*, Manchester University Press, Manchester, 1964; and K.O.L. Burridge, *Mambu: A Melanesian Millennium*, Methuen, 1960.

39. 'Cargo Cult Movements in Melanesia', *The Listener*, Vol. 54, No. 1389, 1955, pp. 97–98.

40. *The Trumpet Shall Sound: A Study of 'Cargo' Cults in Melanesia*, MacGibbon and Kee, 1957; Shocken Books, New York, p. 168; 2nd augmented edition, with new Introduction, Paladin, 1970.

41. In Bob Mullan (ed.), *Sociologists on Sociology*, Croom Helm, 1987, p. 94. Mullan also interviewed me (pp. 59–91).

42. Norman Dennis, Fernando Henriques and Clifford Slaughter, *Coal is our Life: An Analysis of a Yorkshire Mining Community*, Eyre and Spottiswoode, 1956.

43. As well as the article on the anatomy of Mau Mau, I contributed another on 'Albert Schweitzer and the Liberal Conscience', Vol. 1, No. 3, pp. 39–54; the chapter on 'Imperial Retreat', in E.P. Thompson (ed.), *Out of Apathy*, Stevens, 1960, pp. 101–40, and 'Non-alignment and the New Left', in *Out of Apathy: Voices of the New Left 30 Years On*, Verso, 1989.

44. 'Britain: Unknown Country', *New Reasoner*, Vol. 1, No. 6, 1958, pp. 53–64.

45. Jennifer Platt, *The British Sociological Association: A Sociological History*, Sociology Press, Durham, 2003, pp. 34–35.

46. 'The Distribution of Power in Industrial Society', in P. Halmos (ed.), *The Development of Industrial Societies*, Keele, 1964, pp. 15–34.

47. 'Material Symbols of Human Beings among the Wanindiljaugwa', *Man*, 1964, 261.

48. 'Millenarian Movements in Melanesia', *Rhodes-Livingstone Journal*, Vol. 21, 1957, pp. 18–31.

49. 'La répartition des mouvements millénaristes en Mélanésie', *Archives de Sociologie des Religions*, Vol. 3, No. 5, 1958, pp. 38–47.

50. 'Cargo Cults', *Scientific American*, Vol. 200, No. 55, 17, 1960, pp. 87–93.

51. 'The Analysis of Rebellions and Revolutions in Modern British Social Anthropology', *Science and Society*, Vol. 25, No. 1, 1961, pp. 26–37.

52. 'The Concept of Populism', in Ghiţa Ionescu and Ernest Gellner (eds), *Populism: Its Meanings and National Characteristics*, Weidenfeld and Nicolson, 1969, pp. 212–50, and Chapter 4 in *The Third World*.

53. 'Groote Eylandt Totemism and *Le Totémisme Aujourd'hui*', in Edmund Leach (ed.), *The Structural Study of Myth and Totemism*, ASA Monograph No. 5, 1967, pp. 141–59.

54. Murray Dobbin, *The One-and-a-Half Men: The Story of Jim Brady and Malcolm Norris, Métis Patriots of the Twentieth Century*, New Star Books, Vancouver, 1981.

55. *Interim Report No. 1: Economic and Social Survey of Northern Saskatchewan*, Center for Community Studies, Saskatoon, 1961 (with H.L. Buckley and Arthur K. Davis).

56. Irving Louis Horowitz (ed.), 'Bureaucracy and Decolonization: Democracy from the Top', in *The New Sociology: Essays in Social Science and Social Theory in Honor of C. Wright Mills*, Oxford University Press, New York, 1964, pp. 370–90.

57. My kinship analysis is in Chapter 5 of my Ph.D., *The Changing Social Structure of the Wanindiljaugwa*, Australian National University, 1954.

58. G.A. Acquah, *The Fantse of Ghana* (Foreword by Dr P.M. Worsley), Hull (n.d.).

59. Peter Worsley and Paschalis Kitromilides (eds), *Small States in the Modern World: The Conditions of Survival*, a book so badly published that a revised edition had to be published by Zavallis Press only a few months later. Kitromilides wrote the Preface (pp. x–xv) and I wrote an introductory essay on 'Communalism and Nationalism in Small Countries: The Case of Cyprus' (pp. 1–17).

Chapter 6

60. *The Third World: A Vital New Force in International Affairs*, Weidenfeld and Nicolson, 1964.
61. *Report of the British Economic Mission on the Tanzania Five Year Development Plan*, December 1965. Chapter 12, 'The Transformation Approach: Village Settlement', was by me.
62. 'The End of Anthropology?', *Transactions of the Sixth World Congress of Sociology*, Vol. 3, International Sociological Association, Milan, 1970, pp. 121–29.
63. *Introducing Sociology*, Penguin; *Modern Sociology: Introductory Readings*, and *Problems of Modern Society*, all published in 1970. Editing is not fun, and academia has its quota of people who may be good teachers but who have the greatest difficulty writing anything and need a lot of encouragement and assistance. Completely re-editing these three books, in 1977, as *The New Introducing Sociology* left me, as editor, with having to produce two chapters other people had been scheduled to write, one on social class, myself, with only a month to go to the publisher's deadline. All this involved as much work as some of the contributors have produced during their lifetimes.
64. 'Frantz Fanon and the Lumpenproletariat', *Socialist Register 1972*, Merlin Press, pp. 193–230.
65. 'Revolutionary Theory: Che and Régis Debray', in L. Huberman and P. Sweezy (eds), *Régis Debray and the Latin American Revolution*, Monthly Review Press, New York, 1968, pp. 118–38.
66. 'The Revolutionary Party as an Agent of Social Change', in Nancy Hammond (ed.), *Social Science and the New Societies: Problems in Cross-cultural Research and Theory Building*, Social Science Research Bureau, Michigan State University, East Lansing, 1973.
67. 'Authority and the Young', *New Society*, Vol. 6, No. 147, 1966, pp. 10–13.
68. 'Not One, Not Two, But Many Cultures', in Alexander Schouvaloff (ed.), *Place for the Arts*, Seel House Press, Liverpool, 1970, pp. 127–28.
69. 'The Spread of Jazz', *The Listener*, Vol. 19, No. 1772, 1963, pp. 456–58.
70. 'Libraries and Mass Culture', *Library Association Record*, Vol. 69, No. 8, 1967, pp. 259–67.
71. Maya Jaggi, 'Prophet at the Margins', Profile of Stuart Hall, *Guardian*, Saturday Review, 8 July 2000.
72. *Inside China*, Allen Lane/Penguin, 1975.
73. *Two Blades of Grass: Rural Co-operatives in Agricultural Modernization*, Manchester University Press, 1971.

Chapter 7

74. Agustin Cueva, *El Proceso de Dominación Politica en Ecuador*, Solitierra, Quito, 1977, p. 49.
75. Philip Agee, *Inside the Company: CIA Diary*, Penguin, Harmondsworth, 1975.
76. Hugo Burgos Guevara, *Relaciones Interetnicas en Riobamba: dominio y dependencia en una región indígena ecuatoriana*, Instituto Indigenista Interamericano, Mexico City, 1977.
77. I was very keen to make some recompense to Latin America for the hospitality I had received in that continent, and for all that I had learned, so asked an Italian postgraduate, Valentina Napolitano, whom I was supervising for a Ph.D. thesis on Mexico at the School of Oriental Studies in London, to translate this into English as *Guinea-Pigs: Food, Symbol and Conflict of Knowledge in Ecuador*, Berg, 1997.

Chapter 8

78. 'One World or Three? A Critique of the World-system Theory of Immanuel Wallerstein', in John Saville and Ralph Miliband (eds), *Socialist Register 1980*, Merlin Press, 1980, pp. 298–338.
79. 'The State of Theory and the Status of Theory', *Sociology*, Vol. 8, No. 1, January 1974, pp. 1–17.
80. Joanna Holland, 'Conflicts Underneath a Conventional Course', *Times Higher Educational Supplement*, 25 July 1973.
81. Sydel Silverman (ed.), *Totems and Teachers: Perspectives on the History of Anthropology*, Columbia University Press, New York, 1981, p. xiii.
82. Eric R. Wolf and Joseph G. Jorgerman, 'Anthropology on the Warpath in Thailand', *New York Review of Books* special supplement, Vol. 15, No. 9, 19 November 1970, pp. 26–36, subsequently posted on the website of *Public Anthropology* and rightly entitled 'Anthropologists Who Have Spoken Out'.
83. Stanley Diamond, 'The Situation in Nigeria', *New York Review of Books*, Vol. 18, No. 2, 4 May 1972; and 'The Ibos' Plight', Vol. 18. No. 3, 24 February 1972.

Chapter 9

84. *On the Brink: Nuclear Proliferation and the Third World*, Third World Communications, 1987. 'Introduction', pp. 17–43.
85. Ellen Godfrey, *By Reason of Doubt*, Clarke-Irwin, Toronto, 1981.
86. '"Non-Western" Medical Systems', Frazer Lecture, University of Glasgow, March 1981; *Annual Review of Anthropology*, Vol. 11, 1982, pp. 315–48.
87. 'Classic Conceptions of Culture' (pp. 13–21), and 'Culture and Development Theory' (pp. 30–41), in Tracey Skelton and Tim Allen (eds), *Culture and Global Change*, Routledge, 1999.
88. 'The Nation State, Colonial Expansion and the Contemporary World Order', in Tim Ingold (ed.), *Companion Encyclopaedia of Anthropology: Humanity, Culture and Social Life*, Routledge, 1994, pp. 1040–66.
89. *Marx and Marxism*, Ellis Horwood, 1982; revised edition, Routledge, 2002.
90. *The Three Worlds: Culture and World Development*, Weidenfeld and Nicolson, 1984.
91. Mary LeCron Foster and Robert A. Rubinstein (eds), *Peace and War: Cross-cultural Perspectives*, Transaction Inc, New Brunswick, New Jersey, 1986 (my contribution was 'The Superpowers and the Tribes', pp. 293–306); and 'Images of the Other' in Robert A. Rubinstein and Mary LeCron Foster (eds), *The Social Dynamics of War and Peace in International Relations*, Westview Press, Boulder/London, 1988, pp. 69–80).
92. *Knowledges: Culture, Counter-culture, Subculture*, New Press, New York, and Profile Books, London, 1997.
93. J.B. Peires, *The Dead Will Arise: Nongqawuse and the Great Xhosa Cattle Killing Movement of 1856–7*, Ravan Press, Johannesburg, 1989.
94. M.N. Pearson, *Merchants and Rulers in Gujarat*, University of California Press, Berkeley, 1976, cited in L.S. Stavrianos, *Global Rift: The Third World Comes of Age*, Morrow, New York, 1981, pp. 144–51.
95. John Sharp, 'Two Separate Developments: Anthropology in South Africa', *RAIN* (Royal Anthropological Institute Newsletter), No. 36, February 1980, pp. 4–6.
96. Robert Hughes, *The Fatal Shore: A History of the Transportation of Convicts to Australia, 1797–1808*, Pan Books, 1988.
97. Tim Smit, *Eden*, Corgi, 2002.
98. Daniel Tumarkin, 'Miklouho-Maclay, 19th Century Russian Anthropologist and Humanist', *RAIN* (Royal Anthropological Institute Newsletter) August 1982; Peter Worsley, Letter, Summer 1982, *RAIN*, No. 53.

99. '"Cargo" Cults: Forty Years On', in Christin Kocher Schmid (ed.), *Expecting the Day of Wrath: Versions of the Millennium in Papua New Guinea*, NRI Monograph 36, Port Moresby, 1999, pp. 146–55.

100. 'Continuity and Discontinuity in New Guinea Religion', in *Vital Matters III: Emergent Societies and the Post-nation State: Religious Movements*, Bergen 2006.

101. 'Work, Wealth, and Knowledge: Enigmas of Cargoist Identification', in Holger Jebens (ed.), *Cargo, Cult, and Culture Critique*, University of Hawai'i Press, Honolulu, 2004, pp. 209–26.

102. The main works I drew on were the collection edited by Christin Kocher Schmid cited above; Andrew Lattas' *Cultures of Secrecy: Reinventing Race in Bush Kaliai Cargo Cults*, University of Wisconsin Press, Madison, 1998; Helen Aquart's 'The Pomio Kivung Association, East New Britain', Ph.D. thesis, Newcastle University, New South Wales, 2001; Martha Kaplan's *Neither Cargo nor Cult: Rural Politics and the Colonial Imagination in Fiji*, Duke University Press, Durham and London, 1995; Alexander Wanek's 'Fighting Lucifer: The State and its Enemies in Papua New Guinea', Ph.D. thesis, Department of Social Anthropology, University of Stockholm, 1993; and three articles by Ton Otto: 'Paliau's stories', *Focaal, Tidjdschrift voor antropologie*, No. 32, 1998, pp. 71–87; 'Cargo cults everywhere?', *Anthropological Forum*, University of Western Australia, Vol. 9, No.1, 1999, pp. 83–98; and 'From Paliau Movement to Makasol: The Politics of Representation', *Current Anthropology*, Canberra, Vol. 15, No. 2, 1992, pp. 49–68.

103. 'The Telefomin Case', *Anti-slavery Reporter and Aborigines' Friend*, January 1956, Series 6, Vol. 10, No. 4, pp. 74–76.

104. Andrew Strathern, *Ongka: A Self-account by a New Guinea Big-man*, Duckworth, 1979.

105. Dan Plesch, *The Future of British WMDs*, Foreign Policy Centre, 2005.

106. Praful Bidwai and Achin Vanaik, *New Nukes: India, Pakistan and Global Nuclear Disarmament*, Signal Books, Oxford, 2000.

107. Germaine Greer, 'For Whom the Bells Toll', *Guardian*, 14 September 2005.

108. Jared Diamond, *Collapse: How Societies Choose to Fail or Survive*, Penguin, 2005.